The Visit

JER

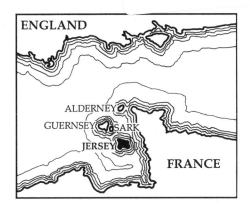

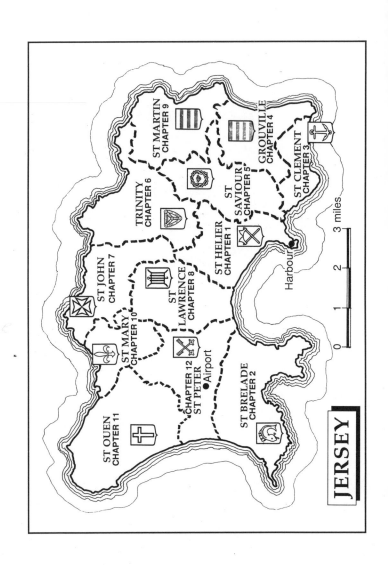

ST OUEN
CHAPTER 11

ST JOHN
CHAPTER 7

ST MARY
CHAPTER 10

ST MARTIN
CHAPTER 9

TRINITY
CHAPTER 6

ST
LAWRENCE
CHAPTER 8

CHAPTER 12
ST PETER
Airport

ST HELIER
CHAPTER 1

ST
SAVIOUR
CHAPTER 5

GROUVILLE
CHAPTER 4

ST CLEMENT
CHAPTER 3

ST BRELADE
CHAPTER 2

Harbour

0   1   2   3 miles

JERSEY

VISITOR'S GUIDE

JERSEY

Sonia Hillsdon

MPC

Published by:
Moorland Publishing Co Ltd,
Moor Farm Road, Ashbourne,
Derbyshire DE6 1HD England

ISBN 0 86190 374 9

Ist edition 1988
2nd revised edition 1994

British Library Cataloguing in Publication Data:
A catalogue record for this book is available from the British Libary

Colour and black & white origination by: Quad Repro Ltd, Pinxton, Notts

Printed in Hong Kong by: Wing King Tong Co Ltd

Front cover: Mont Orgueil, Gorey (*International Photobank*)
Rear cover: Gréve de Lecq (*Jersey Tourism*)

Photographs have been supplied by: Fort Regent p31, *The Jersey
Evening Post* p41; the remainder by Jersey Tourism.

Acknowledgements
The author would like to thank the following for help with the preparation
of this book: the Constables of the twelve parishes; the Town Greffier
Mr P. Freely; Centenier A. Vibert, Miss Jean Arthur, Mr R. W. Le Sueur,
Mr Leslie Sinel, Mrs K. Paget-Tomlinson, Mrs Rosemary Hampton, Mr L.
Hamon of Jersey Motor Transport and Mr M. K. Doong.

CONTENTS

Key to Symbols Used in Text Margin and on Maps

🚶 Recommended walk

🍀 Parkland

Π Archaeological site

🦌 Nature reserve/Animal interest

🐦 Birdlife

🌼 Garden

🌳 Beautiful view/Scenery/Natural phenomenon

♿ Access for disabled

⛪ Church/Ecclesiastical site

🏛 Building of interest

🏰 Castle/Fortification

🏛 Museum/Art gallery

✳ Other place of interest

🎾 Sports facilities

⛵ Watersports

⛳ Golfing course

U Horse riding/Pony trekking

Author's Note
Different spellings and the choice, in some instances, of either French or English for island place names on maps and signposts and in written material only serve to illustrate the bi-lingualism of Jersey and the influence of both Normandy and England on the island.

Note on the Maps
The maps drawn for each chapter, while comprehensive, are not designed to be used as route maps, but locate the main towns, villages and places of interest. Perry's Guide Maps of Jersey are available in handy pocket form from newsagents and bookshops in Jersey and the Ordnance Survey 1:25,000 Official Leisure Map is recommended.

INTRODUCTION

J ersey — a small island in the English Channel which has given its
name to a jumper, a breed of cows, a potato, a lily and even an
American state! The French writer Victor Hugo considered it *un ravis-
sant pays*; the English novelist George Eliot delighted in its 'glimpses of
the sea at unexpected openings'. Between the wars, in the 1920s and
30s, young UK couples chose Jersey as their 'honeymoon island'; in the
1980s television viewers all over the world saw its scenery as a splendid
backdrop for the exploits of their detective hero Jim Bergerac.

Part of Jersey's charm for the million or so visitors it attracts each
year is its special blend of things French and British. Many roads have
French names — La Grande Route de St Martin, Rouge Bouillon, Le
Mont Sohier, La Rue des Landes — but traffic still drives on the left. In
the shopping centres, near branches of well known British stores, stand
the Jersey shops of Voisin, De Gruchy, Elégance, Le Riches, yet the
assistants speak English and the currency is sterling. Visitors can feel
abroad one minute, sampling *fruits de la mer* at a pavement café, or
quite at home the next, enjoying a Jersey cream tea in one of the island's
colourful gardens.

This dual flavour comes from Jersey's history but also, in part, from
its geographical position. The largest and most southerly of the Channel
Islands, it lies in the Bay of Mont-St-Michel, only about 30 miles from the
Breton port of St Malo. From its northern cliffs not only can the other
Channel Islands of Guernsey, Herm, Sark and Alderney be seen but
also, to the east, the long stretch of the Normandy coast — at its closest
only 14 miles across the water. The south coast of England, on the other
hand, is nearly 100 miles away to the north.

The island itself measures only 9 miles by 5 or, in the traditional
Jersey measurement, covers about 65,000 *vergées*, so nowhere is
more than 2½ miles from the sea. It owes its favourable climate and
sunshine records both to the presence of the Gulf Stream and to the fact
that the land slopes from its precipitous cliffs in the north to sea level in
the south.

Its 50 miles of coastline, including 20 miles of sandy beaches, is not
only extremely varied but is also subject, at full moon and at the equinox,
to unusually low and high tides. The network of caves and sheltered
coves on the north coast results from the erosive action of the sea over

7

the centuries on the island's predominantly granite rocks, whose warm, pinky tones feature in so much of Jersey's architecture.

Jersey's History

Traces of Jersey's prehistory still exist today. From the time when the island was part of the continent, there are remnants of a great French forest. These black stumps of trees, when there is an exceptionally low tide, can be seen sticking through the sand at St Ouen. Flints and crude stone tools were left by hunters in La Cotte à la Chèvre (Goat's Cave) — now perched 60ft above the present level of the sea on the north coast of St Ouen — and in La Cotte de St Brelade, one of the most important Palaeolithic sites in Europe. The impressive stone monuments which have overlooked the sea round the island since Neolithic times were an integral part of the burial rites and religious ceremonies of Jersey's first farmers for over a thousand years.

If the Romans ever came to Jersey, nothing substantial remains of their time here, though there is a building at the base of the huge Pinnacle Rock in St Ouen which some suggest was a Roman-Celtic shrine to a local deity.

One of the earliest holy places to which Christian pilgrims came was the rocky outcrop, south of where Elizabeth Castle now stands, on which the hermit and martyr St Helier lived and preached to the islanders in the sixth century. Six hundred years later the oratory, known today as the Hermitage, was built on the rock to honour the saint.

It was probably Saxon pirates who murdered St Helier on the beach of the town which now bears his name, but it is certainly to the later Viking pirates that Jersey owes its longstanding French connection. All during the ninth century these marauders from the north, or Normans as they were called, came in the summer months to plunder the Channel Islands *en route* to and from their coastal raids on England and France. They even sailed up the river Seine to beseige Paris.

This was when the French king, Charles the Simple, realised that to stop the pirate chief Rollo and his followers from terrorising his subjects, his only recourse was to bargain with him. In the treaty of 911, Rollo agreed to keep the peace in exchange for the region around Rouen which today is known as Normandy — the land of the Normans. Thus was forged an important link in Jersey's connection with France, for Rollo's son William, when he became Duke of Normandy, incorporated the Channel Islands into the duchy. So from 933 to 1204 Jersey was ruled from Normandy.

The results of these centuries of direct French rule can still be seen in the Jersey of today. Jersey men and women who claim Norman ancestry often share with their Norman counterparts the same traits of self-reliance, industry, reticence and thrift. The so-called local 'patois' some Jersey families still speak among themselves is correctly known as Jersey-Norman French; their granite houses are reminiscent in their architecture of the farmhouses in Normandy.

That the island is divided into fiefs, as well as into twelve parishes each with its church, and that several fiefs still have their manor house — some with their Seigneur, or Lord of the Manor — also harks back to the days of Norman feudal rule. Many Jersey laws, too, go back to that time, being based on Le Grand Coutumier de Normandie, and are written in French.

One such law is the right to raise La Clameur de Haro. This is done when an islander wishes to stop someone from harming his property. He falls down on his knees in the presence of two witnesses and calls out *Haro! Haro! Haro! à l'aide mon prince, on me fait tort.* (Haro! Haro! Haro! to my aid, my prince, I am being wronged.) Nothing further may be done to his property until the case has been heard in a court of law. Some believe that the word 'Haro' is a direct appeal to Rollo or Rou, the first Duke of Normandy.

The Dukes of Normandy, including William the Conqueror and his descendants who were also Kings of England, continued to rule Jersey and the other Channel Islands from Rouen until war broke out, at the beginning of the thirteenth century, between King John and France. In this war, King John lost all his French possessions, including Normandy. So, in 1204, when they were given the choice, Channel Islanders elected to owe their allegiance to the English throne and break their ancient tie with France. Centuries later, an English monarch who had good cause to be grateful to the continued loyalty of his Jersey subjects, was Charles II. During the English Civil War, knowing himself to be safe from Parliament's troops, he twice took refuge in Elizabeth Castle, first as Prince of Wales and then as the proclaimed but still exiled King of England.

This change in allegiance, however, put Jersey in a vulnerable position for the perpetual hostilities between England and France continued right up to the nineteenth century. Not only was the island in danger because of its own proximity to the French mainland, but also as the first line of defence against a French invasion of England. So fortifications against the French can be seen all round the island. Mont Orgueil Castle, by the order of King John himself, was built in the thirteenth century to guard the approaches to the island's east coast; Elizabeth Castle, named after Elizabeth I, was started in the sixteenth century to defend the growing town of St Helier. The various towers round the coast were part of the defence against a much-feared French invasion between 1778 and the Napoleonic Wars.

These defences were, however, penetrated by the French on several occasions. In 1461 French troops seized, through the treachery of a Jersey man, Mont Orgueil Castle itself and from it ruled the island with great severity for 7 years. In 1781 an expedition, led by the French adventurer, de Rullecourt, landed at La Rocque one January night and marched as far as the Royal Square without a shot being fired against them. It was only the bravery of Major Peirson, an officer of the English garrison stationed in Jersey at the time, that prevented a further French occupation.

The most modern fortifications to be seen all over the island are German. They date back to World War II when the only part of Great Britain to be occupied by the Nazis was the Channel Islands — after Churchill decided they could not be defended and declared them demilitarised. The bunkers and the gun emplacements were constructed on Hitler's orders to make Jersey part of an impregnable fortress against the enemy — the British. Some of them, together with the German Underground Hospital, are open to the public who want to know more about the almost 5 years of German occupation, when the islanders suffered such great deprivation, and came near to starvation before the long-awaited Liberation Day, 9 May, 1945.

No survey of Jersey's history, however brief, would be complete without considering the important part religion has always played in the lives of the islanders. Until the sixteenth century all the parish churches and the various chantry chapels built round the island were, with those in the rest of Western Europe, Roman Catholic. Such ecclesiastical items as the holy water stoups to be found just inside the door of several churches and chapels, date back to this time, together with the place names which commemorate where wayside crosses once stood. There are, for example, four roads called La Rue de la Croix, as well as a Le Mont ès Croix.

At the time of the Reformation, when some Catholics wished to return to the simple faith of the early Church, these protestors were often persecuted by the Roman Catholic Church and burnt. Many of the French protestors, known as Huguenots, fled to Jersey for safety and introduced a very strict form of Protestantism — Calvinism. This, backed up by various royal injunctions from England to destroy all objects of so-called Catholic superstition, turned every parish church and surviving chapel into an austere whitewashed Huguenot temple.

For nearly a hundred years, until the mid-seventeenth century, Calvinism was the state religion of Jersey and its most dominant characteristic — discipline — is said by some still to be evident in the island today. Those who rebelled against the strict régime for whatever reason were often labelled as witches and one of the most serious blots on the island's history is the series of witch trials which took place in the sixteenth and seventeenth centuries, the worst year being 1648. The punishment for witchcraft was burning, but Jersey judges were more merciful than their Guernsey counterparts in that the victims of their death sentence were strangled first. Their bodies were burnt in what is now the Royal Square in St Helier.

The next important factor to affect the religious life of the island was a visit in 1787 by the founder of Methodism, John Wesley. Methodism had already been introduced to the island 4 years earlier, but it was given tremendous impetus by the preaching of Wesley in what is now the United Club at the west end of the Royal Square. Two chapels, which testify by their size to the importance of Methodism in the island are the tall chapel on the border of St John and St Helier at Sion, and the largest place of worship in the whole island, Wesley Grove in St Helier. It is interesting to note that nonconformist, Church of England and Roman Catholic services were, with one or two exceptions, taken in French until the present century.

The Government of Jersey

A fact of which all islanders are justifiably proud is that Jersey's internal affairs have never been administered by Parliament in Westminster. Jersey has, since the time of King John, always had independent home rule, while larger issues, such as the ratification of laws and foreign policy, are dealt with by the Queen and her Privy Council. The important link between the island and the United Kingdom is through the Crown. Its two representatives in Jersey are the Bailiff — a Jerseyman who usually comes to the office through the island's legal system — and the Lieutenant-Governor, a member of the British Armed Forces, whose term of appointment is 5 years. The Bailiff takes precedence in the States Assembly, the island's government, and the Royal Court, the island's supreme court, while the Lieutenant-Governor, who is the island's commander-in-chief, takes precedence elsewhere.

The States, when in session, normally sit in their chamber in the Royal Square every Tuesday and their debates can be heard from the public gallery. The fifty-three honorary members, under the presidency of the Bailiff, comprise twelve Senators, the twelve parish Constables and twenty-nine Deputies — all elected on non-party political platforms to serve terms of office from 3 to 6 years. From their number committees are drawn up to put forward policies on such aspects of island life as education, finance, social security and tourism. Once approved by the States, their directives are carried out by a staff of civil servants.

The Royal Court, the island's court of justice, is made up of the Bailiff and twelve honorary, elected judges, known as Jurats. They hear the civil and criminal cases brought before them, which are of too serious a nature to be dealt with by the magistrate's court, in the Royal Court Chamber in the Royal Square. The Royal Court is also the island's final court of appeal. Anyone wishing to take his case further has then to ask leave to appeal to the judicial committee of the Privy Council. Two interesting traditions dating back to Norman times are that Jersey juries for assize cases number twenty-four — though that is in the process of being changed — and that the passing of contracts for the buying and selling of property is still conducted in French. Stipendiary magistrates, members of the legal profession, preside over the police and petty debts courts. Visitors may attend the sittings of the Royal Court but it is not generally open to visitors.

Local as opposed to central government in Jersey is administered through the Parish Assembly in each of the twelve parishes. It is presided over by the Connétable, or Constable, the most important man in the parish, whose honorary elected position dates back at least to the fifteenth century. Its members include Centeniers, Vingteniers, the Constable's Officers, and the Procureurs de Bien Publique, who decide such matters within the parish boundaries as finance, rates, parking and the social welfare of their parishioners.

The Constable also heads the non-uniformed honorary police force in his parish — the Centeniers, Vingteniers and Constable's Officers — but is in no way the equivalent of an English constable. The Centeniers carry a warrant and have the power to order an enquiry into traffic accidents and institute criminal proceedings. So, for example, should a visitor be involved in an infringement of the traffic regulations outside St Helier, the incident could be dealt with on the spot by the honorary police of the parish where it took place, or at a subsequent parish hall enquiry.

Centeniers are helped in their duties by the Vingteniers and Constable's Officers and work in close conjunction with the island's uniformed police force who have their headquarters in Rouge Bouillon, St Helier.

Trade and Industry

Islanders have never relied on one main source of income. The Jerseyman is nothing if not flexible and has turned his hand to many trades over the centuries, a number of which have left a permanent mark on the island.

One of the first outlets for the Jerseyman's initiative and enterprise was, naturally, fishing. The main catch in the Middle Ages was the conger eel. This was caught locally, salted and then sold to the Catholics on the continent for their fish-only-Fridays and other fast days. Conger eels continue to be displayed, often in their traditional tail-in-mouth way, in St Helier's fish market and conger eel soup remains a popular dish with many Jersey families.

From the seventeenth century onwards, a more complicated trading pattern emerged. Many a young Jerseyman would first plough and sow his land in Jersey and then sail a mixed cargo across the Atlantic to Newfoundland. Once there he would fish for cod and sell it salted in South America or Spain, finally sailing home with a cargo such as the much prized mahogany from Brazil. Many of the island's fine Georgian houses were built with the wealth accrued by these adventurous Newfoundland fishermen and are still known today as 'cod houses'.

From fishing in boats to actually building them was a natural progression and for 50 years, 1820-70, Jersey was, incredible as it may seem, one of the most important ship building areas in the British Isles. Memorials to the busy shipyards which proliferated all along the south coast from Gorey to St Aubin can be found along the fronts at Gorey and Havre des Pas. One of the rope walks where the ropes for the rigging used to be made — parallel to Green Street in St Helier — still bears the name Rope Walk, and several buildings are called 'Sail Loft' to this day.

From the mid-seventeenth century, byproducts of all this nautical activity were smuggling and privateering. False bottoms to boats, for instance, helped hide many an illicit cargo of tobacco, wine or brandy; while letters-of-marque in times of war enabled even Jersey fishing smacks to become auxiliary boats of the British Navy. Under this cover, Jerseymen patrolled the English Channel to capture enemy ships with impunity and kept their cargoes as a well earned prize. Several island families were able to increase their wealth and social status through this legalised piracy!

Apart from the fishing, the main local industry in the sixteenth to seventeenth centuries was the knitting of stockings by both sexes. At its peak about 6,000 pairs of stockings were exported in a week; while a sad footnote in history records that at her execution Mary Queen of Scots was wearing stockings 'with silver about the clocks and white jersey under them'. The knitted woollen shirt that took its name from the island, gained popularity later, particularly among fishermen. The traditional 'Jersey', which, unlike its Guernsey counterpart, has an anchor incorporated in a front panel under the neck, is on sale in most clothing shops, in bright colours as well as the usual navy blue.

Agriculture, because of the island's productive soil, has always been a way of life for islanders. They have also been able to keep the land in good heart through the extensive use of a natural fertiliser—seaweed, known locally as vraic.

The strong centre of the farming scene has been and still is the Jersey cow, famous for its high milk yield and ability to adapt to different climates. Records show that it was exported as early as 1700, but the real peak of the island's cattle trade was in the 1850s. Now there are herds of the pure Jersey all over the world. Certainly the gentle Jersey, with its beautifully marked eyes, not only provides all the milk, butter and cream that islanders need but is one of the island's attractions. The various parish and island cattle shows retain their popularity with locals and visitors alike.

On the arable side of farming, crops have varied over the centuries. In the seventeenth century it was apples for the lucrative cider trade — to such an extent that one writer in 1682 thought that the island was in danger of becoming one huge orchard. Although most of the orchards have now gone, the high banks surrounding many fields go back to that time, as they were originally built up as windbreaks to protect the apple trees. Also part of the industry were the large circular stone apple crushers which now ornament several large gardens and farmyards.

The potato was the next money-spinner — quite by accident. In 1880 a Mr de la Haye cut a freak potato with sixteen eyes into pieces and planted them. In the spring of 1881 up came large kidney-shaped potatoes, and, most importantly, they were ready for sale much earlier than the normal potato crop. They were given the name Royal Jersey Flukes and, ever since their discovery, it has been the aim of every Jersey farmer who grows them to get them to the English markets as early in the spring as possible — before other types grown by competitors. Visitors to the island in March and April will notice how the farmers' efforts include covering whole fields with sheets of transparent polythene — a stranger sight from the air than through a gap in the hedge!

With the potatoes in the ground only half the year, tomatoes make an excellent second crop. These can be seen ripening on the *côtils*, the steeply sloping hillsides, throughout the summer, attached in their rows to wooden cross supports. Farmers with glasshouses grow tomatoes during the winter too, so that they can be exported throughout the year.

Since 1945, more new crops have been tried, two of the most successful being flowers and calabrese, both of which can be seen growing, together with cauliflowers, courgettes and parsley, all over the island. In fact, there are still 534 farms and glasshouse units in Jersey, with twenty-five holdings having a St Helier address — statistics which give Jersey her continuing rural charm.

Today's boom industry, however, is tourism. Until 1824, crossing the Channel to get to Jersey from the English mainland was a hazardous business. In that year, however, two rival companies started a weekly steamship service, one from Southampton, the other from Portsmouth, and the influx of holiday visitors began. Then in 1937 the airport in the parish of St Peter was opened and an alternative route to the island developed. Now over a million visitors each year choose Jersey for their holidays and new or extended hotels and guest houses to accommodate them all continue to proliferate. The island is also attracting more people in the out-of-season months, who see Jersey as an ideal conference centre, with all the up-to-date specialist facilities, together with an island-based conference bureau as co-ordinator.

The island's latest source of revenue and an important contributor to its present state of affluence is the finance industry. It is the growing source of both income and employment, providing a wide range of job opportunities for Jersey's school leavers each year and equalling tourism in its contribution to the island's buoyant economy. Unlike the agricultural and tourist industries, whose main trading partner is the UK, the finance industry is now wholly international in its dealings, which is to Jersey's further advantage. So yet again the island is shown as adapting to and taking advantage of the business opportunities being presented in the last decade of the twentieth century.

Useful Information for the Visitor

To find examples of the island's sturdy independence one need look no further than its money, highway code, media, social security and postage stamps.

Currency
The island, although using the sterling denominations of pounds and pence, has its own distinctive currency which is only legal tender in the Channel Islands. UK currency is also accepted everywhere in the island. The pound note is still retained here and depicts St Helier Parish Church, the £10 note Copley's famous illustration of the 1781 Battle of Jersey, while on the 10p piece is the Faldouet Dolmen. Commemorative coins are also minted for special events, such as the £2 coin for the twenty-fifth anniversary of the World Wildlife Fund. For further information contact The States Treasury, Cyril Le Marquand House, The Parade, St Helier ☎ 603000.

Highway Code
There are two major points from Jersey's highway code for visiting drivers to remember. The first is that the MAXIMUM SPEED LIMIT IS 40MPH. Lower speed limits apply on certain stretches of road in built-up areas. The second applies in the case of an accident. The duties of any driver involved in an accident are threefold:

1 To stop immediately.
2 To leave the vehicle where it has stopped, unless given police permission to remove it.
3 To notify the police or, in a country area, the nearest local Centenier, whose name can be found at the front of the telephone directory.

Riders of motor cycles or mopeds are required by law to wear a helmet and anyone on the road coming across the sign 'Filter in Turn' should negotiate the junction in turn with other vehicles in joining or crossing any stream of traffic. A yellow line across the road at a junction is a stop sign; it indicates entry to a main road. Where there is a single yellow line parallel to the kerb or roadside, parking is prohibited AT ALL TIMES.

Jersey's Flag and Arms

With Jersey having so many of its services to the public administered locally, with distinctively island features, it is not surprising that the island also has its own flag. This is a red saltire on a white background to which has been added the Jersey arms surmounted by the Plantagenet crown. This has flown from island flagstaffs on festive and important occasions, together with the Union Jack, for over 200 years.

Jersey's arms, which often appear on public buildings and smaller items, such as tourism information and coins, are the three royal leopards. They originate from the seal granted to the Bailiwick by Edward I in 1279, a replica of the armorial bearings of every English monarch since Richard I, still to be seen on today's royal standard.

Newspapers, Television & Radio

The *Jersey Evening Post* is published every day except Sunday and is on sale from about 3.30pm on weekdays and noon on Saturdays at all newsagents. As well as reporting the local news and giving a summary of national and international news, its other daily features include the weather, times of high and low tides, together with the evening's programme of listening and viewing on radio and television. The Friday and Saturday editions of the *JEP*, as it is known locally, carry the times of the next Sunday's religious services and the Saturday edition 'The Island Diary' — a synopsis of 'What's On' for the following week.

Channel Television is the smallest station in the Independent Broadcasting Authority's network and has four local news and weather reports: at 9.50am, 1.05pm, 6pm and 10.30pm. It also relays local features from time to time. Channel Television is located on the ITV waveband and starts broadcasting at 5.30am, carrying on throughout the day.

Radio Jersey, BBC local radio, has the highest listener population ratio of any of the UK local stations. It broadcasts on VHF 88.8 mHz and 1,026 kHz (292m) and its main programmes are 'Jersey Today' 7-10am, followed on weekdays by the 'Morning Magazine', 'Jersey at One' and finally 'Jersey at Five'. Its programmes include the international, national and local news, the local weather and shipping forecasts, tide times, together with an extensive list of 'What's On' round the island. 'Morning Thought' is broadcast each weekday after 7.30am and the 'Service on Sunday' after 7.45am. A rare listening pleasure is the short 'Lettre Jerriaise', broadcast in Jersey Norman-French by one of the local speakers, every Sunday morning shortly before 9.30am. Channel 103.7 FM radio has special holiday 'What's On' at 9.30am and 4.30pm daily.

Medical Care

The island's social security system only affects visitors who are in need of medical attention. Accidents and emergencies can be dealt with at the Casualty Department of the General Hospital in St Helier, free of charge. There is also an Open Morning Clinic at the hospital during the summer months from 9am-12noon, Saturdays 10-12noon, where treatment given by local GPs is also free and where the clinic's prescriptions can be dispensed at the hospital pharmacy at £1.50 per item. OTHERWISE VISITS TO DOCTORS' OR DENTISTS' SURGERIES AND PRESCRIPTIONS DISPENSED IN LOCAL CHEMISTS HAVE TO BE PAID FOR IN FULL.

Parking

Payment for parking in St Helier is by Pay Card (20p, 60p or £1.20) at 20p per hour 8am-5pm Monday-Saturday. Pay Cards are valid in car parks where the special sign is displayed. Parking disks are available for other areas on the outskirts of the town, but visitors are best advised to use one of the ten public car parks in St Helier if they wish to spend any length of time in the shopping centre.

Disabled drivers can obtain Orange Badges for special parking facilities from the Town Hall (☎ 25251). A copy of Jersey's highway code and other information can be obtained from the Motor Traffic Department, La Collette, St Helier ☎ 22431.

Postage Stamps

Jersey has also been issuing its own postage stamps since 1969 and these are much admired and widely collected by philatelists. The commemoratives have portrayed famous Jersey personalities such as actress Lillie Langtry, artist Edmund Blampied and golfer Harry Vardon. The current definitive stamps depict local scenes. 'Europa' is a popular theme, in which contemporary art was a recent subject. The philatelic display and sales counter at the Main Post Office, Broad Street, St Helier is open 9am-5pm (earlier closing on Saturdays) ☎ 26262. It should be noted that JERSEY STAMPS MUST BE USED ON ALL OUTGOING MAIL.

Telephone Numbers

Airport Directory 1819
Daily Diary 1882
Fort Regent daily events 1887
Special Events 1886
Weather Jersey 06966 0011
Weather Shipping 06966 0022

Facilities for the Holidaymaker

Jersey is not just an island for basking on the beach in the sun, attractive and varied as its beaches are, for there are so many other activities on offer for the holidaymaker to enjoy.

Indoors

Art exhibitions are held in several places in the island and, in the summer, even in the Royal Square itself. Plays and concerts — from classical to pop — are held in the large Gloucester Hall in Fort Regent, the Opera House which dates back to 1900, or the recently built Benjamin Meaker Theatre in the Arts Centre.

The island's two cinemas often feature top pre-release films at the same time as West End openings, with tickets at a fraction of London prices. Many restaurants and pubs have live entertainment, so there are plenty of opportunities to enjoy an evening watching a cabaret turn, joining in a sing-along, taking part in a talent contest or listening to country, Western or folk music. There are also venues for discos and ballroom dancing. Public house opening hours are from 9am-11.30pm, with Sunday opening from 11am-1pm and 4.30-11.30pm.

For book lovers, the two adult libraries, one in St Helier, the other in St Brelade, together with the children's library in St Helier, will lend books to visitors on payment of a returnable deposit. They open at 9.30am and close 5.30pm Monday, Wednesday and Thursday, Tuesday 7.30pm, Friday 8pm, Saturday 4pm.

Out of Doors

To begin with, there are all the water sports from sailing to scuba diving, with wind surfing and surfing two of the most popular. Fishing can be carried on the whole year with, for example, pollock to be caught when sea temperatures are at their lowest in January, February and March; ling, prolific in high summer; and large size mackerel among many other fish to be caught in the last 3 months of the year. For freshwater fishermen there are opportunities for both fly and coarse fishing.

Sea bathing in Jersey is a great attraction, and it is the most varied in the British Isles. However, moderate swimmers and more especially non-swimmers should exercise reasonable care so as to ensure complete safety when bathing. The following bays are suggested for:

Non-Swimmers. Grève d'Azette, St Catherine, St Clement, St Aubin, Grouville, St Brelade and Anne Port.

Moderate Swimmers. The bays mentioned plus Fliquet, Bonne Nuit, Rozel, Grève de Lecq, Bouley, Plémont, Giffard and Portelet.

Strong Swimmers. All the bays previously mentioned, plus St Ouen.

The last mentioned is unequalled for its surf bathing but, owing to the undercurrent, experienced swimmers only should engage in this sport.

Bathing is dangerous when the red cone is flying; safe bathing area is between red and yellow flags.

The coastline of Jersey experiences one of the largest movements of tide recorded in the world. The vertical rise of tide between low water mark and high water mark during periods of spring tides can be as much as 40ft. During the third and fourth hours of a rising spring tide, the rate of rise can be as much as 2in per minute. These large tides cause strong tidal currents around the coastline and adjacent waters and care must be exercised by visitors when swimming or exploring the rocky foreshore, although of course, the bays indicated are quite safe for the type of swimming mentioned.

The Tourism Committee employ a fully professional team of Beach Guards, who man the modern life saving centre at St Ouen's Bay, and also keep watch at St Brelade's Bay, Plémont and West Park, maintaining constant communication with HQ by means of radio telephone. Beach Guard Service, St Ouen's Bay (June to mid-September) ☎ 482032; Plémont Bay (June to end September only) ☎ 481636.

Land sports include golf, tennis, climbing, horse-riding and walking. There are two 18-hole golf clubs for visitors who are members of a recognised golf club, two public golf courses, and three venues where mini-golf can be enjoyed. There are sixteen public hard tennis courts, three bowling clubs, a newly formed climbing association, plus at least four riding stables which welcome visitors. Cliff paths for the keen walker stretch from Grosnez Castle in the north-west to Rozel in the north-east — a stretch of more than 20 miles.

For those interested in history there are several museums, two castles, a couple of manor houses and German Occupation relics to be visited, as well as guided tours to be joined.

For the nature lover there are the natural flora and fauna of the island to enjoy, from the yellow lent-lilies (*Narcissus pseudo-narcissus*) in the spring to the pink Jersey lily (*Amaryllis belladonna*) in the autumn, while the cliff tops are covered in yellow gorse for most of the year. To the west of the island there is Kempt Tower with all the information about the island's only designated conservation area, Les Mielles, a sand dune landscape of ecological importance; to the north-east there are the exotic, richly perfumed orchid blooms of the Eric Young Foundation Centre. In the spring, bird watchers can see brent geese feeding on the water's edge and in the woods hear or catch sight of a blackcap or greater spotted woodpecker. Puffins, shags and fulmars can be spotted on inaccessible cliff ledges along the north coast. For visitors who just prefer sitting, there are several public parks, including Howard Davis

Park in St Saviour, where visiting bands play during the summer months.

Shopping

Shopping on holiday never seems to be the rushed chore it is back home and this is particularly true for visitors to Jersey. St Helier has a fine shopping precinct as well as quaint back streets where there is a wide range of goods and services — all VAT free. Jewellery and perfume are especially good buys and there are plenty of places to get those holiday snaps printed. There are also the covered Central Market in Halkett Place and the Fish Market in Beresford Street to wander round. The flowers, the umbrellas of the cafés, the benches set out at regular intervals, all give St Helier a leisured, continental air and make it a pleasurable centre for shopping.

Disabled Toilets

Disabled toilets have Rador locks. For £5 deposit keys can be borrowed from St Helier Town Hall ☎ 25251.

Transport

Access to Jersey

Access to Jersey itself from the British mainland is frequent and direct from most of the major airports during the summer months. Ferry services operate from Weymouth and Poole. Details of charter flights, winter breaks, package holidays, hotels, guest houses, self-catering accommodation and camping facilities can be obtained from any UK travel agent or by applying direct to Tourism, Weighbridge, St Helier (☎ [0534] 500700). For details of conference facilities contact the Conference Bureau, Weighbridge, St Helier (☎ 500700).

By Air

Direct passenger services to the island are available from the following places in the UK:-

Aberdeen, Belfast, Birmingham, Blackpool, Bournemouth, Bristol, Cambridge, Cardiff, Coventry, East Midlands, Edinburgh, Exeter, Glasgow, Humberside, Leeds/Bradford, Liverpool, London/Heathrow, London/Gatwick, Luton, Manchester, Manston, Newcastle, Norwich, Plymouth, Southampton, Southend, Stansted, Staverton, Teeside

By Sea

British Channel Island Ferries from Poole.
Condor from Weymouth
Torbay Seaways from Torquay (cars can be carried on all ferries).
Further details can be obtained from travel agents.

In the Island

Getting about the island for visitors who do not bring their own car is no problem. Not only are there several car hire firms but rates are low and petrol cheaper than on the mainland. Most car hire operators are also prepared, at no extra cost, to deliver the hired car to the visitor at the airport, harbour or hotel and collect it from there at the end of the holiday.

Otherwise there are taxis available at the harbour, the airport and at the taxi ranks in St Helier at Broad Street, Snow Hill and the Weighbridge, or there is public transport. The Jersey Motor Transport Company provides an all island bus service from the Weighbridge, St Helier (☎ 21201) with buses to and from the airport every 15 minutes during the season. A bus timetable is available from the enquiry desk at the Weighbridge bus station.

Moped and motor cycles, including helmets, can also be hired, but perhaps the best way of exploring Jersey is to hire a bicycle. This is simple, inexpensive and a marvellous way to have a healthy holiday.

The names, addresses and phone numbers of all the many car and cycle hire firms, together with the taxi firms can be found in the Yellow Pages of the Jersey Telephone Directory.

Day Trips from Jersey

Jersey is such an attractive holiday resort, that it might seem strange to mention a day away from it, but one of its further attractions is its proximity to the other Channel Islands and to France. There are frequent sea and air trips to Guernsey, from where the smaller islands of Herm and Sark can be reached. There are also boats and hydrofoil trips to Herm and Sark and Alderney from Jersey, and a direct Aurigny flight to Alderney, the only one of the smaller islands to have an airport.

France can be reached either from Gorey Harbour, to Normandy, or from St Helier Harbour to St Malo and Brittany, while Cherbourg is only 20 minutes flying time away. Visitors should remember, however, that PASSPORTS ARE NOW ESSENTIAL FOR GOING TO FRANCE — even on a day trip. Currency, though, is no problem, as sterling can be changed into French francs at any of the main clearing banks or bureaux de change in Jersey.

Information about inter-island travel and trips to France can be obtained from any travel agent, or any of the addresses below:

Jersey Airport St Peter ☎ 46111

Aurigny Air Services, Weighbridge, St Helier ☎ 35733, 43568

Ferry Centre Travel, 5 Esplanade. Ticket reservations for all car ferries ☎ 26452.

Emeraude Ferries, Albert Quay, St Helier ☎ 66566, 856792 (Gorey only)

Commodore Shipping (Hydrofoil), 28 Conway Street, St Helier ☎ 71263

1 ST HELIER

Around St Helier

(Bus Town Services 18, 19, 20)

Despite its present size and importance as the capital of Jersey, St Helier was not always the centre of island affairs as it is today. For one thing, the island's only castle in medieval times was Gorey Castle, in the parish of St Martin, and from it the island was governed for several centuries; for another, the most sheltered and easily accessible port was at St Aubin, in the parish of St Brelade, while St Helier harbour was not completed as a commercial port until well into the last century.

The earliest settlement in the eastern corner of St Aubin's Bay, probably in the sixth century, was on a marshy plain between Mont Millais in the east, Westmount in the west and Mont au Prêtre in the north. The settlement also included the rocky outcrop jutting out into the sea towards the south-east, where Fort Regent now stands. The whole area was named after the saint who for 15 years lived the life of a hermit on the small islet just south of this marshy coast, whose martyrdom has given the present town its emblem of two axes.

Many legends have been told about St Helier himself, but it is known that he was born in Tongres in Belgium and that he came to Jersey in about AD540. It is said that his pagan parents had named him Helibert, but that after he had been cured of paralysis at the age of 7 by the Christian missionary Cunibert, he was called Helier, which means pity, because God had obviously taken pity on him.

When Helier grew up, he served as a missionary under St Marculf who had a Christian centre at Nanteuil and it was St Marculf who suggested that Helier came to live and preach in Jersey. When Helier arrived, the settlement on the marsh numbered only about thirty people, probably mostly fishermen, and he decided to minister to their spiritual needs from a small cell he built on a high rock about a mile-and-a-half from the coast, quite surrounded by the sea at high tide and reached at low tide by a natural causeway. The site of the cell, and the oratory afterwards built on L'Islet, is known today as the **Hermitage Rock**.

Tradition has it that from that natural vantage point of his hermit's cell, St Helier was able for 15 years, with God's help, to keep marauding Norman raiders from attacking and stealing from his small flock. At last,

22

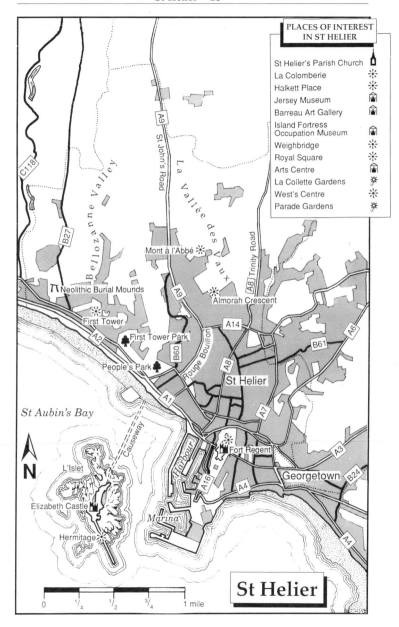

PLACES OF INTEREST IN ST HELIER

St Helier's Parish Church
La Colomberie
Halkett Place
Jersey Museum
Barreau Art Gallery
Island Fortress Occupation Museum
Weighbridge
Royal Square
Arts Centre
La Collette Gardens
West's Centre
Parade Gardens

St Helier

however, the legend tells of how in that fifteenth year, some of the Norman raiders, despite being blown out to sea by an offshore wind through the prayers of Helier, did manage to land. When they saw Helier praying alone on the seashore they swung their axes against him and cut off his head.

In Helier's memory, St Marculf founded a monastery on the islet where he had lived for the 15 years of his ministry — where Elizabeth Castle now stands. Today, in memory of St Helier, a pilgrimage — led by the dean and clergy of Jersey and the Constable of St Helier — is made on the Sunday nearest to 16 July, tide permitting, to the Hermitage Rock and any visitor is welcome to join.

The history of L'Islet 400 years after St Helier's death is a chequered one, because in another Norman raid in the tenth century the monastery of St Helier founded by St Marculf was sacked and destroyed. It remained in ruins until a wealthy man in Normandy, in whose dukedom Jersey then was, decided in about 1125 to build an abbey in its place. Fifty years or so later the abbey was demoted to become a priory but still had to pay revenues to Normandy. A priory it remained until Henry V of England (for by this time Jersey owed allegiance to the English Crown) confiscated all property belonging to priories held by foreigners. Without its wealth, which had been considerable, the priory could not carry on and soon fell into disrepair.

When Queen Elizabeth's military engineer, Paul Ivy, came to Jersey in 1594 to update the island's defences, he immediately saw L'Islet with its ruined priory as the obvious site for a new castle. When it was completed in about 1600, official documents named it the New Castle; local inhabitants called it Le Château de L'Islet; today it is known simply as **Elizabeth Castle**. So any of the thousands of holidaymakers who visit it every year are not only looking over a sixteenth-century castle but are also walking over the site — in the great courtyard of the castle — of a Christian centre which remained an important force for the religious instruction and secular organisation of islanders for over 400 years.

There are two ways to get to Elizabeth Castle, both starting from the slipway at West Park. One is to walk the mile-long causeway from the slipway which is dry enough to use for about 5 hours between high tides; the second is to use the regular amphibious DUKW service. A bell is rung half an hour before the causeway is due to be covered, which can be by as much as 15ft of water on a high spring tide, to warn walkers to start back.

The first gate of Elizabeth Castle the visitor passes through is guarded on the west side by Fort Charles and on the east by the northeast bastion.

The bell in the belfry above the gate is the one which gives half an hour's warning of the incoming tide. The turnstile for admission to the castle just inside the gate is housed in the old port guard house.

Hermitage, L'Islet

The second gate leads to the first of the three sections into which the castle is divided — the outer ward. This owes much of its strength to the fact that the castle's original builders made good use of the rocks that projected naturally round the edge of the narrow islet, thereby also giving the sentries guarding the landward side of the castle an uninterrupted view of its walls right round to the central lower ward. Within the outer ward, around the green, were erected, in the 1700s, such necessary buildings to a garrison force as a lime-kiln, stables, workshops, general store and even a hospital.

The castle's third gate leads from the outer ward to the more important lower ward. Here are the barracks, the officers' quarters, the canteen and cook houses, the early eighteenth-century gymnasium, now a militia museum, storerooms and the seventeenth-century magazine, in the south-west corner of the ward. Visitors will also notice the huge iron water storage tanks which were the only way to ensure a fresh supply of water for the garrison before 1874, when a mains water pipe from the town was finally laid.

The iron gate, with its typical Jersey granite arch, the fourth gate through which the visitor passes, leads to the oldest part of the castle, the upper ward, the only part of the rock fortified by Ivy, Queen Elizabeth's chief engineer. This was originally guarded in Elizabethan times by fifteen cannon. The fifth and final gate, named after the Queen, is arguably the most architecturally perfect of them all. Visitors can see not just the coat of arms of the English Queen on the gate but also, to the left, the arms of Jersey's Governor from 1590-1600, Sir Anthony Poulet. For in the upper ward or keep was built the Governor's house, first lived in by Sir Walter Raleigh, when he was the island's Governor from 1600 until 1603, after which he was deprived of his governorship by James II and imprisoned in the Tower of London. Now this typically seventeenth-century Jersey granite house is where visitors can see tableaux depicting some of the famous events which took place in the castle during the several centuries of its development.

There was the seige of the newly-enlarged castle during the English Civil War when, in 1643, the Parliamentary Lieutenant-Governor Major Lydcott unsuccessfully besieged the Royalist Sir Philippe de Carteret. Three years later, the fleeing Prince of Wales, later to become Charles II, took refuge in the castle from his father's enemies for 10 weeks. He returned to Jersey as the newly proclaimed king in 1649, staying 20 weeks. After the restoration of the monarchy, Charles gave land in America to Sir George Carteret as an expression of his regard for his loyalty to him and his father. This land was named New Jersey.

Whilst Charles was in the castle, eleven people suffering from the skin complaint scrofula went for a healing session in the old abbey church where, it was said that just a touch from King Charles and the words 'May God heal thee' cured them of their disease immediately.

*Elizabeth Castle
Museum*

CHARLES Ⅱ

GEORGE CARTERET

Then for the 9 years between 1651 and 1650, Royalist sympathisers had to lie low in Jersey, for the island Governors who lived in Elizabeth Castle during that time were all Cromwell's men. The castle's next excitement was over a hundred years later, when the French adventurer, de Rullecourt, invaded Jersey in 1781. As he rode out with his forces from St Helier and along the causeway to demand the surrender of the castle, the only reply he got was cannon fire, one ball amputating the leg of one of his officers. So de Rullecourt wisely decided to retire. With the victory of Major Peirson later in the day, no further action from the castle was needed.

The breakwater which joins the upper ward to the Hermitage Rock and St Helier's Oratory was a nineteenth-century attempt to give the town of St Helier a proper harbour. The arm which juts out nearly 700yd further into the sea was designed to meet a similar arm from La Collette. But as this was smashed by south-westerly gales 3 years running, the whole idea of the new harbour was eventually abandoned.

When the Germans occupied Jersey, 1940-5, Elizabeth Castle had its final reconstruction as a fortress. Visitors will notice in the outer ward the concrete base in the centre of Fort Charles' tower where a gun was positioned, and the underground shelter near the hospital; in the lower ward, the machine gun and searchlight post on the green bastion, together with the one gun casemate, for which part of the eighteenth-century canteen was demolished. In the upper ward no-one can fail to notice the concrete fire-control tower which is so ill-matched with the seventeenth-century keep, the original of the castle which Sir Walter Raleigh proudly named 'Fort Isabella Bellissima', the 'castle of Elizabeth the most beautiful'.

Such have been the efforts in recent years to restore this historic monument set so magnificently in St Aubin's Bay that in 1987 Elizabeth Castle was awarded a Civic Trust commendation. So holidaymakers will find a visit not only enjoyable but informative as well. There is, for example, an exhibition called 'Granite and Gunpowder', plus an audio-visual presentation, which traces the whole 400-year-long history of armaments and fortifications used to defend the island, as well as the tableaux with their taped background information. Visitors should be ready, by the way, if in the vicinity of the castle at noon to put their hands over their ears — for that is when one of the guns at the castle is fired in a daily salute!

Because of the number of stone steps within the castle precincts, it is unfortunately, not suitable for the disabled to visit.

St Helier has two distinctive natural features, both eventually utilised for its defence: the first, the tiny island over a mile out to sea where, as previously mentioned, a religious community and then a garrison force were housed; and the second, the hill to the south-east which was first known as Le Mont de la Ville, later as the Town Hill, and on whose furze-covered top Neolithic settlers had buried their dead and where later parishioners had the right to graze their sheep.

The military potential of Le Mont de la Ville had been realised as early as 1550, when Henry VIII suggested that the townsfolk set about making a stronghold on the hill in case they needed a refuge if the island should be invaded. But the townsfolk ignored his advice and did nothing. Only after de Rullecourt's invasion in 1781 did parishioners stir themselves. Then they levelled the top of the hill for a drill ground for the St Helier militia and surrounded it with a low wall of turfs, mounted by several guns.

It was while at this defence work that the levellers discovered an extensive passage grave. The 15ft-long covered passage led to thirty upright stones surrounding five large cells, each one with its own capstone. The Governor of Jersey in 1785, when this archaeological find was made, was General Conway and he was so convinced of its importance that he had two scale models made of the grave, one of which can still be seen at Jersey Museum.

The grave itself can no longer be seen — at least not in Jersey. The constructors of the drill ground wanted it out of the way and, since General Conway had shown such considerable interest in it, it was decided to present it to him on his retirement — an eighteenth-century equivalent of 'the golden handshake'! The passage grave still stands on General Conway's property, Park Place, near Henley-on-Thames, in Berkshire, to where it was gradually removed, heavy menhir by heavy capstone.

The proper fortifications of Le Mont de la Ville were only begun after 1804, when the Crown bought Town Hill from that part of St Helier known as Le Vingtaine de la Ville for the then magnificent sum of £11,280. This sum was immediately put away by the thrifty Procureurs and the income from it is still used today for improvements in the town.

One can judge how imminent a French invasion was thought to be at that time, on learning that when General Don was appointed Lieutenant-Governor in 1806, he at once set up a signalling system to give advance warning.

If the French fleet left St Malo, news was to be flashed from a nearby look-out ship to Mont Orgueil, from there to Grosnez and finally, via Sark, to Guernsey, where the British fleet lay in wait. So no wonder that General Don also made haste to lay the foundation stone of the fort that was to guard the southern approaches to St Helier on Le Mont de la Ville. The stone can still be seen above the main entrance and as well as General Don, Lieutentant-Colonel John Humfrey, the fort designer, is also named.

The fort was completed 8 years later, just a year before Napoleon's defeat at Waterloo. It was named after the Prince-Regent, later to become George IV and is still known today, though in quite a different context, as **Fort Regent**. Visitors to it will see how skilfully its builders have used the rock of Le Mont de la Ville to make the fortress impregnable and what a vantage point there is to be had from any of its ramparts. It did not, however, serve the defence purpose for which it was originally built — despite its having the most up-to-date design in fortifications at the time of its building and being continuously garrisoned by units of the British Army until 1927 — until 120 years after its completion. This was when the Germans used Fort Regent as an ordnance depot and sited anti-aircraft guns on its summit to be fired against British and Allied aircraft.

The British government sold Fort Regent back to the States of Jersey in 1958 — for just £3,220 more than they had bought it from St Helier in 1804. Then came the problem of what to do with a Napoleonic fortress which had outlived its usefulness. Nine years later, in 1967, it was decided — after much heated debate — to convert Fort Regent into a leisure centre providing amenities for both residents and tourists. So now, in the unique setting of a nineteenth-century fortification, with panoramic views over the sea and the town, there is a leisure complex that includes everything from concerts and cabarets to swimming and sports and much more besides.

Access to Fort Regent is either by the stone steps in Pier Road for the energetic, or there are lifts and escalators in the adjacent multi-storey car park. In the season (April-October) a road shuttle operates between the fort and Snow Hill from 9.45am to 5.30pm. Here there is a diverse range of leisure facilities and attractions for all ages. Children will love the indoor and outdoor adventure playgrounds, both with sections for the under fives. For the sports enthusiast there is the chance to try something new or to have a game of an old favourite: the range indoors includes bowls, table tennis, snooker, badminton and squash — and there are changing and shower facilities. Those who have come to Jersey to get or keep fit will want to find their way to the weight training and fitness rooms, the swimming pool — a six lane x 33½m indoor heated pool with spring boards, leading to a sun terrace overlooking the sea. There is, by the way, a smaller pool in the swimming complex for young children.

Anyone visiting the pool in January or February may be amazed at the amount of activity surrounding it. This all stems from the fact that over the February half-term weekend the island holds a swimarathon in aid of charity and as about 400 teams of six enter, there are plenty of swimmers of all ages wanting to put in a few practice laps in readiness. This fun event is open to visitors to watch from the gallery and to support as it is in the Guinness Book of Records for its level of fund raising, which is over £70,000.

The Piazza is buzzing with activity, especially from Easter to October when there are live daytime shows for all the family on the Piazza stage. In the rooms around the Piazza there are displays and exhibitions ranging from an aquarium to an exhibition of a German Bunker. The 2,000-seater auditorium of the Gloucester Hall is the venue for some fifteen concerts and shows a year, covering pop, classical and comedy. Three or four exhibitions are staged here, such as the craft fair in September.

As the Gloucester Hall also makes a perfect conference hall — every year Jersey hosts at least one or two conferences of over a 1,000 delegates and several smaller ones — just opposite is the Don Theatre Conference Suite, with a 150-seater audio-visual theatre, plus a room suitable for receptions and another for board meetings. The Don Theatre is where the lottery draw is held every other Thursday.

In between the Piazza and the Gloucester Hall there is the newly developed Queen's Hall which has been built over the former parade ground. This huge area of 27,000sq ft below the dome of the roof provides a wide range of sports and other leisure activities, including a roller skating rink. The Queen's Hall also gives a permanent home to the

Attractions for all the family at Fort Regent

Compton cinema organ which used to be in the now demolished Forum Cinema. To complete the attractions of Queen's Hall, a balcony goes right round it at rampart level with space for exhibitions, lounges and viewing areas.

Outside the fort itself are more attractions for visitors. The World of Fun, open in the season, offers a variety of fairground rides especially popular with youngsters. There is also crazy golf, a play area for children and Quasar, a popular action game with harmless laser guns. More restful is a stroll through the rose garden and the aviaries, or a picnic with a panoramic view over the ramparts.

It is true to say of Fort Regent that there is seldom a week of the year when there is not something special going on — even out of season with such events as the Darts Festival in October. It is also an ideal spot for spending a whole day, as there are bars serving pub meals, snack bars and a restaurant, all within the complex.

It is also an ideal spot for spending a whole day, as there are bars serving pub meals, snack bars and a restaurant, all within the complex. With such a wide variety of interests catered for, from a video on the life-story of Lillie Langtry to children's shows, there is enough here to keep every member of the family happily occupied for hours.

The Town of St Helier

Between the time of St Helier in the sixth century and General Don in the nineteenth, the development of the town was a surprisingly slow one. Until the Middle Ages there was still only a small community of fishermen living near the shore, with two small chapels for worship: the earliest, La Chapelle de la Madelaine, just north-west of where the present parish church is now, and La Chapelle de Notre Dame des Pas on the eastern slope of Le Mont de la Ville, near the sea end of Green Street. The town's turning point only came when the monks of the abbey on L'Islet obtained a royal licence to hold a market in St Helier, where the Royal Square is now.

Then, where the farmers congregated every market day, usually a Saturday, first taverns and then shops were built for their convenience. Later still, the growing St Helier was found to be more central than Gorey for the hearing of court cases, so a primitive Royal Court was built next to the market place. However, there were, in the fourteenth century, still fewer people living in St Helier than in the country parishes of St Saviour, Grouville, St Martin, Trinity or even St Ouen. In 1593 there were still only 300 households in the town.

Until as late as the eighteenth century the extent of St Helier from east to west was marked by its pumps: La Pompe de Bas at Charing Cross and La Pompe du Haut at Snow Hill. To the south of these two landmarks was La Muraille de la Ville, the town wall, built in a vain endeavour to stop sand from the dunes to the south getting into the streets and shops of the town. Behind La Rue du Milieu, now Queen Street, and La Rue de Derrière, now King Street, were only gardens and fields.

An extremely narrow strip of a town and, apparently, none too clean, Sir Walter Raleigh, from his experience of being the island's Governor for 3 years, spoke of St Helier as a 'mean and dirty place'. Eighty years later a special official was appointed to keep the town clean, but still complaints were made about the filthy state of the streets — in which much more than litter was deposited — and about pigs running loose round the Market Place and through the nearby cemetery. The present-day Church Street was called La Rue Trousse Cotillon (Tuck Up Your Petticoat Street) because to go along its dirty length ladies had to tuck up their skirts!

In 1685, when the revocation of the Edict of Nantes meant the persecution of Huguenots in France once more, many fled to French-speaking Jersey and no doubt accounted in some measure for the increase in the population of St Helier to 5-6,000. Another influx of French refugees, this time political, came with the French Revolution, so that by 1800 the population of the town was about 8,000.

Most of the fine, large buildings of the present town, therefore, were not put up and the harbour not built until the last century. In fact, the accessibility and size of St Helier's harbour had a great deal to do with the growth of the town. Only in 1700 was the first small harbour built, known as La Folie and hence the name of the pub that overlooks it; the extensions to it, of the New North Quay and South Pier, came over a hundred years later in 1813. But even these were unable to cope with the great number of Jersey ships involved at this time in the Newfound-land fishing trade, so the States decided to treble the harbour's size. One of the first people to step ashore on the new south pier in 1846 was the young Queen Victoria, and it was named Victoria Pier. Her husband's name of Albert was given to the second, north pier, completed in 1853.

Despite these enlargements of the harbour, the central problem of the town's port still remained — at low tide it had not sufficient water for ships to enter! In fact, when the royal couple landed, Prince Albert asked 'Why do you Jerseymen always build your harbours on dry land?'

In the 1990s there have been further extensions to the harbour to accommodate today's larger container ships and car ferries.

THE MARINA

Already built, for much smaller craft, is the Marina. Conveniently placed in the Upper Harbour, opposite the harbour office, the Marina is, literally, only a few minutes from the town centre.

Opened in 1981, the Marina provides permanent berths for about 180 local craft, leaving 200 berths for visitors. (Approaches to St Helier are described in detail in the following Channel Pilot and Admiralty Charts: 3655,1137 and 3278 refer and visiting craft should keep a listening watch on Channel 14 VHF, *not* Channel M, when approaching.) Once in, visiting crews will find that all their needs are met within the Marina complex. Fresh water is laid on to all pontoons and, providing that there is a suitable point, electric power can be supplied. In a purpose-built amenity block on the New North Quay there are toilets, showers, laundry and telephones. The Marina shop, where a full range of provisions can be bought, is open all year.

During July and August the demand for berths can exceed supply, so it is wise before crossing the sea to Jersey to check by telephone (☎ [0534]79549) or radio to make sure that a berth is available. Advance bookings cannot be made. Once here, visiting yachtmen will receive a warm welcome at either St Helier Yacht Club, on the South Pier, or the Royal Channel Islands Yacht Club, at the Bulwarks, St Aubin.

For those without boats of their own, there are several possibilities. At the kiosk at the north end of the Albert Pier bookings are taken for *Pride of the Bay*. She has a lounge bar, sun and shelter decks and starts to cruise along Jersey's picturesque southern coast at 11.30am and at 2.30pm daily. On Wednesdays there are romantic sunset cruises, starting at 7.30pm.

If you want to go the whole hog and sail a boat of your own why not charter one? Jersey Cruising School and Yacht Charters at the New North Quay, can offer bare-boat charter on a range of quality power or sailing yachts, all equipped to exceptionally high standards. As navigating the strong tidal waters of the Channel Islands calls for a detailed knowledge of the area, an inexperienced visiting yachtsman might prefer to hire the services of an experienced, professional skipper who knows the local waters, who could also give instruction, should this be required. For boating beginners there is a full range of RYA instructional courses. For further information visit the office/classroom on the New North Quay, or ☎ 888100.

For those visitors who like the sea but prefer to stay on *terra firma*, a compromise is to walk the length of the Albert Pier. Here, with the sea on both sides, the manifold activities of the island's only commercial port unfold. Not only do tourists land here in their thousands from the UK and France, but all Jersey's exports and imports arrive here too. The visitor can watch the daily renewal of Jersey's life lines. A harbour scene to marvel at!

SHOPPING IN ST HELIER
Many visitors comment on the town's fresh, clean appearance and they crowd its streets looking for items that are both different from back home and, because VAT does not apply in Jersey, often at least 15 per cent cheaper. St Helier is made even more attractive by the numerous first-class restaurants, inexpensive cafés and snack bars — often with tables outside — and public houses, whose licensing hours are from 9am until 11.30pm daily, and 11am-1pm and 4.30-11.30pm on Sundays. Flagging spirits on shopping sprees are always lifted by the sound of one of the many bands which visit Jersey during summer on their daily march through the town, and by the colourful sight of street entertainers.

Most of St Helier's shops are in the pedestrian precinct of Queen Street and King Street, which runs east from Snow Hill westwards towards Charing Cross. The chief shopping streets coming into the precinct from the north, are — starting at Snow Hill — Bath Street, Halkett Place and New Street. To the south of the precinct are the Royal Square and the States Offices, Conway Street and Broad Street, where there is the General Post Office. There is plenty to delight the visitor, though, who wanders away from the pedestrian precinct and main shopping area to explore the many little byways that go to make up St Helier.

The best bargains to be found in St Helier are perfume, cosmetics, jewellery, cigarettes and tobacco, alcohol, electrical goods, cameras, watches, sports equipment, china and glass — all because they are VAT-free and almost duty-free as well. So the visitors should not be surprised at the number of shops they see specialising solely in cosmetics, toiletries and perfume — all at a fraction of the UK price. Even more noticeable, are the number of shops selling watches and jewellery, again at competitive prices, which fall even lower during the winter, for off-season visitors to take advantage of. Not only is there new as well as antique jewellery on offer in St Helier, but there is at least one jeweller in town, who will make items to suit the customer's own individual requirements.

When it comes to buying clothes, not only will holidaymakers find the shops they are used to in their own High Street on the mainland, but also individual and specialist boutiques for every member of the family. There are plenty of places selling fashionable smart and leisure clothing. There are also two first-rate department stores situated in the pedestrian precinct. Many of the shops in St Helier have been run by Jersey families for several decades, all of them offering friendly service, as well as the best of local, English and Continental goods.

When it comes to hunting for souvenirs or presents, the most popular are those with a local flavour. So look out for silver spoons which bear the parish crest, copper milk cans and churns, miniature reminders of how milk used to be collected on Jersey farms, sets of local coins and stamps. Also available are items made by local artists and craftsmen, such as paintings depicting local scenes, with a starting price as low as £10, pottery, wooden artefacts and the warm oiled-wool sweater, the genuine Jersey.

LEISURE ACTIVITIES

Fitness fanatics and keen sports players are also catered for in St Helier. Snooker and pool can be played at **Funland** on the Esplanade — Jersey's largest family amusement complex, and at the 147 Snooker Club in Wharf Street. Players in the latter must be members, but visitors can join by the day and so enjoy the facilities of the sumptuously furnished lounge, and play on one of the twelve tables. The club also has pool tables and a fully licensed bar with snacks available.

Football fans will enjoy watching the island's principal matches up at Springfield but the event which commands the largest crowds there is the Muratti, a competition between Jersey, Guernsey and Alderney. When the final is held in Jersey, it takes place in early May.

Dining out is a must, as there is so much to tempt both the gourmet and the family who want a cheap meal. Diners will find restaurants specialising in French, Italian, Portuguese, Greek, Chinese, Indian and even Malayan dishes. There are those, too, which offer more traditional English fare, but a feature of most eating places is their use of fresh local produce, such as Jersey Royal potatoes, cauliflower and tomatoes and, in particular, locally caught seafood. Many visitors comment with amazement that their excellent meal has cost them only about half of what a similar meal in the UK would have done.

There are two cinemas, the Odeon in Bath Street, simultaneously showing two programmes nightly, and the Ciné de France in St Saviour's Road — just over the border in the parish of St Saviour — where the latest films can be seen. Live shows can be enjoyed at either the Opera House or the Arts Centre throughout the year, either put on by local artistes or professional UK performers. These range from concerts and cabarets to full length plays.

Other musical events to which visitors are made welcome are the concerts and recitals put on by the Jersey Music Club, once a month from October to May, at the Jersey College for Girls in Rouge Bouillon. For ballroom dancers there is a dance from 8pm till midnight every Thursday at the Royal Hotel, David Place. In spring there is the Jersey Jazz Festival, and in the autumn the Festivals of Folk and Blues and Country Music.

Those who enjoy disco dancing have at least nine discothèques to choose from, all with their own particular brand of night life. Some have restaurants, others have sparky light shows, as well as the latest from the top of the pops. All are lively and just right for the young as well as the young at heart.

Details of where to eat and what to do in St Helier on any night of your holiday can be found in the leisure pages of the *Jersey Evening Post*, which is on sale from mid-afternoon, giving plenty of time to make a choice.

At certain times of the year St Helier is quite transformed. In May there is the month-long Spring Festival, when shops vie with each other in eye-catching shop window displays with a springtime theme and the streets are liable to be filled with morris dancers and brass bands. Also, about this time of the year, is the Good Food Festival, including an

St Helier Marina

Italian street Food Fair as a special feature, with regional food and wine to sample and traditional music to listen to.

Later on comes the Portuguese Food Fair (there is a sizeable population of Portuguese in the island) and then the France-Jersey Festival. This last festival has proved so popular that it has been extended to last more than its original week and during it Wharf Street is closed to create a typical French market. The festival includes concerts of French music at different venues, as well as street theatre — in fact, the whole town is *'en fête'*!

In July and August, flowers are the theme in St Helier. In July is Floral Island Week, during which shops, banks, hotels and private houses and flats in town compete against one another in a floral competition, beautifying St Helier in the process. Then, of course, at the beginning of August is Jersey's Battle of Flowers. The floral floats parade up and down Victoria Avenue, delighting the crowds that line both sides. Even taxis and coaches are decorated on the Thursday of the Battle of Flowers!

Throughout the summer there are bargains to be had in the Hope Street Open Air Market every Saturday.

At the end of the year comes the town's final transformation — at Christmas. A huge tree is placed in the Royal Square, together with a nativity tableau, and the lights and decorations strung across the streets and the precinct make a veritable fairyland of St Helier after dark. Carols are sung in the Royal Square, the market and the pedestrian precinct to complete the yuletide scene.

Tours of St Helier

For those interested in historic places and buildings in St Helier, here are six short tours of the town, each one starting from a different car park, beginning with Green Street in the east and finishing with Patriotic Street in the west. Bus users who come to St Helier's terminus at the Weighbridge (also site of the Tourism Information Centre) can join or walk to the start of any tour from there. In general terms, as has been seen, most of the old buildings in St Helier date only from the nineteenth century, but even where modern shop fronts line the streets a glance above could reveal interesting architecture from another age, often with a distinct French influence. Visitors might also find the tours more useful if they read them first in their hotel or guest house before starting out.

1 GREEN STREET NORTH TO LA COLOMBERIE OR SOUTH TO HAVRE DES PAS

Turning north and then east from the car park just beyond where Green Street makes the fork with Grenville Street, is Green Street cemetery. Not only is this a peaceful place to sit, but it also has a memorial at its southern end to the only St Helier official to be killed in the course of doing his duty. The 25ft-high granite monument was erected by the citizens of St Helier to the memory of Centenier George Le Cronier.

With the Constable's Officer, he had gone on the 28 February 1846 to arrest a couple in Patriotic Street for keeping a house of ill repute. When the two men arrived at the house, only the wife was at home but, as the Centenier was about to arrest her, she suddenly took up a carving knife and thrust it into Le Cronier's stomach. The poor Centenier died from his wound next day and his murderess was banished from the island for life.

There is a short cut from the cemetery into Roseville Street, where there is, to the left, both a post office and a chemist. A walk north up Roseville Street leads to La Colomberie, at the eastern end of which is the famous Howard Davis Park (St Saviour), while a walk south down Roseville Street, past houses with interesting features such as towers, wrought iron balconies, Victorian paving tiles and typically Jersey dormer windows with decorated barge boards, leads directly to the Havre des Pas Swimming Pool and the sea.

La Colomberie, which can be reached via Roseville Street, Green Street or Grenville Street going north from the car park, takes its name from the time when the road was bounded by fields on both sides. The farm on the south side was owned by a family called Coullomp or Coulomb and so it was called in traditional Jersey fashion La Coulomberie, and gave its name to the road which led to it. This was eventually modified to Colombarie. Now virtually every type of small shop and business can be found down this narrow street running from Howard Davis Park into the centre of St Helier.

A couple of interesting architectural details to notice on the way down into the centre of town are both on the right. The first is the exuberant woodwork on the house called St Ives, which sets off the textured granite so splendidly. Both the stained glass and the gold lettering over the front door are typical of the Victorian period when it was built. Further down the road is Colombarie House, opposite the end of Grenville Street, built, as its fine proportions would suggest, at the beginning of the last century. It was originally the home of the Hemery family, distant ancestors of the present-day athlete David Hemery and then housed the Jersey High School for Girls, the Girls' Collegiate School and, lastly, Colombarie House School.

An alternative to turning north from Green Street car park is to turn south and walk down Green Street itself towards the sea. On the right is Jersey's only tunnel road, a continuation of La Route du Fort giving easy access from the south-east to the south-west of the island. Work was started on the short tunnel, which goes from Green Street to the Weighbridge and the harbour area, only shortly after World War II.

Further down the road, after the tunnel and opposite the small row of shops known as Clos des Pas, is a stone commemorating the chapel on the south-eastern slope of Le Mont de la Ville which could have given the area of **Havre des Pas** its name, as it was called La Chapelle de Notre Dame des Pas. Now whether this twelfth-century chapel, demolished in 1814 lest it should give cover to an enemy attacking Fort Regent, was dedicated to our Lady of the Footsteps or Our Lady of Peace is a moot point. Certainly tradition has it that Our Lady appeared near the bottom of Green Street and left her footprints on a rock there, but the small harbour that the bay affords would also have been a peaceful one, after negotiating the fearsome rocks that strew its entrance. Whatever its origin, that part of the coastline to the left of Green Street is called Havre des Pas.

Right on the corner, turning left, is a public house whose architec- tural details, including the two dormer windows, are made the most of by its exterior decoration. Next door is a row of typical fishermen's cottages, dating back to the time before 1824 when Havre des Pas was still a tiny village. After 1824, when a regular steamboat ferry was started between England and Jersey, the elegant Regency houses, which give such period charm to the north side of the coast road to St Clement, were built to accommodate the visitors who began to flock to the island. Particularly attractive are their finely decorated balconies.

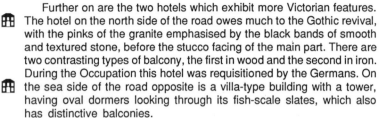

Further on are the two hotels which exhibit more Victorian features. The hotel on the north side of the road owes much to the Gothic revival, with the pinks of the granite emphasised by the black bands of smooth and textured stone, before the stucco facing of the main part. There are two contrasting types of balcony, the first in wood and the second in iron. During the Occupation this hotel was requisitioned by the Germans. On the sea side of the road opposite is a villa-type building with a tower, having oval dormers looking through its fish-scale slates, which also has distinctive balconies.

Still on the sea side, walking east, on the way to the Dicq slipway is the Silver Tide Guest House which, during the 5-year Occupation of Jersey, was the headquarters of the hated German Secret Police. A few doors further on is a plaque to mark where the twentieth-century playwright and librettist, Frederick Lonsdale, used to live.

After a stroll round the corner to read the plaque commemorating the rock at Le Dicq just in St Saviour, where Victor Hugo and other political refugees met to put the world to rights, retrace your footsteps back along the sea front — a delightful example of a Victorian promenade, complete with the original iron railings — and to Jersey's only pretence of a pier. It leads to the outdoor swimming pool — the headquarters of the Jersey Swimming Club who organise frequent competitions and special events here — which is open all the summer for swimmers and sunbathers and which provides a variety of light refreshments. A little further on, the promenade leaves the road to follow the coast. As it does so, it passes where, in the eighteenth century, a guard house was built by Major General James d'Auvergne to keep a look out for a possible French invasion.

A few steps beyond this is a memorial — in the shape of an anchor and a keel — to one of the many south coast shipyards that carried on Jersey's profitable shipbuilding in the nineteenth century. If you look over the railing down at the sea wall, just in front of where the yard was, you will notice that the slipway that used to be there to launch the ships has been filled in with much smaller stones than those in the rest of the wall. A typical journey for one of these Jersey-built ships would have been to Newfoundland to fish for cod.

At Green Street slipway, as well as noting the finely cut granite paving stones and border of the slipway itself, you will see three interesting houses across the road. A little way up Mount Bingham is the imposing villa, Seaview, on whose side wall a prow-shaped window has been added to take every advantage of the sun. A few steps further down is Bramerton House, where Lawrence of Arabia stayed when he was a boy and, no doubt, played on the beach of Havre des Pas. Next door is Du Heaume House where, 40 years earlier, Victor Hugo, during his exile in Jersey, kept his mistress, Juliette Drouet.

Still following the line of the beach along the promenade, you come

A plaque commemorating the Battle of Minden, Minden Place

LA VINGTAINE DE LA VILLE

MINDEN PLACE
NAMED TO COMMEMORATE THE
BATTLE OF MINDEN 1759
CAPT. CHARLES W. LE GEYT
COMMANDED A GRENADIER COMPANY OF
25TH FOOT, KING'S OWN SCOTTISH BORDERERS
ALSO
37TH FOOT, ROYAL HAMPSHIRE REGIMENT
AND ROYAL ARTILLERY
PARTICIPATING IN THIS HISTORIC BATTLE
IN 1794 CAPT. LE GEYT
WAS APPOINTED THE FIRST
POSTMASTER IN JERSEY

to La Collette, a small neck of land which juts out into the sea, where among the shingle can still be seen bits of rusted twisted track from the railway the Germans built from Grouville to St Helier. It was laid to carry the sand needed to make the concrete to turn Jersey, under Hitler's own direct orders, into an impregnable fortress and ran right past the north gate of the swimming pool and along the bottom of La Collette Gardens. The tower which dominates the skyline ahead — behind the nineteenth-century barracks — is part of Jersey Electricity's power station, while the squat tower to its south is a pre-1830 defence tower, which the Germans adapted in 1944 so that two anti-aircraft guns could be mounted on its top.

To return to Green Street car park, cut up through La Collette Gardens, cross Mount Bingham and walk up South Hill past the gym. Then follow the road as it forks down to the right to Rope Walk, where in the island's ship-building days, long twists of hemp were laid out to make ships' ropes. Continue north along Rope Walk, past the Cheshire Home — which often has hand-made items for sale — through a small turning to the right and back into Green Street, where several yards ahead on the right, is the multi-storey car park.

The beach along Havre des Pas is popular both with town residents and visitors from nearby hotels and guest houses but it never becomes overcrowded. Bathing is quite safe and is even possible, for those who do not mind a long trek across the sand, at low tide. The strange rock formations which are a feature of this bay afford opportunities for both rock climbing — the Three Sister rocks stretching out to sea are a favourite clamber — and low water fishing, but be careful not to be caught by an incoming tide. At high tide anglers fish from Green Street slipway and supplies of bait etc can be bought down Green Street in Clos des Pas.

2 SNOW HILL PARK TO THE ROYAL SQUARE AND HALKETT PLACE

Before leaving the car at Snow Hill it is interesting to know the origin of this plot of land at the northern foot of Fort Regent. When Jersey had a railway it was the town station until 1929 for the Jersey Eastern Railway and also the place where the buses which replaced them were turned on a revolving turntable.

Walking west down Hill Street, noted for the number of lawyers practising here, turn right at the lights and cross the road into the Royal Square which is so packed with memories of the past that a little time should be spent exploring it. To begin with, this is where the original market in St Helier was always held from the Middle Ages down to the nineteenth century. The market cross was destroyed at the Reformation but is thought to have stood where the statue of George II is now. From its foot were proclaimed all new laws and public announcements and in the market square itself many criminals, including alleged witches, were pilloried or put to death. The twelfth-century Jersey poet, Maistre Wace, would have been well acquainted with the sight of stalls piled high with dairy and vegetable produce from the country parishes, locally caught fish laid out on slabs of stone, the open brook running through it and the noise and bustle of the island's only shopping centre. In his *Roman de Brut* are the earliest surviving references to several facts about King Arthur and his Round Table; his *Roman de Rou* Wace tells of the Norman conquest of England. A plaque on the wall of the States Buildings facing into the Royal Square honours the memory of this Jersey-born poet.

These public buildings round the old market place were only built gradually. The present **Royal Court** — the island's court of justice — is about the fourth replacement of the original cohue, as the courthouse was then called, and was completed in 1866. The arms of George II, from the former building of 1760, are above the public entrance. Inside, the Bailiff's chair with its heraldic carvings dates back to as early as the turn of the sixteenth century. The Lieutenant-Governor's chair which sits beside it is of a slightly later date. The silver gilt mace, which is always laid before the Bailiff both in court and in the States, was presented by Charles II to the island in recognition of the fact that twice he had found safety there. Its inscription reads 'Not all doth he deem worthy of such a reward'. The oil paintings which line the walls include portraits of George III and General Conway, the latter by Gainsborough, and a copy of the famous *The Death of Major Peirson* by Copley, the original of which hangs in the Tate Gallery. Once a year, at the beginning of the Michaelmas Law Term, the Seigneurs of the island's fiefs swear allegiance to the Queen, and Royal Court Advocates reaffirm their oaths in the presence of the Bailiff. This sitting of the Assize d'Héritage, thought to be the oldest-surviving court in Europe, is preceded by a ceremonial inspection of the Guard of Honour by the Lieutenant-Governor and is followed by a service at the Town Church.

To the east of the Royal Court, with its main distinctively decorated entrance in Halkett Place, is Jersey's seat of government—the island's legislative body — the **States Chamber,** which was built in 1887. Inside, the banner, which is above the Bailiff's chair, is of three leopards passant which feature on the Bailiff's official seal as well as in the heraldic arms of the Queen. There is a gallery in the States Chamber from which visitors may watch and listen to States proceedings every Tuesday when the House is in session. The other Royal Square buildings house the island records.

Three events worthy of note took place in the Royal Square in the eighteenth century. The first of these was in 1751 when, to the deafening roar of cannon, the gilded statue of George II — still in the square today—was unveiled. The king is dressed as a Roman senator and rumour at the time had it that the statue was none other than a looted Roman emperor from a Spanish ship that the local hotelier, who presented the gift to St Helier, had got at a bargain price from a sea captain! This tale, though, does not take into account the fact that the supposed Roman emperor happens to be wearing the Order of the Garter, a distinction unknown to the Romans. Whoever the spindle-shanked statue really represents, it was erected in gratitude for the £300 given by the monarch towards the building of the harbour. The Market Place was renamed in honour of George II and his statue as the Royal Square.

The most dramatic, and finally tragic, episode of the island's history that took place in the Royal Square was the Battle of Jersey. At the beginning of 1781 the French adventurer Baron de Rullecourt, as was mentioned in the history of Grouville, invaded Jersey at La Rocque and marched unchallenged through the night until he reached St Helier. Here de Rullecourt bluffed the Governor Moses Corbet into surrendering the island and all might have been lost for Jersey, if the British forces and the Jersey militia under the command of the young English officer Major Peirson had not disobeyed Corbet's command to surrender too.

Major Peirson swept down from Westmount and through the streets of St Helier in two columns and blocked de Rullecourt and his forces in the Royal Square. Shot marks from the ensuing battle can still be seen on the walls of the public house at the corner of Peirson Place. Sadly, just as the French were being routed from their position in the Square, Major Peirson was fatally wounded and did not live to see the final victory. Baron de Rullecourt also died from wounds sustained in the fierce fighting and now both victor and vanquished lie at rest in the town church opposite the scene of the Battle of Jersey, which Copley has depicted so dramatically in his painting *The Death of Major Peirson*. A stone commemorating the event is on the ground in the centre of the Royal Square.

Six years after the Battle of Jersey had been fought and won, John Wesley paid an 8-day visit to Jersey during his tour of the Channel Islands. The room in St Helier in which the 81-year-old founder of Methodism preached in 1787 was a privately owned hall above the corn market at the west end of the Royal Square. The corn market is now the Registrar's Office and above it, where Wesley spoke to his Jersey followers, is the United Club.

The visitor will see also, at his or her feet, carved on the paving stones 'Vega + 1945' now suitably bordered by a black band of stone that was unveiled by HRH The Duchess of Kent in 1985, 40 years after it had been written. The *Vega* was a Swedish ship, sent by the Red Cross, loaded with food parcels and medical supplies for the island's starving inhabitants in the last months of the Occupation. So deeply grateful for the visits of this mercy ship were the islanders, that not only was one baby (born in 1945) actually christened after the Swedish ship but more permanently — underneath the very noses of the occupying German forces — what was forever etched into their memories was set in stone in the Royal Square — V for Vega but also for Victory.

The final end of the Occupation is still remembered by those who crammed into the Royal Square on Tuesday 8 May 1945, to hear the Bailiff, later Lord Coutanche, tell them from the balcony over the Royal Court that shortly there was to be a broadcast from England, relayed to them through the huge loudspeakers hoisted in the trees. Then the crowds heard the well known voice of Winston Churchill proclaim that the war in Europe had just ended and that later that day 'our dear Channel Islands' were to be freed. In fact Jersey was not liberated by British troops until the following day, 9 May, and it is fitting that on every anniversary of that Liberation Day, which is always kept as a public holiday, a service of thanksgiving is held in the Royal Square where the joyful news was first announced. There is a plaque beneath the balcony to tell of that historic occasion in May 1945.

The Royal Square is no longer quite the focal point of island life that it once was but, besides the many stories of the past it has to tell, it is also the venue for several special events. In May and September one of the local artists' guilds holds outdoor exhibitions here; this is where the Variety Club of Jersey set up their annual Town Fayre; and, most appropriately, where the 'Vier Marchi' the old market, with stall holders in their traditional Jersey sunbonnets is still held during Battle of Britain week in September. In between these special events, there are always

Public entrance to States Chambers

the seats under the chestnut trees to sit on and contemplate the amount of history crammed into such a small place.

Leaving the Royal Square by its south-east entrance, opposite the side of the States Chamber, is the office of the Jersey Chamber of Commerce, the first, in 1768, to be founded in the English-speaking world. Turn left and you have a view of the whole width and length of Halkett Place. Look at the wall to the right on which the street's name is placed and you will see how rich it is in architectural motifs, complete with grotesque faces carved on top of the window columns.

Further down on the left is the **Central Market**, which was finally banished from the Royal Square in 1800. This perfect example of a Victorian cast iron market hall is a great favourite with visitors who enjoy its rich architectural detail: noting the gates at the Hilgrove Street and Market Street entrances decorated with the fruit, vegetables and poultry on sale inside; the coats of arms of the various parishes above their heads; and the much photographed central fountain as well as the fresh wares piled up on the stalls to tempt them. It was opened in 1882 and, despite the food shortage during the Occupation, has been trading ever since in meat, bread, fruit, vegetables and flowers. The smaller fish market is opposite the north side of the large market, in Beresford Street, and visitors will be amazed at the variety of fish it has on offer. There is everything here from dried salted cod, a favourite with old Jersey families and the Portuguese population alike, to conger eel for the traditional Jersey dish of conger soup, as well as all the shellfish, including the popular spider crab, and other fish, such as mackerel, caught in local waters.

Further down Halkett Place, on the left, is the ornately decorated Mechanics Institute, next to the soon to be built Central Library. Across the end of the street is the eye-catching Methodist church, known as **Wesley Grove**, with its mixture of classical and Gothic detail. Originally seating 1,600 worshippers, this huge building was first opened in 1847 and now seats about 1,000. It is, therefore, the ideal venue for the concerts of religious music usually given at Christmas and Easter by local and visiting musicians and singers. From Halkett Place the visitor can turn left into Vauxhall Street, left into New Street, left again into Burrard Street, to find the out-of-the-way shops, along Minden Place, and turn right into Bath Street. At the top of Bath Street, turn left and then right, back to Snow Hill car park.

3 PIER ROAD TO THE MUSEUM, TOWN CHURCH AND MOUNT BINGHAM

Walking north down Pier Road, on the left-hand side is the entrance to the Société Jersiaise Library. This is often used by visitors wishing to research either the island's past or — if they have Jersey connections — their own family tree.

On the other side of the road to the library is the oldest building in the town, the **parish church of St Helier**, usually simply called the 'Town Church'. There has been a place of worship on its site at least since the eleventh century and a look at the outside walls will show the different developments that have taken place in the subsequent centuries. So the walls of the chancel — originally a small chancery chapel — are made of rough boulders brought up from the beach, while local granite squares were used in the fifteenth century to add the south aisle and south chancel.

Time past, the Town Church was not just used for Sunday services, it was the centre of parish life everyday of the week. When news spread that any French raiders were approaching the island, the town's people would lock themselves into the church for safety. Until 1830 all parish assemblies, dealing with such civic matters as rates and drains, were held here, parishioners casting their vote by raising their hats. Until 1844 the church also served as somewhere for the Jersey militia to keep their cannon. Neither was the church bell ringing just a Sunday occurrence: it rang on market day to start buying and selling in the Royal Square opposite, it was the fire alarm and the call to civil defence. In the church porch elections for Jurats and Constable were held after Sunday morning service and miscreants were placed in the stocks at the church gates to serve as a warning to the rest of the congregation.

Perhaps one of the most prestigious worshippers the Town Church has had was Charles II, in 1649, when he was still Prince of Wales and 3 years later when he was King. Nothing demonstrates so well Charles' easy going nature than the story of his unofficial jester trying to preach a sermon there one Sunday. This jester was, in fact, a dwarfish French doctor of divinity whose mind had become unbalanced. On that day it came into the dwarf's mind to pretend to be a monkey and preach a monkey's sermon in front of his master, King Charles.

So, much to the monarch's surprise, during the service the ugly little face of the dwarf peeped over the edge of the pulpit and he began his gibberish. Immediately the Lieutenant-Governor, who was also present, dashed to the pulpit, ejected the furious little man and the service continued. But then, hurtling through the church window came three large stones, one just missing the King's head. The dwarf's punishment? The King just sent him back to France, complete with a new suit of clothes and a full purse.

All round the church are memorials to parishioners, such as the one in the Lady Chapel to Madeleine Durrell, who married into the famous island de Carteret family, or the one to General Anquetil who died in an earlier Afghan war, in the retreat from Kabul in 1842. At the foot of the pulpit is the memorial that everyone wants to see — given by the States of Jersey to the hero of the Battle of Jersey, Major Peirson. A granite stone in the churchyard marks the grave of his adversary, Baron de Rullecourt.

During the Occupation of Jersey the Town Church was also used by the German troops. Services were conducted by their own chaplains, using their own altar ornaments and the soldiers attending them were always well behaved. As the Occupation diarist Leslie Sinel commented: 'They left quietly and we went in quietly, for it surely must have been patent to many in the two distinct congregations that we were all worshipping the same God!'

For the faithful witness of the clergy and their congregations during the 5 long years of the Occupation and as a thanks offering for the island's liberation, the Queen Mother, when she was Queen Elizabeth, presented the island with a fine crucifix and candlesticks which are on the altar. Other gifts of church plate are on show in the church, while the beautiful processional cross and the Bailiff's chair show the continued links between the island and the New World, as they were presented by the diocese of New Jersey.

Opposite the north entrance of the church is St Helier's **Church**

🏠 **House**, completed in 1970 on the site of the former rectory garden. Its façade is of very pale grey granite quarried at L'Etacq, demonstrating that Jersey's distinctive stone is still being utilised, even if its cost nowadays prohibits more than a mainly decorative use. Church House is often the venue for charity sales, coffees, lunches and teas, so it might be worthwhile for visitors who would enjoy light refreshments served by friendly helpers to call in to see if there was anything on there during their stay.

For the visitor who still has energy, there is a pleasant walk back to Pier Road car park round the harbour and the west flank of Fort Regent. From the Town Church walk down Mulcaster Street to the Weighbridge: ahead is the harbour, to the right across the road is the Tourist Information Centre and just 50yd round the corner on the Esplanade, 🏰 well worth deviating from your route for, is the **Island Fortress Occupation Museum**. This exhibition, for which there is an admission charge, features uniformed dummies and various pieces of equipment from World War II. One of the most recent finds is of two field kitchens which have been carefully restored. So that the visitor can understand the full implications of all that is on show, including guns, vehicles and authentic documents, there is a video cinema where a clear explanation of Occupation events is shown.

🏠 From the Occupation Museum, walk back to the **Weighbridge**, noticing as you do the decorative architecture of some of the buildings which flank it, in particular the Southampton Hotel, the only Victorian building which remains just as it used to be, down to the detail of its trefoil balustrades, when first built in 1899.

🏰 On the northeast side of Liberation Square you will find the new **Jersey Museum**. Once inside you will realise why in 1992 the Guild of Travel Writers voted it 'The most outstanding tourist attraction in the British Isles'. In 1993 it received the National Heritage/IBM 'Museum of the Year' award, while its restaurant won the Gulbenkian 'Best Museum Restaurant' award.

Starting on the ground floor you should go straight to the Audio Visual Theatre to enjoy a 12-minute 'Jersey — a Place in History' to get a brief outline of what exactly Jersey was and now is. A simultaneous French translation is available through headphones. Then there is an information station, testing local knowledge for two minutes at a time, which always has a huddle of excited youngsters round it.

What also catches everyone's attention on this floor is the imaginative reconstruction of an Ice Age hunting scene. Here is a craggy rock face down which are climbing some ragged-looking hunters to where their dinner awaits them below.

On the next floor up you will find out how they came to be so lucky in their day's hunting. Here are the mammoths and woolly rhinos that the hunters managed to manoeuvre — perhaps by the strategic use of

Shopping in St Helier

fire — over the edge of the cliff to their deaths at the bottom. Some of the bones found at the Ice Age site of La Cotte at St Brelade have been placed in position at the base of the reconstructed cliff, just as the archaeologists would have found them.

The whole of the museum's first floor is, in fact, devoted to the 'Story of Jersey'. As well as these 250,000-year-old bones and several artifacts, there are different displays dealing with the island's earliest industries of fishing and farming, Jersey's special relationship with the Crown, archive film, old photographs and, of course, there are several displays dealing with the island's military history, including the Occupation. On the second floor is the Barreau-Le Maistre Art Gallery where, from an art collection of 4,000 items — mainly paintings, prints and drawings by local artists or depicting Jersey subjects — a changing exhibition is held.

The final floor gives a link with two important examples of Jersey's past. The first is the viewing window through which can be seen one of the first signal stations in the British Isles, with a guide to what the flags flying by Fort Regent actually mean. There is also a glimpse into the first room to be restored to its former use in No 9 Pier Road, which used to house the old museum. This is a typical bedroom of a merchant's house in 1865, furnished in the style of the period. For children there is also a splendid doll's house on this top floor, made in 1914.

The museum is open daily, with a reduced admission charge for senior citizens and students, while children under 10 years old are free. To visit the fully-licensed café for tea, coffee, lunch or a snack, or to the gift shop, featuring a wide range of local books, there is no admission charge.

On the summit of Town Hill behind the bus terminus can be seen the Lieutenant-Governor's personal standard and the flags fluttering from Great Britain's oldest signal station. Walk round the south of the bus terminus and then cross over by the entrance to the tunnel to Commercial Buildings which runs along the side of the old harbour, across which a glimpse of the ferries from England and France can often be seen. Follow the road round the corner till it comes to the huge wall which separates Commercial Buildings from Pier Road above, opposite Le Quai des Marchands. As the plaque on the wall explains, this wall is 1,000ft high, was built in 1820 and there are over thirty steps to take you up to Pier Road. If you ignore the steps up and continue along the road past the many openings in the wall on the left, for tools and oakum used in the adjacent shipyards, also on the left you will see on **Mount Bingham**, two memorials, one to an Englishman and the other to a Jerseyman, both lost at sea over a hundred years ago.

The tragedy happened in the early morning of 17 March 1870, when in thick fog the Southampton mail packet, the *Normandy*, bringing mail and passengers to Jersey, was rammed by the Baltic trader *Mary*, 13 miles off the Isle of Wight. Captain Harvey, from the time his boat was struck until she foundered 20 minutes later, never left the bridge. From it he instructed that the ship's head be kept to the sea as much as possible so the lifeboats could be launched. As they left filled with terrified passengers, his last words were 'Return quickly for we are sinking fast.' But when the lifeboats did return, of the *Normandy*, her captain, his mate and the ship's boy who all stayed at their posts till the last minute, there was no trace.

These three, however, were not the only ones who showed heroism that terrible night. There were also two passengers, Harry Kinloch and John Westaway, son of a Jersey advocate, who, during the panic and confusion, helped many of the passengers to find their way to the boats, while John Westaway was personally responsible for saving the life of one of the terror-stricken women passengers. But their action was at the cost of their own lives, for when the *Normandy* suddenly sank, they were among the thirty-two who went down with her.

In memory of the brave men, there is a commemorative tablet to Harry Kinloch at Sandhurst and the two memorials on Mount Bingham to John Westaway and Captain Henry Beckford Harvey. The Westaway memorial, designed by the French sculptor Robinet, was originally intended as a drinking fountain and has a sea serpent on top of its octagonal column, through whose body an anchor is thrust and it was first placed at the Weighbridge. The Harvey memorial is in the form of an obelisk and honours both the captain and the men who went down with him. It was originally sited at the back of the Victoria Pier, but it is fitting that the two impressive monuments should now share the same spot overlooking the sea and the harbour of St Helier.

For a spectacular, panoramic view of the harbour the visitor should follow Mount Bingham — named after a popular former Lieutenant-Governor — round the bend to the left and on and up round the next bend to the right and then look back down at the busy scene below. Here there are attractive terraced grounds and a children's playground.

At the top of Mount Bingham are **La Collette Gardens** beautifully laid out — a green oasis with the sea on three sides — in memory of one of Jersey's benefactors Benjamin Meaker. Here, apart from the spring and summer bedding plants, the observant visitor will discover the sweet scented violets and the buds of pink japonica in spring and the cascades of mesembryanthemums in summer. Look east and there through the trees is the bay which stretches from Havre des Pas across to Grève d'Azette. Ahead to the far south is Icho Tower and Green Island and, further north, the four modern tower blocks, one of twentieth-century Jersey's architectural mistakes.

After a rest here to admire this view, continue on down Mount Bingham and cross over the road to go up South Hill, which passes behind both the swimming pool and Fort Regent. For the keen explorer of byways, the lane called East Road, that runs south to north just before the swimming pool, follows the ramparts of Fort Regent and leads to the crossroads where Green Street meets the tunnel and continues over the bridge into Regent Road — a pleasantly quiet way into town by way of Colomberie.

From the Glacis field, next to the path which leads up to the back of the swimming pool but which does not give an entrance to it, there is another fine view — this time over the east of the town and up to the Gothic building on the skyline, Victoria College for Boys, founded in 1852. This is sometimes the venue for both concerts and cricket matches open to the general public. The first turning after this leads to Fort Regent, where there is a lift down to Pier Road car park, the second road also winds down to Pier Road with the car park to the right.

4 SAND STREET TO ROUGE BOUILLON

From Sand Street car park turn left and go down the short cut on the right to Seale Street which passes by the side of the **Town Hall**. This nineteenth-century building, which acts as St Helier's Parish Hall, is unmistakably French in tone, from the vertical linking of its windows to the garlands and swags running all round the building at the top of the second storey. Here parish rates and parking fines are paid, St Helier's Centeniers hear cases of infractions of the law that have taken place in St Helier, which they either deal with themselves or refer to the magistrate's court, also at present in the same building, according to the seriousness of the case. Parish meetings to debate such issues as rates, assessments, roads, traffic, parks and the upkeep of public buildings are also held here — the centre of civic affairs in St Helier. In the spacious Assembly Room are pictures by well known Jersey artists such as *The Boyhood of Raleigh* by Millais.

Across the road from the Town Hall, in the Parade, is the island's cenotaph. The La Moye granite pedestal was unveiled on 11 November 1923 and today the sarcophagus holds the roll of honour not just of the 862 Jerseymen killed in World War I but the 458 killed in World War II as well. Incredibly, even throughout the German Occupation, the ritual of placing wreaths of poppies at its foot on the anniversary of the 1918 Armistice was allowed to continue.

The **Parade Gardens** beyond the cenotaph were once, as their name would suggest, the parade ground when St Helier had its own regiment of militia. This is a very pleasant open space — with well tended flower beds offering a feast of colour for most of the year — on the west edge of town, just opposite the shops and the General Hospital — in which to rest, amuse the children in their special playground area, or have your photograph taken near the cannon which guard Robinet's statue of Jersey's great defence builder and road maker, the English General Sir George Don, Lieutenant-Governor of Jersey from 1806-14, which was unveiled in 1885. The attendant figures represent Ceres, the goddess of Agriculture, and Mercury, the god of Commerce.

The **General Hospital** opposite has had a chequered career. It was built as a poor house, between 1765 and 1772, with money left expressly for the purpose by a wealthy widow in St Aubin. Seven years after it had opened, it was requisitioned by General Conway for his troops. So, at the time of the Battle of Jersey in 1781, a Highland regiment was billeted there and it was the regiment's gunpowder which exploded, bringing down, in 1783, about two-thirds of the building. The poor house was not rebuilt and used for its intended purpose until 10 years later. Six years after that, in 1799, the poor were once again evicted, this time to billet Russian soldiers, who could not be sent back to Russia until the following spring, when weather conditions improved.

Once the Russians had left, a new wing and a chapel were added, only for the rest of the building to be gutted by a serious fire in 1859. In the rebuilt poor house, not only were the paupers cared for but also an increasing number of sick and mentally ill patients. Eventually this intolerable situation was eased by sending the orphans and the mentally ill to other establishments on the island, though the paupers remained.

During the Occupation, the hospital was once more commandeered, as half of it was used for German troops. After the Liberation, however, the poor were finally found alternative accommodation and the hospital was able to concentrate solely on caring for the sick and injured. The 1980s have seen major rebuilding projects carried out in the General Hospital complex, as anyone sitting in the Parade can see for themselves.

After a wander round the Parade Gardens, turn left into Elizabeth Place which soon becomes **Rouge Bouillon**. This unusual name, which means Red Spring, came from the fact that the spring which used to flow along Queen's Road brought iron oxide down with it, giving the mud at the bottom of the stream a reddish tinge and so from Elizabethan times the whole area was known as 'La Contrée du Rouge Bouillon'. Now Rouge Bouillon is famed for being the base of BBC Radio Jersey, which is on the left-hand side of the road walking north. Further up on the same side is the ambulance station, while on the opposite side of the road are the headquarters of Jersey's paid police force.

The visitor who wishes to make the circular trip into town, should follow Rouge Bouillon round the bend to the right and then take the first right turn at the traffic lights, down Midvale Road, which first becomes David Place and then Bath Street (where the public baths used to be) which in turn leads straight into, on the right, the pedestrian precinct. Sand Street car park is at the western edge of town, after Charing Cross, with its distinctive granite monument marking the spot where King Street and Broad Street meet, and commemorating the Silver Jubilee of Queen Elizabeth in 1977. The flower beds at Charing Cross are constructed with granite from each of the island's quarries and two of the offshore reefs. On the cross are depictions of St Helier (from a Normandy statue) the Town Church, the Hermitage, the old prison, the Mont de la Ville dolmen, an ormer and the Jubilee emblem itself.

For anyone who wants a short out-of-town walk, follow Rouge Bouillon as far as the turning to the left after the traffic lights, called Undercliffe Road, and enjoy the walk — with its view across to Elizabeth Castle — down St John's Road towards the sea. At the bottom, turn left into Cheapside, which eventually becomes the Parade and follow your tracks back to the car park.

5 MINDEN PLACE TO THE JERSEY ARTS CENTRE AND ST THOMAS CHURCH

Minden Place was so named in commemoration of the Battle of Minden fought in Saxony, north Germany in 1759 which brought an end to the Seven Years' War. The plaque in Minden Place also commemorates the part played in that battle by the Royal Hampshire Regiment, the

King's own Scottish Borderers and the Royal Artillery, under the command of the Jerseyman Captain Charles Le Geyt, who later became the island's first postmaster.

Leaving Minden Place car park, walk east towards Bath Street and cross the road into Phillips Street, where a little way down on the left is the **Jersey Arts Centre**. Opened in 1982, the complex includes a theatre, a gallery, a bar and a restaurant. The Benjamin Meaker Theatre was the last part of the Centre to be completed and is a compact venue for plays and concerts, from classical to folk and jazz, seating 250. In the Berni Gallery on the first floor regular exhibitions are shown of both local and international artists which can be viewed by visitors without an admission charge.

On the ground floor are the rooms where various courses in dance and crafts take place, as well as the well appointed bar and restaurant. This is a favourite place for local people to relax in over a drink or a meal and visitors are welcome too. Pre-theatre suppers or suppers after the show are also available, but it is advisable to book these in advance.

There are special provisions in the Arts Centre for the disabled, as wheelchairs can come through the main entrance on the ground floor, where the toilets are also situated. Advance notice, or arrival half an hour before the performance starts, however, is advisable for anyone in a wheelchair who wants to go to the Benjamin Meaker Theatre. For the hard of hearing, there is a hearing loop throughout the theatre for every seat, so no advance notice need be given.

Leaving the Arts Centre, turn left into Providence Street, where one comes across a small modern town housing estate which must be second to none for the number of keen gardeners who make the most of every inch of their tiny gardens. From Providence Street turn right into Charles Street, where the *Jersey Evening Post* have their offices, and straight on into Bath Street. To the left, at the junction of Bath Street, Beresford Street and Peter Street, is **West's Centre**. Here, under the shade of young trees, one can sit and watch the world go by. West's Centre is sometimes the venue for the Jersey Art Exhibitor's Guild to display a selection of local art. Pictures in any medium, from pastels to oils, can be enjoyed at this open-air exhibition and also be bought.

After a rest in West's Centre, walk a little further up the precinct into Hilgrove Street, which used to be known as French Lane, because French farm workers used to congregate here on a Saturday afternoon. To the right is Halkett Place, but if you take the left turning into Hilgrove Street and then the first turning to the left again into Hilary Street, the square has been made with Peter Street and one is ready to walk north up Bath Street. As you walk, note the fine top half of many of the buildings: such as the one at the corner of Charles Street on the east side of the road and the French-style roof on the corner of Minden Place opposite. Continue walking up Bath Street, which becomes David Place, until the crossroads with Victoria Street and Stopford Road. On the right is the Royal Hotel, fronted by its elegant standard roses, which has ballroom dancing every Thursday.

At the bottom of Victoria Street is the Catholic **church of St Thomas**, built in 1887 in the style of the thirteenth century. This is the largest Roman Catholic church in the Channel Islands, where over 1,000 people worship every Sunday during the summer and where the island's main ecumenical carol service, complete with several choirs and an orchestra as well as the organ, is held at Christmas. There is also a community centre at the church — built to mark its centenary and officially opened by the Roman Catholic Bishop of Portsmouth — which is a recreation venue for groups ranging from mothers and toddlers to senior citizens.

From St Thomas' church, turn south down Val Plaisant which becomes **New Street**. This hotch-potch of a road was, in the eighteenth century, mainly gardens, where the townsfolk used to grow their vegetables when their day's work was over. It was laid in the nineteenth century to join Val Plaisant in the north to La Rue de Derrière in the south which is now known as King Street. The pharmacy at the junction with Devonshire Place has been dispensing drugs since that time, as the sign outside shows, though it no longer includes the painless extraction of teeth among its services! CSP Furnishers used first to be a chapel and then, in 1937, was converted into The Playhouse. On the east side of the street, are two more nineteenth-century buildings: the Trustee Savings Bank built in 1870, now with an 1987 extension, and St Paul's church which was built in the Gothic revival style popular in 1891. Visitors are most welcome not just to the services at St Paul's, but also to take tea with their sandwiches on week days between 12 noon and 2pm.

Opposite St Paul's notice the fine side entrance to de Gruchy's which was opened by the merchant Abraham de Gruchy in 1826. In 1854 the store was thought comparable 'to the best in London'. Its founder died in 1864 and was buried in Green Street cemetery and the store is no longer owned by the family. Burton's, on the same side of the road and making the corner with King Street, was requisitioned during the Occupation so that the Germans could sell inexpensive goods from it to their troops.

Next door to the church is Voisin, the family firm that was begun as a tiny back street shop in 1837 by François Voisin. That it grew to its present-day proportions is largely due to the fact that Mr Voisin left the selling to his assistants and gave his own personal attention to the buying of goods for his shop to sell. In his diary he records his journeys all over Europe, as well as his regular visits to the great fur fair in Russia and his search in the East for silks and damask. After being the most travelled Jerseyman of his time, François Voisin became Constable of St Helier in 1878 and in that capacity completed the levelling out of the Parade and the landscaping of Westmount, begun but abandoned in the 1850s.

To get back to Minden Place car park, walk up King Street as far as Don Street, turn left and walk past the two pavement cafés and on to the junction of Don Street and Burrard Street. Turn right here and the multi-storey car park is on your left, opposite the rear entrance to the fish market.

6 PATRIOTIC STREET TO VICTORIA AVENUE

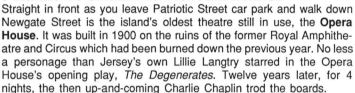

Straight in front as you leave Patriotic Street car park and walk down Newgate Street is the island's oldest theatre still in use, the **Opera House**. It was built in 1900 on the ruins of the former Royal Amphitheatre and Circus which had been burned down the previous year. No less a personage than Jersey's own Lillie Langtry starred in the Opera House's opening play, *The Degenerates*. Twelve years later, for 4 nights, the then up-and-coming Charlie Chaplin trod the boards.

During the Occupation, putting on amateur shows every fortnight at the unheated Opera House and going through the blacked-out streets to see them was a most important morale booster for islanders. The only snag was that the Commandant had to have a German translation of everything that was put on, even if the lyric were only 'O dear, what can the matter be!'. Only one part of one of the shows put on, however, met with real criticism from the Germans. The actor who played Shylock in Shakespeare's *Merchant of Venice* was informed that his delineation of the character of the Jew was not considered sufficiently 'repellent' and he was asked to remedy the situation. The actor ignored the order, but no further measures were taken against him.

For a time after the Liberation, the Opera House was converted into a cinema but reverted to its original use in 1958. Since then it has been used by both amateur and professional companies with many household names appearing in the summer shows which run throughout the season.

At the sea end of Gloucester Street, turn right into the Esplanade and cross the road to the Promenade. By the causeway to Elizabeth Castle is the open-air swimming pool, ideal for children and non-swimmers to practise their first tentative strokes. There are always plenty of deck chairs put out here for visitors to use either on the prom or the sand and close by is an open-air café for light refreshments.

Across the road from the slipway, between Peirson Road and St Aubin's Road in the newly landscaped Triangle Park, now renamed Victoria Gardens, are more deck chairs and a statue of Queen Victoria, gazing out to sea as if she is definitely not amused by what she sees going on around her. On the west side of St Aubin's Road is the **People's Park**, now sadly denuded of its many old trees after the hurricane in October 1987. This is a favourite venue for impromptu games of football and in June for the Waiters and Waitresses Race, which promotes such keen support from the hotels and guest house guests. There is a quiet paved area near the fountain at the back of the park, where parents can sit while their children play on the grass or in the playground on the slopes behind.

Behind the People's Park is **Westmount**, which used to be known less pleasantly as Le Mont ès Pendus or Gallows Hill. For this 250ft-high hill was where the death penalty of hanging was carried out for hundreds of years, until as recently as 1829. The small summer house at the top is on the actual site of the gallows. Hangings were not just to punish the criminal, who might only have stolen something worth as little as a shilling, but also to serve as an example to the general public. So hangings always took place on Market Day, having been well advertised the Sunday before in every parish church, and school children were brought by their teachers to be taught a lesson on what happens to law breakers.

Today, though Westmount lost some of its pine trees in the 1987 hurricane, the steep hill gives a marvellous view of St Aubin's Bay and Elizabeth Castle, while at its foot is one of St Helier's most popular nightspots. It is also very pleasant to wander up and down its paths or sit in the shade of one of its remaining tall trees.

One such walk leads to the **Jersey Bowling Club** at the top of Westmount which celebrated its 75th anniversary in 1987. The club welcomes visiting bowlers. The green fee per session includes the use of new woods and footwear, while weekly membership of the club is available on request. It is preferred that intending players should not wear jeans or shorts. Those who enjoy watching a bowls match, in which international players often take part, should look in the local paper for the dates and times of forthcoming fixtures. Certainly a more idyllic spot in which to play or to watch bowls would be hard to find.

From the top of Westmount one can also look down on the Lower Park, a safe playground for children which runs parallel with **Victoria Avenue**, and the avenue itself. This is Jersey's only motorway, though the island's overall speed restriction of 40mph still applies. It is here that spectators crowd both sides of the avenue to watch the highlight of Jersey's summer season — **The Battle of Flowers** which takes place on the second Thursday in August.

This island spectacular began as long ago as 1902, to mark the coronation of Edward VII and Queen Alexandra. In honour of the King's mother, Queen Victoria, it was staged along the avenue named after her, with a gun positioned on Westmount to signal the beginning and close of the procession of decorated carriages.

Following continental tradition, there really was a battle when it all began, waged with true Edwardian decorum. 'Occupants of the carriages were well supplied with ammunition in the form of tiny bunches of flowers and at once opened a fusillade on their friends in the stands.'

Sadly, as the years went by, the battling crowds got over enthusiastic and at the end of the procession tore apart the beautiful floral floats they had come to see. So now there are new features to entertain the crowds: there is a Miss Battle who is always escorted by a popular show business personality; music is provided by marching bands and movement by baton twirling majorettes; for the week there is a fair in the People's Park. In the evening there is a floodlit procession of the floats. Next day the floats are exhibited for admiring throngs to notice the careful attention to detail and the thousands of flower heads used to create the overall effect. Certainly an occasion when locals and visitors alike have their cameras at the ready to capture for posterity the stunning results of months of hard work.

A way back from Westmount and Victoria Avenue, for the visitor who does not wish to follow the coast line to the other end of St Aubin's Bay along the prom, is to walk down Westmount Road which borders the north edge of the People's Park. From there cross the road into Cheapside, walk along the Parade past the hospital and take the turning to the right which runs by the side of the hospital, Gloucester Street. Patriotic Street car park can be reached by turning right into either Newgate Street or Patriotic Place.

Other Places Of Interest in the Parish

There is more to the parish of St Helier, though, than the town. Incredible as it may seem there are still farms and small holdings with a St Helier address, so anyone who wants to sample the countryside of the parish should go north up Val Plaisant and Trinity Road (A8) and then turn left into **La Vallée des Vaux**, where there is a tranquil walk past the water meadows, where the cows graze, the brooks and gardens and a pond where local children come to feed the ducks. A circular walk back into St Helier can be taken by walking up the stone steps about half-way along La Vallée des Vaux on the left, going along the narrow footpath called Highfield Lane and then turning left into La Pouquelaye. On the way you pass the UK's smallest independent television station, Jersey's Channel Television which goes out on Channel 3. La Pouquelaye is another pleasant walk, though more built up, which takes its name from the fact that a menhir — a fairy stone or *pouquelaye* — stands in a nearby farm. This menhir, though, is on private property and access is not given to the general public to view it.

Walk down La Pouquelaye, past the D'Auvergne playing fields and

Jersey Bowling Club, Westmount

Almorah cemetery on the left, and pass by the side of **Almorah Crescent**. Take a moment to look through the gateway, for this crescent of ten houses though built, between 1845-50, is probably the most distinguished example of Regency architecture not just in Jersey but in the whole of the Channel Islands. From its commanding position its distinctive design can be picked out across the plateau of the town from as far away as Elizabeth Castle. The name Almorah for both the crescent and the cemetery behind it comes from the fact that the wife of the speculative builder who put up the crescent was born in Almorah in the Himalayas.

The walker can get into town by walking across the front of the crescent and down — taking the furthest one of the pair of steps that lead up to the crescent — into Upper Midvale Road. By following Midvale Road into Bath Street, one is back in the centre of town. The car driver continues down La Pouquelaye and turns left into Queen's Road, past one of Jersey's most interesting Victorian properties, Le Chalet, on the left. The three-house terrace is wholly built of granite — the shaping and placing of the blocks is outstanding — and has some of the most spectacular timber fretwork, originally done by hand, on the island.

Another way in to the less urban parts of St Helier is to go north up St John's Road. On the way up on the right are the display beds with their contrasting colours of both St Helier's and the States nurseries, from whence come the plants to beautify the public parks and gardens

PLACES OF INTEREST
IN THE PARISH OF ST HELIER

Hermitage
L'Islet
Site of the cell of St Helier himself
and monastery. Elizabeth Castle
also stands on this islet.

Elizabeth Castle
L'Islet
Sixteenth-century castle. Includes
militia museum.

Fort Regent
Le Mont de la Ville
Named after the Prince Regent,
later George IV. Now a leisure
centre — all sports and entertainments, concerts, cabarets,
adventure playground.
Conference facilities.

St Helier Marina
St Helier harbour
Boats for hire, pleasure cruises.

Funland
Esplanade
St Helier
Snooker and pool facilities.

St Helier Parish Church
St Helier
Oldest building in the town.

147 Snooker Club
Wharf Street
St Helier
Sumptuously furnished snooker
hall. Visitors can join by the day.

Colomberie
St Helier
Narrow street containing architecturally interesting buildings, and
every type of shop.

Havre des Pas
Coastline of St Helier with
interesting buildings including
nineteenth-century fishermen's
cottages, Regency houses.

Royal Square
St Helier
Site of original medieval market.
Home of the Royal Court and the
States Chamber. Scene of the
Battle of Jersey, 1781.

Jersey Museum
Weighbridge
St Helier
Story of Jersey, art gallery, audio-
visual show, exhibitions, walled
garden, restaurant, shop.

in St Helier and the rest of the island. For walkers or drivers who want
to deviate from the main road there is one way to the right and one to
the left before the nurseries to get off it and into the country.

Turn right down La Rue des Côtils and one comes into La Vallée des
Vaux with its gorse-covered *côtils* from its northern end. Turn left down
La Verte Chemin, and you come to the steep hill of La Rue de Moulin
du Fliquet at the bottom of which is **Bellozanne Valley**. This valley,
which comes down to the sea at First Tower, got its name from a
monastery in Normandy called Bellozanne Abbey, to which King John

PLACES OF INTEREST
IN THE PARISH OF ST HELIER - continued

Island Fortress Occupation Museum
Esplanade
St Helier.

Weighbridge
St Helier, near harbour
Architecturally attractive buildings.

Mount Bingham
St Helier
Site of memorials to people lost at sea and La Collette Gardens.

Town Hall
Seale Street
St Helier
French-style nineteenth-century building.

Parade Gardens
St Helier
Attractive gardens, playground.

Jersey Arts Centre
Phillips Street
Theatre, art gallery, bar, restaurant.

Open Air Market
Hope Street
St Helier
Every Saturday

West's Centre
St Helier
Occasional site of open-air art exhibitions.

Church of St Thomas (RC)
Val Plaisant
St Helier
Built 1887 in style of the thirteenth century.

Opera House
Gloucester Street
St Helier
Oldest theatre in Jersey.

Jersey Bowling Club
Westmount
St Helier

Beaches
Havre des Pas.

Activities

Walks — Albert Pier, Bellozanne Valley, La Vallée des Vaux

Ballroom dancing — Royal Hotel

Bowls — Jersey Bowling Club

Cinema — Odeon, Ciné de France

Sailing — Jersey Cruising School & Yacht Charters

of England gave the Jersey valley as a gift. It remained in the control of the Normandy abbey until the time of Henry V and was therefore known as Bellozanne Valley, with the hill behind it being called **Mont à l'Abbé**.

The valley has lost much of its natural beauty because on the left as you go towards the sea, is the marked by the tall chimney, is where Public Services have one of Europe's best waste disposal operations. Where Bellozanne comes into the St Aubin's Inner Road, to the left is the animal cemetery and to the right is a Neolithic burial mound.

The **animal cemetery** was founded in 1928 for owners to have ✳

somewhere special and peaceful to bury their pets. The well tended graves are for pets as small as mice or as large as horses; there is even a monkey buried here and many visitors visit the tiny graveyard to read the loving epitaphs that have been written by grieving owners. The animal cemetery is run by Jersey's Animal Shelter and is open daily between 9am and 4.30pm.

To the right, at **First Tower** (La Première Tour), named after the first in a series of defensive towers in St Aubin's Bay built around 1790, is **First Tower Park**. In the park, side by side, are examples of both pagan and Christian belief and ritual. In the centre of the park, under a grove of trees is both a gallery grave and a cist-in-circle. The gallery grave, dating from about 2500BC, is similar to the one described at Le Couperon but, unusually, it was reused around 1800BC for a Beaker culture burial. The stones it is built of are of L'Islet (where Elizabeth Castle now is) granite and, though it contained no bones, twenty-two beakers, some Jersey bowls and an archer's wristguard were found. The monument itself remained undiscovered, however, for thousands of years, as it was not till 1869 that its existence was suspected and excavations finally begun.

To the east of Ville ès Nouaux, as this dolmen is called, stands the Anglican church of St Andrew, also built in granite. It took its name from a small seaman's chapel built on the Esplanade in 1850 to serve not just the busy port but also the shipbuilding industry which flourished then. When this came to an end, the chapel was closed down and its name and endowments given to the new church, urgently needed to serve the fast growing community to the west of the parish.

In First Tower Park or St Andrew's Park, as it is also called, there is a children's playground and plenty of space for sitting or walking, with the sea and the beach just across two roads.

The best way to explore these outskirts of St Helier is, of course, on a bike. There are many places in town where cycles can be hired at a modest cost, by the day or week as preferred. There is also 'Le Petit Train' — the road train — which has an hourly service along the promenade from West Park to St Aubin, 10.30am-4.30pm and 7-10pm.

2 ST BRELADE

About the Parish

(Bus 9a, 12, 12a, 14, 15)

The parish of St Brelade covers the south-west tip of the island and extends along the coast from St Aubin's, just west of Beaumont, round Noirmont Point, into St Brelade's Bay itself, round Corbière and then to the north up along St Ouen's Bay, just past Le Braye slipway. With such an extensive coastline, it has many attractive beaches to choose from as well as cliff walks with splendid views.

It was once thought that St Brelade might have been the sixth-century saint so famous for his voyages, St Brendan. Nowadays, though, the name St Brelade is thought to be a softened version of the Celtic name Bren Gwaladr or Branwallader. Branwallader was a Celtic monk and companion of the more famous St Sampson, who was supposed to have visited Jersey in the sixth century. St Brendan's personal symbol — a silver fish on a blue background — is (now mistakenly) the parish emblem, as can be seen on the wall of the Parish Hall (*La Salle Paroissiale*) in St Aubin by the harbour.

Prehistoric Remains

For those interested in Jersey's prehistory, the most important site in the parish, as well as in the whole of Jersey, is at the east end of St Brelade's Bay at La Cotte Point. It is a cave, **La Cotte de St Brelade,** ⋔ now some 60ft above sea level, first used in about 110,000BC, where not only food remains and flake tools have been found but also mammoth and woolly rhinoceros bones. It is thought that the ravines in this cliff were used as 'gump traps' to catch these huge animals, as they were forced along the narrow strip of land to the drop below. This camping place for prehistoric hunters can be reached either from the beach or by a steep path down the cliffs from Portelet Common. Many of the items found in the cave are on display in the Jersey Museum in St Helier, as are the pots and implements from a Neolithic settlement excavated at Les Blanches Banques, further to the west of the parish.

Also from the Neolithic age are the heaps of fallen stones on the cliffs overlooking Fiquet Bay which were once two dolmens, while near **La** ⋔ **Sergenté** off Le Mont de la Pulente are the remains of a round hut tomb, the earliest dolmen in Jersey. Several menhirs, or standing stones, among the grass-covered sand dunes of Les Quennevais, the **Blanches Banques Menhirs**, also bear witness to the pagan religious observances of those prehistoric times.

In and Around St Aubin

Whether prehistoric man ever had time to marvel at the many different bays and caves in St Brelade, today's visitors certainly can. Starting at the sheltered east corner of St Aubin's Bay there is the stretch of sand from the Gunsite slipway to St Aubin which is perfect for basking on and quite safe for bathing. Swimmers should take care, however, to avoid the area round **La Haule slipway** (*Bus 12, 12a, 14, 15*) which is reserved for water skiing. For here at La Haule there is a licensed school for water-skiers (Jersey Sea Sport Centre ☎ 45040), staffed by fully qualified instructors. It is open everyday from 10am until 6pm and all equipment is supplied. After two or three lessons even a complete beginner should be able to enjoy the thrills and exhilaration of this increasingly popular water sport. Also available for hire are surf jet and wet jet personal water craft. Surf jets are 30mph jet powered surf boards (the easiest water sport), while wet jets are sea scooters. Banana boat rides and boat trips complete the variety on offer to give enjoyment to the whole family.

Almost opposite St Helier harbour, is **St Aubin** (*Bus 12, 12a, 14, 15*). There is a delightful promenade walk of about 3 miles between St Helier and here, as well as an easy cycle ride along the specially made track. As it is flat all the way, with a wonderful sea view, it also makes a popular course for joggers. In the summer there are water-skiers and other water sporting activities to watch and from November to spring, over-wintering brent geese, oyster catchers, redshanks and dunlin can be seen wading along the shore. The bright lights along the whole length of the prom make a colourful display on summer evenings.

Why this village of St Aubin, first mentioned in the sixteenth century, was named after a Breton saint, no one can be sure, as there was certainly no church in the area till the 1800s, but he was the saint who gave special protection against pirates and invasion by sea. Yet because of its position on the coast and the fort built in the 1540s to protect the ships which anchored there, St Aubin eventually became the island's safest harbour and the merchants who used it and got rich from it built their fine houses round it, which are still in evidence today. There was also a permanent market built over the road from the harbour and the bank which is now on the site has faithfully copied the original design. In fact, St Aubin only ceased playing an important role in the

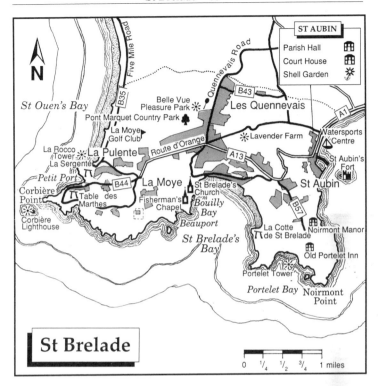

St Brelade

mercantile and trading life of the island when the harbour at St Helier was finally completed in the 1840s. Today the boats moored in the harbour, the nearby boatyards and the Royal Channel Islands Yacht Club are the only remnants of St Aubin's proud seafaring tradition.

The best way for a visitor to enjoy St Aubin is to stroll round it. There is parking on the front to the east of the village from where it is only a step or two to the boatyard and harbour. Facing the harbour is La Salle Paroissiale de St Brelade (**St Brelade's Parish Hall**), which was once the Terminus Hotel and railway station of the Jersey Railway. This ran originally from St Helier to St Aubin and was then extended to Corbière. In 1936 the railway station was gutted by fire and the major part of the line's rolling stock was destroyed. Mystery surrounds the fire to this day. Whatever the cause, the important result was that the company decided to close the railway, and so the bus took over as the island's sole form of public transport from that year.

Continuing along the Bulwarks, formerly known as Le Boulevard, with the harbour to the left, there are several fine houses lying back from

Collecting vraic

 the road which are worth looking at in passing. The **Old Court House** at the very end of the road is particularly interesting, as it was probably here that seventeenth-century privateers brought their booty for auction. Watchers of the television series, *Bergerac*, may also recognise it as 'The Royal Barge' where Diamond Lil used to be the hostess. Locals and visitors enjoy the view from its courtyard over the harbour and the bay beyond. Over the road on the headland is the Royal Channel Islands Yacht Club, where visiting yachtsmen are always welcome.

The next road of architectural interest in St Aubin is the High Street, to the right up Mont les Vaux. The earliest houses, dating from around 1657, are at the bottom of the hill. Those at the top of the High Street were built in the last century. Many of the old granite cottages have 'marriage stones' with the initials of the husband and wife who owned it. The date on the stone could either be that of the marriage or when the house was built. The Sail Loft is a reminder of those days when ship building was an important industry in St Aubin, before the advent of steam-powered boats.

 Continuing up Mont les Vaux there are still two more places to see. On the right-hand side of the hill there is **St Aubin's church** itself, a pleasing example of Victorian Gothic. Inside there is the only pre-Raphaelite stained glass in Jersey — a fine window in the Lady Chapel by Edward Burne-Jones and William Morris.

 On the bend further up the hill is a garden which intrigues everyone who passes it. The **Shell Garden** and all the ornaments in it are

St Brelade's Bay

decorated throughout with the pearlescent shells of the ormer which used to be found so abundantly in Jersey waters. An unusual shot for the holiday album!

In St Aubin, there is a small group of shops, including a bank, a post office and a supermarket. There are also several restaurants, cafés and inns. All in all, a most attractive part of St Brelade's parish.

The Railway Walk

For the keen walker there is a flower- and shrub-lined walk, The Railway Walk, which follows the track where the railway used to run the 4 miles from St Aubin up to Corbière. The number 12 bus goes every hour from Corbière back to St Aubin for those without the energy to walk back. The great block of red granite which lies opposite where the Corbière railway ticket office was, is known as the **Table des Marthes**, as children used to play knucklebones (*marthes*) on it. Originally it was no doubt the capstone of a prehistoric tomb.

Bays, Beaches and Clifftops

BELCROUTE BAY

The next bay round the coast worth a visit is Belcroute (*Bus 12 and walk*). This can be reached by going along La Route de Noirmont and then, just before Portelet, bearing to the left down a steep narrow road, past the magnificently wrought-iron gates of the privately owned Noirmont Manor. From this quiet, east-facing and sheltered bay, with its wooded backdrop, inhabited by tits, flycatchers and goldcrests, the visitor can look right across St Aubin's Bay to Fort Regent.

NOIRMONT POINT

Between the bays of Belcroute and Portelet comes the majestic headland of Noirmont (*Bus 12 and walk*), the Black Mount, of which Jerseymen say that when clouds gather over it, or *'quand Niêrmont met son bonnet'* (when Noirmont puts on its bonnet) it is sure to rain. There is so much of interest here: a wood with holm oaks to wander through and cliff paths to walk along; at the headland's point a German Occupation command bunker, complete with its K18 coastal artillery gun; at its foot Noirmont Tower built between 1810 and 1814 against a French invasion and now used as a lighthouse. In spring, nature lovers can spy the young herring gull and shag in their nests on the cliff ledges; inland the nests of the Dartford warbler; and all summer enjoy the sight and smell of its gorse- and heather-covered slopes. On the grass-covered cliff slopes the rare autumn squill with its blue/white bells can be seen from July to September and, at its best on a sunny morning, the yellow spotted rock rose can be found. By the small pond to the south-west of the headland grows the unique, but sadly fast-declining, Jersey forget-me-not. Most importantly there is plenty of space for parking. The whole headland is kept by the States of Jersey as a war memorial to those who perished in World War II.

A Walk over Noirmont Point (Approx 1½ miles)

Take the bridle path on the left of the rustic stile, which follows the perimeter of the conifer plantation and leads to Noirmont Point. There are trees on either side, so you will expect to see and hear many more birds, including tits, warblers, robins, wrens, thrushes and blackbirds. The fence on the left surrounds the property and grounds of **Noirmont Manor**. The original house was built in 1700 by Philippe Pipon. In 1810 it was demolished and rebuilt by the Pipon family and purchased in 1909 by Guy de Gruchy. Lillie Langtry spent her honeymoon there and scratched her name on a window pane with her diamond ring. The manor is not open to the public.

Walking forwards and along the east side of the Point, you can glimpse through the trees, Belcroute Bay, where ships from the 'plague ports' had to anchor during their time in quarantine.

Follow the path, which is very well maintained by the Public Works Department — even in wet and muddy conditions wood chippings are laid on it, which makes it very comfortable to walk along. Looking east there is a good view of St Aubin's Bay and across to the rocky outline

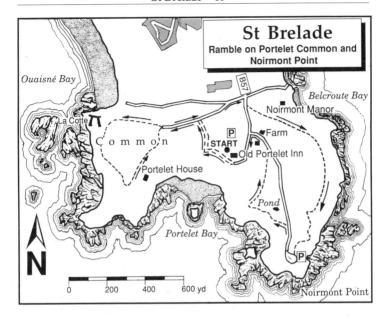

St Brelade
Ramble on Portelet Common and
Noirmont Point

of Grève d'Azette.

Take the path back to the car park on the Point and walk to the west, looking directly over Portelet Bay and the Ile au Guerdain. This is one of the most beautiful views on the island. In June and July the pink and yellow mesembryanthemums cascade down the cliff to the mellow pink granite shoreline below. Golden sand, turquoise sea, blue sky and the green of the isle make it a popular vista for artists and photographers.

Walk along the road for about 200yd, turning on to a grassy footpath, where there is a delightful pond, ringed by willows and a resting place for mallard. Looking across the bay you can see the Ile Percée and the tunnel made by the sea constantly thundering through it. Just ahead is a seat and another extremely good viewing point.

Take the grassy footpath back to a fork, turn left, and, finally, join the road through Warren Farm. This is a small preserved Jersey farm, owned by the States and tenanted. Behind the barn is an attractive area of woodland, mainly evergreen conifers, but with some deciduous trees. It was planted in 1950-2, and gives excellent shelter for many birds and, possibly, the red squirrel. It can be very bleak and windswept particularly in winter. Immediately after the farm, turn left and follow the road back to the bus stop, or the car park behind the Old Portelet Inn.

Gunsite at St Aubin

PORTELET BAY

Returning from Noirmont Point towards La Route de Noirmont, there are two beaches and two commons to choose from. The first turning to the left leads down Portelet Lane to Portelet Bay (*Bus 12*). This is approached from the road by steep steps — not for the unfit — leading down to the beach which is surrounded on three sides by tree-covered cliffs. The sandy beach is small but charming and, despite the steep climb down, popular, because of its south-facing sheltered aspect.

A tragic tale is associated with the tiny **Ile au Guerdain** which lies in the centre of this small bay. A certain Philip Janvrin, born in the parish of St Brelade, sailed to Nantes in his ship the *Esther* but when he came back in 1721 and wanted to anchor in St Aubin, he was refused permission to do so for fear of infection from the bubonic plague, then raging in that part of France. Instead his ship and its crew had to remain in quarantine in Belcroute Bay. Unfortunately, Philip Janvrin had indeed been infected by the plague and it was not long before he died of it, still aboard his ship.

The authorities continued to be adamant that even his dead body could not be brought ashore. Then, after intercession from his widow, a compromise was reached. Permission was given for him to be buried on the Ile au Guerdain, in sight of his St Brelade home. So today the island is known locally as 'Janvrin's Tomb', though Portelet Tower built over the grave a hundred years later is part of Jersey's defence against the French and not part of the memorial to poor Janvrin. He was later buried in St Brelade's cemetery. It should be noted that swimming in the waters round Janvrin's Tomb can be dangerous.

The second turning, down Portelet Road, leads to **Portelet Common**, an ideal spot for family picnics and rambles. The third turning to the left is the narrow Mont de Ouaisné (pronounced 'waynay') which leads down to the sandy beach of Ouaisné and the common. They can also both be reached by climbing down the cliff slope from Portelet Common by La Cotte Point, where the Palaeolithic cave is.

At **Ouaisné** (*Bus 12*), large gatherings of the great crested grebe have been seen in the spring, taking advantage of the bay's shelter. In the summer this south-west-facing beach is a favourite spot with families, as there is a large car park and a café serving the area. Then as well as the fine stretch of sand, there is the common behind the beach for picnics or exploring. The toilets have easy access for wheelchairs.

A Ramble on Portelet Common (Approx 2 miles)
(see map page 69)

This ramble is notable for its spectacular coastal views. It also has a good variety of flowers, mosses, lichens and birdlife. Start from the car park behind the Old Portelet Inn and at the side of Janvrin's Restaurant. Turn right on leaving the car park on to a footpath, passing stables on the right. Turn right at the end of this lane, onto a road with the hotel on the left. Turn left at the 'T' junction, which is the lane leading to Portelet Common. The Portelet Hotel is now on the right. Bordering the lane on the right is an old bank, with a nice mixture of small wild flowers. Continue along the lane through the high hedges of privet and macrocarpa. The lane opens out onto the common and forks, so take the right-hand path through high gorse. In early summer this is a mass of yellow and highly scented flowers; in the mid-summer heat you will hear the popping of seed pods as they burst. The low-growing gorse, which grows with heather on a large area of the common, comes into flower a little later. From this headland there is a fine view over Ouaisné, St Brelade's Bay, and across the bay to Battery Point. Below is the cave known as La Cotte, mentioned earlier.

From here take the path towards the wall which runs out to the end of the cliff. If you are lucky you will see the stonechat, chaffinch, sky lark, linnet and the Dartford warbler.

Now walk parallel to the wall until you come to the iron gate of Portelet House grounds, turn left, following the path which winds down through the evergreen holm oaks. There is a broken-down fence along the edge of the path. As you proceed, the pathway is straddled with large roots, weaving patterns on the surface of the roadway, which come from the large pines on the right. Rejoin the road at the fork which began the walk on the common. Walk back to the Portelet Hotel on the left and turn right to rejoin the route to your car.

ST BRELADE'S BAY

After the small, unspoilt bays of Belcroute and Portelet, the sweep of St Brelade's Bay (*Bus 12, 14*) next to Ouaisné is quite a contrast but it is also one of the most photogenic bays in the island, with its palm trees, colourfully laid-out gardens and extensive stretch of sand. St Brelade's beach can be reached from Ouaisné either by walking along the beach at low tide, or over the common which borders the beach. The approach to St Brelade's Bay by road is along the B57 from Noirmont and then down Mont Sohier (B66). There is plenty of space for parking in the car parks on the right-hand side of the road. The number 12 and 14 buses give a frequent service from the Weighbridge to St Brelade's Bay.

St Brelade's parish church (*Bus 12, 14*) dedicated to St Brelade is at the west end of St Brelade's Bay. Built of local La Moye granite, with the sea coming up to the churchyard, it is probably the most picturesque church on the island. It dates from as early as the eleventh century and the south, east and west walls of the original Norman building are still standing. Since then, however, numerous changes and additions have been made, including, at the end of the nineteenth century, church pews in the then contemporary art nouveau style, which are still in use.

Two memorials distinguish the churchyard. The first is the obelisk

Portelet Bay

given by the States of Jersey to commemorate the generous founder of the General Hospital, Mrs Marie Bartlet, who lived in the parish in the eighteenth century. The second belongs to our own century and was given by Lady Trent in memory of her husband, Jesse Boot, the famous chemist, the first Lord Trent. The attractive lychgate makes a popular backdrop for the photographing of those married in the church.

Outside the church is a short footpath leading from the south door, down some granite steps, to the sea. This is the *perquage* or sanctuary path, which every island church had in the Middle Ages. It offered to those members of the parish who had broken the law, a way of escape from the harsh torture and imprisonment that would await them if they were found guilty at their trial. Many criminals chose to go down the *perquage* path to perpetual banishment from Jersey rather than face the rigours of the medieval penal system.

Right alongside the parish church is what is known as the **Fisherman's Chapel** (*Bus 12, 14*), which may, in fact, mark the site of the original church. It too is built of local granite and dates back to the twelfth century, when it seems to have been used as a mortuary chapel and then as a chantry chapel, where mass was said for the family who owned it. Its historical importance stems from the fact that it has the finest medieval wall paintings in the Channel Islands, which people from all over Europe come to see.

It was during the fourteenth and fifteenth centuries that the south and north walls of the chapel were painted with biblical scenes from the Old and New Testaments including the Fall, Cain and Abel, the Annunciation, Palm Sunday and the Crucifixion. Over the altar is painted God the Father, appearing in the heavens and, below, the Virgin Mary with the sons of the owner's family kneeling on her left, and the daughters kneeling on the right. On the west wall, opposite the altar, is a depiction of the Last Judgement, reminiscent of the style of Stanley Spenser, with the medieval parishioners, complete with hats of the period, rising from their tombs to be judged by the figure of Christ.

This chapel may at one time have served as a place of worship for a guild of fishermen but after the Reformation it was no longer used at all for religious purposes. In fact, for 300 years it was totally neglected, finally being used as a workshop. Only in 1933 was it restored as a place of worship, when an old altar slab with five consecration crosses, commemorating the five wounds of Christ on the cross, was brought from Mont Orgueil, and erected as the altar.

A history of both the church and the chapel can be found just inside the west door of the church, while an illustrated summary of the restoration of the wall paintings inside the Fisherman's Chapel can be seen on the outside of the north wall of the chapel itself.

Lining the front of St Brelade's Bay are hotels, restaurants and cafés; on the beach there are deckchairs and windbreaks for hire and trampolines to exercise on. Here too is a **Watersports Centre** catering for sports of all kinds and of all standards, from pedaloes to waterskiing. Pedaloes can be hired and would-be and experienced water-skiers will find a licensed school staffed by fully qualified instructors.

There is also a **Windsurfing and Sailing School** at the Wayside slip in St Brelade's Bay. Here beginners can enjoy tranquil sea conditions in Mediterranean-style surroundings. There are canoes, sailing dinghies and windsurfer equipment to hire as well as instruction in sailing and windsurfing.

St Brelade's Bay is an extremely popular beach, perfect with its sheltered position for both sunbathing and safe swimming at all stages of the tide as well as watersports. During the summer the beach is patrolled by beach guards. It also looks most picturesque from the sea during one of the boat trips that can be taken round the bay. For anyone who wants a change from sea and sand, there is the **Winston Churchill** **Memorial Park** on the other side of the coast road, with its climbing roses, miniature waterfall and seats in the sun or shade.

From the far west end of St Brelade's Bay there is easy access to an ideal and quiet picnic spot. Follow the white railings by the jetty up to a signpost which reads Le Coléron and walk up the narrow path by the side of it and out on to the headland. Here there is a seat surrounded by gorse, broom and other wild flowers from which St Brelade's Bay can be viewed to the left and Bouilly Port (above which is the resting place of the famous chemist Jesse Boot) lies overlooking the bay, to the right.

BEAUPORT (*Bus 12*)

This south-west corner of the island has three more beaches which are worth a visit; the next round the coast is Beauport. From the footpath between St Brelade's church and the new cemetery a little way along it, there is a well signposted 20-minute walk over the cliffs to Beauport, or it can be reached by car from either end of Mont ès Croix. The eastern end goes past St Brelade's church hall, opposite the church, and the western end is reached from Route Orange. Both approaches are clearly signposted. There is a car park but no toilet facilities above Beauport and the beach is reached by going down a path which winds for about 5 minutes' walk through the bracken to the golden sands below. This bay, with its sparkling sea, has been kept unspoiled and is well loved for its seclusion and good swimming by locals and visitors alike. It should be noted that no refreshment facilities are available either on the beach or on the cliffs above it.

CORBIERE (*Bus 12*)

Before coming to the next small beach along the parish's Atlantic coast,

Ouaisné

Windsurfing, one of the many watersports on offer in Jersey

St Brelade offers the visitor the lonely splendour of the **Corbière lighthouse** (*Bus 12*) on its extreme south-western tip. Its name comes from *corbeau*, the French for a crow, rook or raven, once considered birds of ill omen, and therefore appropriate for dangerous rocks that brought many a ship to disaster and many a sailor to a watery grave. Yet a lighthouse was not built to warn of their danger until 1873. The States chose Imrie Bell to construct it and he built a 35ft-high concrete tower on a 9ft-high concrete platform — the first concrete lighthouse in the British Isles. The beam from its powerful, automatic light can be seen over a distance of nearly 20 miles.

The rocks are still a hazard to those on foot, however, because although there is a natural causeway to the lighthouse at low tide, when the tide turns, the seas cover the path at an incredible speed. There is a memorial stone at Corbière which acts as a constant reminder of the dangerous rush of the tide and reads 'Peter Edwin Larbalestier, assistant keeper at the lighthouse, who on the 28th of May, 1946 gave his life in attempting to rescue a visitor cut off by the incoming tide. Take heed, all ye that pass by!'

The second tower on the headland was an observation tower built by the Germans with the help of their slave labour force during the Occupation. It is now used by Jersey Radio as a marine coast station. The headland can be reached by car along La Rue de la Corbière, by the number 12 bus, or on foot up The Railway Walk from St Aubin, which is even pleasanter to walk down. The tower south of La Rue de la

Corbière is part of the sea water desalination plant which ensures a constant water supply for islanders, even in time of drought.

THE ATLANTIC-FACING COAST

The last two beaches to visit in the parish face due west. First comes **Petit Port** *(Bus 12)*, just round the road from Corbière, which can be reached on the B44 Corbière-Petit Port road which comes sweeping down past gorse-covered hills to the no-through road on the left, where there is the car park for the beach. When the tide is out this is more a beach for sunbathing on, or rock clambering, rather than swimming, as the receding tide leaves only small rock pools behind.

Petit Port is a good starting point, though, for a short cliff walk around the headland to St Ouen's Bay, the largest bay in the island. The walk starts either past four concrete posts at the entrance to the car park or by the sea wall. If the latter is taken there are extensive German fortifications to the left of the path and then the sweep of St Ouen's Bay from L'Oeillère (the 'Look Out') along the 5 sandy miles to Etacquerel, with La Rocco Tower in the foreground and, on a clear day, Sark and Guernsey on the distant horizon. This footpath is lined here and there with the fragantly scented white-flowered burnet roses and leads to La Pulente in about 20 minutes.

La Pulente is an ideal beach for the active visitor as well as the sunbather, because of its extent both across and down to the sea. Once famed for its seaweed or vraic gatherers, and still plentifully covered with small shells, La Pulente is now a favourite spot for all-year-round jogging, which can continue right round the bay. To the north at Le Braye slip *(Bus 12a)* sand car and motor cycle races are held, while further along the beach the Atlantic rollers make this the best spot on the island for surfing. There is parking, as well as toilets and refreshments, at both La Pulente and Le Braye. Nature lovers may like to note that to the north of Le Braye slip, behind the sea wall, grows the saltmarsh species of sea purslane together with the South African 'mesem' Diophyma, which are obviously not to be picked.

The dunes behind these west-facing beaches belong to one of the most extensive dune systems in the British Isles. Springing through the coarse turf is an abundance of wild flowers; some so small that one has to kneel down to spot them. Here grow different kinds of orchid, including the early purple, the green winged and the pyramidal, as well as hare's-tail grass, Atlantic clover and the sand crocus.

Les Quennevais (Shopping Centres)

(Bus 12, 12a, 15)

It would be a mistake to think that St Brelade offers only seaside pleasures. On the contrary, it offers at Les Quennevais the largest shopping complex outside St Helier. The name Quennevais comes from *chènevière* or *chanevière*, meaning a place where hemp is grown, for this was an important crop when ropes made of hemp were needed for the island's shipbuilding industry.

A chilling legend has grown up to explain why so much of Les Quennevais' once fertile soil has become covered in sand. The tale goes that on St Catherine's Day in 1495 local wreckers lured five Spanish ships, laden with cargo from the New World, to their doom on the rocks. Just before the last of the ships sank, without any of the Jerseymen going to the aid of the drowning seamen, one of the Spaniards cursed the pitiless wreckers, prophesying that within the year they would suffer God's wrath because of what they had done.

With one day to go before the end of the fateful year, the wreckers decided to celebrate their escape from the curse of the Spaniard. Just as they were sitting down to their feast, however, a most terrible storm arose, with gale force winds lashing the sea right over the land. Every wrecker was drowned and, as the tide retreated, it left the whole of Les Quennevais covered with sand.

To return to the shopping facilities at Les Quennevais, there are, in fact, three distinct centres, all developed in the 1950s or 60s. Driving south from the airport, along L'Avenue de la Commune and then La Route des Quennevais, the first shops on the left, built round three sides of the car park with a large supermarket in the centre, are known as Les Quennevais Parade. Tucked just behind the Parade, on the right, is Les Quennevais Precinct, whose shops have the advantage of a large car park at the back. Then, on the four corners of the crossroads where Route d'Orange meets La Rue Don is the third shopping and parking area (complete with toilet facilities) known as Red Houses. Together these three centres will provide for almost every shopper's needs from banking to DIY, including clothes, food, hairdressing, chemists, travel agents, record centres, cleaners, cafés and restaurants — even dentists and doctors. So comprehensive is the range of goods and services on offer and so convenient the parking at Les Quennevais, many islanders do their shopping there in preference to the busier St Helier.

Other Places to Visit

As well as opportunities to delve into the past, sample coves and beaches, and to shop, St Brelade still has more to tempt the visitor.

The entrance to **Pont Marquet Country Park** *(Bus 15)* is on the right down La Petite Route des Mielles travelling north and it has its own car park. A ramble round the park with its fine pines and chestnut trees could take anything from half an hour to an hour or the ramble could be

Sailing, another popular pastime in Jersey

extended by walking some distance along The Railway Walk from St Aubin to Corbière, which lies by the side of the park. It is also an ideal spot for a picnic, with its wild flowers and tranquil atmosphere.

For children who might be too young to enjoy the unspoilt pleasures of the park, on the other side of La Petit Route des Mielles there is a playground. This has a sand pit, climbing frame, swings, seesaw and chute for the youngsters to play on, with sheltered seats where parents can sit. There are also toilet facilities.

 The **Lavender Farm** is on La Rue du Pont Marquet, 5 minutes' walk from the bus stops at St Brelade's camp site and Red Houses, which are served by the 12, 12a and 15 buses. The most interesting time to visit is when the lavender is harvested in July and August. Then visitors can see the cutting and gathering of the crop from the fields, watch the steam distillation of the lavender oil and go through the room where the perfume is bottled. A full range of the Jersey Lavender products, including potted lavender plants, are on sale in the Lavender Shop.

But even when it is not harvest time there is still plenty to do and see. For the energetic there are the three main lavender fields to walk round, with benches for those who want to enjoy the view, or the woodland walk to wander down and try to name some of the sixty varieties of trees on the farm. There is also a genuine gypsy caravan, over 150 years old, as well as a herb garden and a dovecote, not forgetting the beehives, from which comes the lavender honey on sale in the shop. There is a restaurant with a verandah from which to view the fragrant fields.

Beauport

PLACES OF INTEREST
IN THE PARISH OF ST BRELADE

La Cotte de St Brelade
La Cotte Point
Cave, first used about 110,000BC,
with mammoth and woolly rhino
remains.

La Sergenté
Off Le Mont de la Pulente
Simple passage grave (from
3600BC).

The Blanches Banques Menhirs
Les Quennevais
Standing stones on the sand
dunes.

Parish Hall
St Aubin
Nineteenth-century former
Terminus Hotel of Jersey Railway.

The Old Court House
St Aubin
Once frequented by seventeenth-
century privateers.

St Aubin's Church
Victorian Gothic, with pre-
Raphaelite glass.

La Haule Slipway
St Aubin's Bay
Jersey Sea Sports Centre.

Shell Garden
Up Le Mont les Vaux
Decorated with ormer shells.

St Aubin's Fort
Sixteenth century. Located on
island in St Aubin's Bay.

Table des Marthes
Corbière
Capstone of prehistoric tomb, used
by children playing 'knucklebones'.

Pont Marquet Country Park
La Petite Route des Mielles
For rambles and picnics.

Noirmont Manor
Near Belcroute Bay
Rebuilt 1810.
Lillie Langtry spent her honeymoon
here. Private.

Noirmont Tower
1810-14, now a lighthouse.

Portelet Tower
Ile au Guerdain (Janvrin's Tomb)
1808, part of Jersey's defence
against the French.

Parish Church
W St Brelade's Bay
Eleventh-century, churchyard and
memorials, *perquage* or sanctuary
path.

Fisherman's Chapel
St Brelade's Bay
Twelfth century, frescoes of
special interest.

For those with specialised interests, there are facilities in the parish
to enjoy indoor and outdoor sport and country music. The **Les
Quennevais Sports Complex** is at Don Farm, Les Quennevais. It now
provides facilities outside for hockey, rugby, cricket, football, tennis and
athletics. There are also a 1,500m road cycle track and bowling greens.
In the indoor sports hall badminton, table tennis, volleyball and basket-

PLACES OF INTEREST
IN THE PARISH OF ST BRELADE - continued

Windsurfing and Sailing School
Wayside slip, St Brelade's Bay
Instruction in windsurfing and
sailing, also hire facilities.

Winston Churchill Memorial Park
St Brelade's Bay
Restful, with view over the bay.

Corbière Lighthouse
South-west tip of parish
The first concrete lighthouse in the
British Isles, built 1873.

Lavender Farm
Near Red Houses, Les Quennevais
Six acres lavender fields and
woods, shop and restaurant.

Les Quennevais Sports Complex
Don Farm, Les Quennevais
Facilities for hockey, rugby, cricket,
football, athletics, badminton, table
tennis, bowling etc.

La Moye Golf Club
Off La Route Orange
18-hole course.

Nashville Country Music Club
La Moye Ballroom
On La Route Orange.

Beaches
St Aubin's Bay
Belcroute Bay
Portelet Bay
Ouaisné
St Brelade's Bay
Beauport
Petit Port
La Pulente

Activities
Promenade walk — St Aubin to St Helier
Cycle track — St Aubin to St Helier
Sailing — Royal Channel Islands Yacht Club, St Aubin
Railway walk — St Aubin to Corbière
Surfing, water-skiing, windsurfing
Cliff path — Portelet to Ouaisné
Coastal walk — Ouaisné to St Brelade's church
Athletics — Les Quennevais Sports Complex
Golf — La Moye Golf Club
Children's Playground — La Petite Route des Mielles
Country music — La Moye Ballroom and Bars

ball can be played. The new changing pavilion includes a large social room as well as a kitchen area and toilets. All these sporting activities are available to visitors during the school summer holidays. Also throughout the season the keenly contested Summer League football matches between local hotel sides are played here, which visitors might enjoy watching.

Corbière Lighthouse

LA MOYE

There is an 18-hole golf course at La Moye, off La Route Orange, but visitors must be members of a recognised golf club. It is at **La Moye Golf Club** (*Bus 12 and 12a to both golf and music club*) that the Jersey Open Golf Tournament is held, usually in June.

During the summer **Nashville Country Music Club** meet every Wednesday and Friday at La Moye Ballroom and Bars on La Route Orange. Meetings, at which both local and visiting groups perform and for which there is an admission charge, start at 8.45pm and continue till midnight. In the winter the club meets on Wednesdays only.

Those interested in croquet might like to have a game with members of the Jersey Croquet Club at Les Quennevais Sports Complex. For further information ☎ 483566.

3 ST CLEMENT

Around the Parish

(Bus 1, 1a, 18)

Covering the south-east tip of the island, St Clement is not only Jersey's smallest parish but also the most southerly parish in the British Isles. With one of the rockiest coastlines and perhaps the most fertile land, St Clement is also noted for its long stretches of sandy beach, its prehistoric remains, a fine manor house and tales of superstition and witchcraft. It was also, for over 3 years, the home of the famous French writer Victor Hugo. Despite the ribbon development along the coast road and the ugly intrusion of the four high-rise blocks of States flats on the Le Marais skyline, making this small parish the one with the fourth-highest population, St Clement is still in many parts — with its small fields and many hedges — a charming part of the island.

St Clement shares its northern boundaries with St Saviour and Grouville and extends from just west of Plat Rocque Point westwards to **Le Dicq** (pronounced dyke) slipway. This dyke was one of the first attempts to combat the devastating effects of so much parish land lying below high-tide level. Before it was constructed, much land was lost, as can still be seen when exceptionally low tides lay bare the remnants of a great forest now lying beneath the sands of Grève d'Azette. In 1811 even the dyke was not strong enough to hold back the seas and the extensive flooding that year forced the States to build the high sea wall along this beach.

Looking seaward from this south-eastern corner the view is of fantastically shaped reefs and broken rocks. The lunar-like landscape stretches from the coast to far out to sea with many of the rocky peaks at the ebb and flow of the tide just below the surface of the water — a constant navigational hazard. Yet defence of 'this terrible coast', as it has been called, was still thought necessary at the time when a French invasion was feared. So in 1780 a tower was built at **Le Hocq** and, in 1811, on the rock islet of Icho a quarter of a mile out in St Clement's Bay, a second tower — 28ft high. In the autumn, on nearby reefs, herons can sometimes be seen waiting for the high tide to ebb.

A third tower, a well known landmark, dating back at least to the

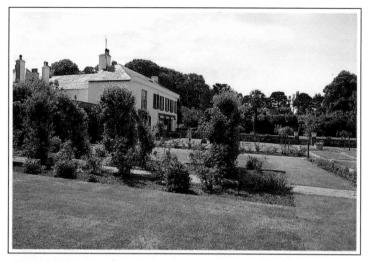

Samarès Manor

eighteenth century, overlooks the parish and its coastline from a high spur land of land to the north-west of La Rue au Blancq. This is known as Nicolle Tower and has been used over the centuries, including the time of the German Occupation, as a look-out station.

Remains of the parish's earliest visitors, from prehistoric times, have been found both on the coast and inland. On the tidal islet 300yd from the promontory that divides Grève d'Azette and St Clement's Bay, eighteen cist or box-like graves were discovered, some still with human remains. This La Motte, or **Green Island** (*Bus 1*) as it is known today, is a grass-covered rock about 200ft long which is surrounded by water only at high tide. Today it is a favourite picnic spot for local families, being within such easy reach of St Helier, while several of the cist graves have been removed to the museum at La Hougue Bie in Grouville to save them from being washed away by the tide. On the beach opposite Green Island there are a licensed restaurant and toilet facilities.

Earlier immigrants went further inland and one of their passage graves is high on **Mont Ubé**, overlooking the coastal plain to the sea. Dating from about 2800BC, it had small stone cists arranged round the end of the chamber and burnt bones, pottery and even a Roman gaming piece have been discovered. However, its religious significance had long been forgotten by the 1800s, when it was used as a pigsty and its capstones broken up for building purposes. Twenty-eight uprights though, still flank the passage to the burial chamber. The wooded *côtil*

Samarès Manor gardens

of Mont Ubé, owned by the National Trust, can be reached by going up La Blinerie, which goes north from La Grande Route de St Clement, or the Inner Road as it is called. It is on the right-hand side of the road, up some stone steps by a stone tablet indicating the direction of this prehistoric tomb, which looks down over Samarès Manor to the west and St Clement's Bay to the south.

Less easy to find, but also of religious significance to early man is the standing stone on almost a straight line between Green Island and Mont Ubé. This is known both as **La Blanche Pierre**, the White Stone, and La Dame Blanche, the White Lady. Twelve feet away from this menhir was found a cache of limpet shells, surrounded by a ring of stones, which would suggest that the sea was a major source of food for these prehistoric inhabitants of Jersey. Starting again from St Clement's Inner Road, turn south down La Rue de la Croix. Go past the length of the long high granite wall on the right, past the first turning into a field and take the second path in. Follow this path which turns to the right, towards the middle of the next field to the west, where there is a gap in the hedge revealing the 11ft-high White Stone, standing in the middle of the field. As these two fields are under cultivation, any visitor wishing to see La Blanche Pierre should remember to keep to the paths.

SAMARES
The salt marsh, which is to the south-west of La Blanche Pierre, was of great significance to much later residents in the parish of St Clement.

It gave its name to the fief (an estate held from the Crown on certain conditions) the manor and the Seigneur (Lord) of the manor. Salt water marsh in old French is *salse marais*, which, corrupted to Samarès (*Bus 1a*), is the name by which all three are now known. In fact, the first Seigneurs of Samarès used to find the salt deposits left by the ebbing tide in the flat marshy ground between the manor and the sea provided an important part of their income.

Several distinguished Jersey families can claim a Samarès Seigneur among their ancestors, but the first holder of the title was supposed to have been a Norman landowner to whom the fief had been given in 1095 by the son of William the Conqueror. His family, the de St Hilaires, held the Samarès fief until the 1330s. In fact, Peter de Sausmarez, as it was then spelled, was summoned in 1300 to explain why he behaved like a king in his fief, that is to say he kept a pair of gallows, had a warren, claimed ships wrecked on his treacherous coastline, chased after rabbits (where Fort Regent is now) and kept hawks — all royal privileges. His confident reply was 'That he and his ancestors were in possession from time immemorial of the said Manor and had free liberty to chase over all the Mount of St Helier with their hunting dogs, ferrets, nets and hunting poles.'

 All that is left today of the de St Hilaires' tenancy of 'the said Manor' is the crypt of their chapel. It is unusual on two counts: instead of lying east to west, as do most Christian places of worship, it lies from north to south, and, secondly, it is dedicated to St Martha. It is quite rare to find a chapel dedicated to the busier of the two biblical sisters who used to entertain Jesus in Bethany. Two other well known island families who held the fief were the Payns and Dumaresqs (pronounced Dumarick) and a stone from their original manor, depicting the Payn trefoils and the Dumaresq scallop shells on the alliance by marriage of the two families, can be seen in the garden of the present manor.

During the English Civil War, the Seigneur of Samarès, Henri Dumaresq, was one of the few islanders who supported the Roundheads. So, immediately he learned in 1643 that George Carteret had won over the island for the king, Dumaresq escaped to London. In his absence his effigy was hanged in the manor grounds by Royalist supporters and George Carteret turned the house into an internment camp for the wives of those Parliamentarians who had fled Jersey!

 It was Henri's son, Philippe Dumaresq, in the second half of the seventeenth century who was the first of the Seigneurs to make the beauty of the Samarès gardens a byword, as it still is today. In a letter to John Evelyn, the well known English diarist, he wrote: 'I have planted a score of cypress from France and some borders of Phillyrea, whereof most were from slips. I have this year begun a little plantation of vineyard.'

Sir James Knott, who bought the fief in 1924, had at one time forty

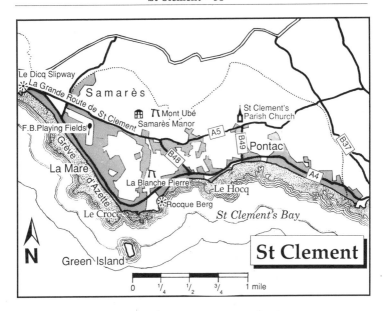

gardeners to carry out his own ambitious plans to drain the marsh so that he could construct unusual rockeries and water gardens as well as a special spot for the sub-tropical plants he collected. To this garden, the largest in Jersey, he also introduced an oriental theme, with a series of waterfalls, a pagoda and a summerhouse in the Japanese style.

Today many of the garden features introduced by the various Seigneurs of Samarès can still be traced. For instance in the spring there is the magnificent sight of over eighty varieties of camellias in bloom. There are also different corners of the grounds made into specialised areas such as a herb garden, a walled garden and a water rock garden. The herb garden itself is sub-divided too, into four different sections of cosmetic, culinary, fragrant and medicinal herbs. All the herbs are set out and labelled to give visitors easy access to them as well as the pleasure of their distinctive scents.

There is also a tea garden where, tea, coffee, home-made cakes and salad lunches are served. In the farmyard there is a craft centre with spinning and weaving to watch, plus locally made goods to buy, as well as an animals corner. There is also a shop selling pot pourris and books about herbs and live souvenirs of Jersey in the shape of potted herb plants. For children there is a playground and the unusual treat of rides in an old restored Jersey van pulled by a shire horse.

Le Hocq

There is no entrance charge for those who only wish to visit the shop, otherwise there is an admission fee.

The manor too, is open to visitors, though, because of successive modernisations only the thickness of the walls and St Martha's crypt testify to its original antiquity. However, across the drive from the manor's front door stands the island's oldest *colombier* or dovecote, dating back to the eleventh century, which only Seigneurs were allowed to have. Tradition has it that owls use the Samarès *colombier* as a base when they fly from Longueville Manor in the parish of St Saviour.

Noteworthy features inside the manor include the fine French walnut panelling in the dining room where there is a Simon Elwes portrait of the present Dame of Samarès in riding habit. The drawing room, with its specially woven carpet of sage green and the Steinway piano, in its ornate case after the Dutch style, is often used for concerts given by both local and internationally known musicians. The intricately carved staircase to connect the dining and drawing rooms was specially ordered by the Dame of Samarès to be in keeping with the two restored rooms.

In the past there were certain services that not only the Seigneur had to give the king but that tenants had to give their lord of the manor. In Samarès tenants in the fief had to defend the person of their Seigneur in times of danger with their own body, even stand hostage for him. Each tenant had also once in his life to ship his lord and master to any one of four Norman ports whenever he wanted a free trip to France. Four 'voluntary' journeys per vassal! As late as 1763 tenants had the menial tasks of making the Seigneur's hay and cleaning out his *colombier*.

The rector of St Clement had his own special duty too, though this by its very nature occurred quite infrequently. If the Dame of Samarès happened to have a baby while living in the fief du Hommet, a subsidiary of the Samarès fief, then it was the rector's task to make sure that the dame had a white horse on which to ride to church for her churching service.

The present Dame of Samarès no longer has the privileges her ancestors enjoyed, such as chasing rabbits over the Town Hill, but she still has a duty in common with some other Seigneurs. Once a year she has to attend L'Assize d'Héritage. This is a sitting of the Heritage Division of the Royal Court, which certain Seigneurs attend and when the name of their fief is called affirm their allegiance to the Queen. This is the oldest court still attended in Europe.

Witchcraft
In the sixteenth and seventeenth centuries the parish of St Clement was

noted for something far less attractive than the beauty of Samarès garden. It became a centre for witchcraft, with the special meeting place of the initiated taking place on the western side of St Clement's Bay at Rocque Berg.

There were witch trials in Jersey right through the reigns of Elizabeth, James I, Charles I and even during the Civil War. They came to a peak, however, between 1548 and 1620, when Jersey was in the grip of Calvinism. Whether those who were tried as witches were serious followers of the organised devil worship that had started in the Middle Ages and which was rampant for several centuries all over Europe, or whether they were simply rebels against the strict discipline of Calvinism and only wanted a bit of excitement in their drab lives, is difficult to judge. Certainly the authorities who sat in judgement on them three or four centuries ago believed in the corrupting power of the devil and felt they had every justification to punish those who seemed to be the devil's disciples.

A look at the trial of five so-called witches from St Clement will give some idea of the supposed crimes and punishment. It was reported of Jean Mourant in 1585 that 'he having been so forgetful of his salvation as to make a contract with the Devil, confessed with his own mouth his dealings with the Devil by mark and pact, confirmed by pledge and gift of one of his members [a finger joint] by means of which he had committed infinite mischiefs, crimes and homicides by reason of which he has been condemned as a criminal to be strangled until he is dead and his body burned until it is entirely consumed and to have all his goods and chattels confiscated.'

Six years later the growth of witchcraft and the increased numbers of those who went to witches for help when they were in trouble were deemed such a threat to the States that a proclamation was drawn up, addressed to all islanders. It declared that 'for all time to come everyone shall turn away from such inquisitions and diabolical practises against which the law of god decrees the same punishments as against witches and enchanters themselves....It is strictly forbidden to all the inhabitants of this island to receive any counsel or assistance in their adversities from any witches or diviners or anyone suspected of practising sorcery under pain of one month's imprisonment in the castle [Gorey] on bread and water.'

This proclamation had no effect on the activities of three female parishioners, for in the witch trials of 1611 Collette Horman was found guilty of witchcraft and executed, as were Isycles Hardyne and Germaine Royl. The fifth witch, Marie Filleul, was aged about 60 when she was sentenced to death, and her trial brought up the grisly right of the Seigneur of Samarès to hang someone who lived in his fief, as Marie Filleul did, on his own gallows and to confiscate all her possessions. So of the five St Clement parishioners who were brought to trial and found guilty of being witches, only Marie Filleul was executed at Samarès. The rest were hung and then burnt in the Royal Square in St Helier.

Whether these five had as the focal centre of their witchcraft the 40ft-high granite rock on Le Nez Point known as **Rocque Berg** is not recorded. But this rock, with its top vitrified by lightning and marked with what looks like the cloven hoof of the devil himself, is known to this day as the Witches' Rock. As late as 1875 Jersey people would go nowhere near Rocque Berg, specially if it was a Friday and there was a full moon because 'The Prince of Darkness has a special fancy for the locality. He frequently came here in former days and still manifests himself!'

Such a terrifying place, now tamed somewhat as it is part of a private garden and can only be viewed from the corner of Green Island car park or the St Clement coast road, obviously attracts legends and two of them are still told. The first concerns the beautiful Madeline and her sweetheart Hubert, who both lived in the fishing community at La Rocque. Hubert had always been interested in the occult and one night found his way to Rocque Berg where he fell asleep. When he awoke the place had been transformed into a beautiful garden and all around him charming girls were dancing. He was attracted by one of the young girls in particular and promised to come again the following night to meet her.

Returning to La Rocque, Hubert was full of all that had happened to him but Madeline begged him not to go again. Hubert ignored her pleas and set off for his tryst at the Witches' Rock. Madeline then sought the help of a priest, who, giving her a cross, said that, with it alone to help her, she could save Hubert from all harm. So Madeline, hugging the cross to her walked through the night to Rocque Berg.

What she saw there filled her with dread, for Hubert stood in the middle of a circle round which savagely danced a group of old and ugly hags. Madeline raised the cross as if to block out the hideous sight and immediately the scene was changed. Hubert, half unconscious from fear, lay at the foot of the rock but the witches were nowhere to be seen, only the sound of their despairing cries faded on the wind.

Victor Hugo

Perhaps the most distinguished foreigner who has ever lived in Jersey was the great French poet, novelist and dramatist Victor Hugo. He spent 3 of his 19 years' exile from France in the parish of St Clement. The reason for his expulsion from France was a political one: he had dared to oppose the ambitious plans of Louis-Napoleon Bonaparte to become emperor.

The first place to which Hugo fled was Brussels, but when the authorities there became nervous of harbouring a pamphleteer who continually vilified the 'Little Napoleon', Hugo decided to come to Jersey where there were already several political refugees from Europe. And it seemed that when he landed at St Helier on 5 August, 1852, most of them were at the harbour to meet him for he said when he saw them: 'I left France on the quay of Antwerp but I find it again on the jetty of St Helier.'

Hugo's wife, their two sons and the brother of his drowned son-in-law were already in Jersey. Until they could discover somewhere more permanent, they all stayed at the Pomme d'Or Hotel in St Helier. Then they were fortunate enough to find a pretty little furnished house to suit their needs at 3 Marine Terrace, on the shore of Grève d'Azette. The family did not mix much with the local Jersey people but preferred to keep their own company. Two favourite occupations were picnics at St Brelade and, for the younger members of the group, steeplechasing on the beach.

This carefree existence on the island after all the political turmoil enabled Hugo to return to his writing. Several of the poems he wrote while he was here were obviously inspired by Jersey scenes and events. He even wrote a poem about a crab which nipped his fingers after he had bought it live from a fisherman at Grève d'Azette. He drew a moral for his readers from the fact that, instead of punishing the crab for biting him, he threw it back in the sea! *'Que l'homme rend le bien au monstre pour le mal'* ('The man gives back good for the evil done by the monster').

In another poem, which appears in the collection of poems he called *Les Châtiments*, he wrote of Jersey *'J'aime cette île solitaire'* ('I love this solitary island'). He also mentions the famous rock near Le Dicq — just in the parish of St Saviour — where he used to go almost every day to listen to the sound of the sea and to talk with other political refugees. So famous a meeting place did this *'roche solennelle'* become, that it is still called 'Le Rocher des Proscrits' (the Exile's Rock) and has a plaque to identify it as such.

In fact, so impressed was Victor Hugo by Jersey's huge rocks and caves that not only did they inspire his writing but he wanted them as a suitable Gothic backdrop for the photographs taken of him by his son, with special equipment brought over from France. A collection of these remarkable photos of Victor Hugo posing in poetic stance on or near rocks on different parts of the island can be seen in the Reference Library in St Helier.

As well as devoting his mornings to writing and his afternoons to walking, Victor Hugo spent many an evening table-turning — the latest Paris craze. He also enjoyed a game of billiards on Sundays — but behind closed shutters, so as not to shock the neighbours! In typical French fashion, which would have shocked the puritanical islanders even more had they known, his mistress Juliette Drouet was also with him in Jersey, as well as his wife and family. He found accommodation for her just along the coast, at the foot of Mount Bingham in what is now Du Heaume House.

This island idyll lasted only 3 years and once again it was political intrigue which ended it. Victor Hugo was still a staunch Republican and delivered the funeral oration at Macpéla Cemetery in St John at the death of most political refugees. He was also a supporter of the exiles' newspaper *L'Homme* printed in St Helier. This had the temerity in October to reprint a scurrilous open letter written to Queen Victoria on the subject of her visit in Paris to their enemy, Napoleon III. For this act of treason the editor, owner and seller of *L'Homme* were all immediately expelled from Jersey.

Hugo thought this expulsion, without a trial, outrageous and wrote a declaration saying so, which he had signed by thirty-five other exiles and posted up in St Helier. Hugo's name topped the list of signatories, while the declaration concluded with the words 'Expel us too!' The next morning the Constable of St Clement on the orders of the Lieutenant-Governor did exactly that. As Victor Hugo set sail for a new asylum in Guernsey, he looked back on Jersey, no longer as 'beautiful and charming' but as a mere 'nothing'.

A Walk to Green Island

Just as Victor Hugo took delight in walking along the beach so can today's visitors to Jersey. One such easy walk which takes about 30 minutes, is that along the beach from Le Dicq to Green Island. At both ends of the walk and all along south-west-facing Grève d'Azette are stretches of sandy beach with safe bathing. Swimming, though, is best at high water before the receding sea reveals the rocks. Great care should be taken, however, not to get stranded while exploring these rocks and gullies by the tide's swift return. At the Dicq slipway there is limited disc parking and a kiosk; there is limited free parking halfway along Grève d'Azette at La Mare and toilets with easy access for wheelchairs; while at Green Island there is a free car park, as well as refreshment and toilet facilities. Green Island is the most southerly beach in the British Isles and is much patronised by locals for its sheltered charm. Even when it is not warm enough to swim or sunbathe, it is restful to sit on one of the seats provided at the edge of the car park.

Anyone wanting to make a round trip back from Green Island to Le Dicq but not along the beach, could walk up La Rue de Samarès, then turn left along La Grande Route de St Clement, continuing along Green Road and then turning down the coast road. This inland route would take almost twice as long as walking along the beach.

Le Hocq

Another beach which is popular with local families is further east around the coast at Le Hocq (*Bus 1*), just opposite St Clement's Parish Hall. It extends quite a distance both sides of the slipway and is sheltered from the north wind by the high sea wall. There is a grassy picnic area for those who do not want sand in their sandwiches and an old coach from which light refreshments can be bought. Bathing here is safe and best at high tide. At low tide this is a favoured spot for those fishing, with salt and plastic bags, for razor fish. Feeding on an incoming tide during the winter months waders are prolific, including plover, red shank, turnstone, dunlin, curlew, oyster catcher and large numbers of black bellied brent geese.

There is also pleasant sailing for windsurfers at high water in St Clement, but sailors should be warned about the dangerous currents at low tide.

Other Places of Interest in St Clement

For those who want something other than windsurfing, swimming or walking there are the **Jersey Recreation Grounds** (*Bus 1a, 1*) which are on the corner made by the Inner Road at Grève d'Azette and Plat Douet Road. Here there is a variety of sports for all ages where the whole family can relax and enjoy a day in the open air. For serious golfers there is a 9-hole course, but they will have to supply their own clubs. Less serious golfers can opt for either mini-golf or putting where equipment is supplied. There are sixteen courts for tennis players and racquets and balls can be hired. There are also bowling greens. Patrons can relax and enjoy a snack or a full meal, hot or cold, from breakfast time onwards, inside or outside on the patio of the fully licensed self service café which is open all the year round. Special parties can be catered for too. There are also changing and shower facilities in the same building.

For those who prefer their sports from a spectator's point of view, further up Plat Douet Road, towards the sea on the left, are the **FB Playing Fields** (*Bus 1a*), named after the wife of the famous chemist Florence Boot. Here, as well as football and cricket pitches, is Jersey's all-weather six-lane athletics track with facilities for all field events which was opened in September 1987 by the Olympic gold medallist David Hemery.

The track can be used by visiting athletes for a nominal payment per hour, payable at the track, but rubber sole shoes or 6mm needle spikes only should be worn. It is available daily till dusk for running, long and triple jump and general training. Hurdles, high jump, pole vault and throwing equipment, however, are available to authorised athletes only.

The final spot for visitors to this parish to make for is its centre — **St Clement's parish church** (*Bus 1a*). It is further to the east, along La Grande Route de St Clement, the Inner Road. The name Clement

PLACES OF INTEREST
IN THE PARISH OF ST CLEMENT

Jersey Recreation Grounds
On the corner of the Inner Road at
Grève d'Azette and the Plat Douet
Road. Nine-hole golf course, tennis
courts, bowling greens, café.

FB Playing Fields
Plat Douet Road
All-weather six-lane athletics track.

Green Island
On tidal islet 300yd from the prom-
ontory dividing Grève d'Azette and
St Clement's Bay
Grass-covered rock where prehis-
toric remains have been found.

Parish Church
La Grande Route de St Clement
(Inner Road)
Eleventh century. Font and frescoes
of special interest.

Mont Ubé
La Blinerie
Passage grave from about
2800BC.

**Samarès Manor, Grounds &
Herb Centre**
Shop, splendid gardens and
tours of the manor house, tea
garden, playground.

Beaches
La Grève d'Azette, Green
Island, St Clement's Bay, Le
Hocq.

Activities
Walk to Green Island from Le
Dicq
Jersey Recreation Grounds

comes from the Latin *clemens*, meaning merciful, and it was a very popular name in ecclesiastical circles in the Middle Ages. The Clement, however, from whom both the church and the parish got their name was probably Pope Clement I, who lived in the first century AD. He is best known for his Epistle to the Church of Corinth and has long been the patron saint of sailors — most appropriate for a parish with such a dangerous coastline. St Clement's special emblem, which is also the parish crest, is an anchor, to commemorate his being condemned to die for his faith by drowning in the Black Sea, with an anchor tied round his neck.

The date of the original St Clement's church is hard to pinpoint, as it has been so altered and added to over the centuries, but it could not have been later than 1067. From 1090 to the time of the Reformation it was owned by the abbey of St Sauveur le Vicomte in Normandy, which was responsible for its upkeep. At this time, in common with the other parish churches, it would have been a building with a low thatched roof and narrow windows, two of which can still be seen in the north wall. That part of the present church where the organ is now was a separate chapel and remained so for about 500 years. The fine sculptured granite font dates from about 1400 and was dumped outside the church during the Reformation, only being found again 300 years later.

In the fifteenth and sixteenth centuries the church gradually took the cruciform shape it has today and added its belfry and spire. The church's renowned wall paintings date back to the fifteenth century and are worth looking at for their period detail. On the west wall of the south transept all that remains of an illustration of an ancient French poem are the legs of two horses, the hand of one of its riders, the head of a dog and the depiction of a boar, which presumably was being hunted. The poem *The Three Living and Three Dead* tells how three successful hunters met three skeletons who warned them of the vanity of worldly success and pleasure. All that is left on the wall of the French text reads 'Alas, St Mary, who are these three corpses who look so grim? It breaks my heart to see them so piteous.'

The walls in the north transept and on the north side of the nave, tell the tales of two vanquished dragons. In the first St Margaret holds the wing of the one she conquered, while St Michael has just slain his in the second.

During the hundred years or so that followed the break from Catholicism in the sixteenth century, St Clement's church, in common with the island's eleven other parish churches, was no longer referred to as a church but as a temple. It was whitewashed every 10 years or so and instead of coming in to worship together, the men of the parish used the west door and the women used a door, now walled up, at the end of the north transept. No equal rights in Jersey's Calvinist period!

Today, the church still retains its rural setting, with cows grazing in the fields that stretch down to the churchyard. The inn which is to the west of the church was built on the site of one of the four priories founded here soon after the original parish churches were built — hence its name The Priory.

4 GROUVILLE

Around the Parish

(*Bus 1, 1a, 2c, 3a*)

Fame has come to Grouville in several guises — from Neolithic times to the present day. For many centuries both pagan and Christian pilgrims came to the parish to worship at La Hougue Bie; today's visitors to the parish come in their thousands especially to watch Jersey pottery being made. And over the intervening years there have been other compelling reasons to come to Grouville.

The most ancient of the landmarks in this south-eastern parish, with its long eastern coastline, is a Neolithic burial chamber, covered by a mound that is over 40ft high. This cruciform passage grave of **La Hougue Bie** (*Bus 3a*) is considered to be one of the finest dolmens in Europe. By the time the site was excavated in 1924, though it had already been robbed, the religious vase supports that still remained suggested that it had been a religious monument of some importance.

The huge mound which covers this ancient burial place has given it its name, as 'Hougue' is a corruption of *haugr* — the Norse word for mound. The meaning of the adjective 'Bie' is harder to trace, but the legend which purports to give its origin, shows the continuing religious tradition surrounding La Hougue Bie down to Christian times.

Apparently, way back in the Dark Ages, the parish of St Lawrence was being devastated by a fire-breathing dragon and there seemed no-one on the island able to stop its devastations. So the Seigneur of Hambye across the water in Normandy came over to pit his strength against the monster, bringing with him his trusted squire Francis. After a great battle, Hambye slew the dragon and cut off his head as a trophy of his victory but, unfortunately, decided to rest awhile before making the return trip to Normandy. Then his servant Francis showed his true colours. He killed his master and set sail for home, hoping to win the hand of the now widowed Dame of Hambye. Kneeling in front of her, with the dragon's head to prove his bravery, Francis persuaded the stricken widow that it had been her husband's last wish for her to reward him with her hand in marriage.

Reluctantly the Dame of Hambye agreed to marry Francis but soon afterwards she learnt the true story of her first husband's death. Francis

104

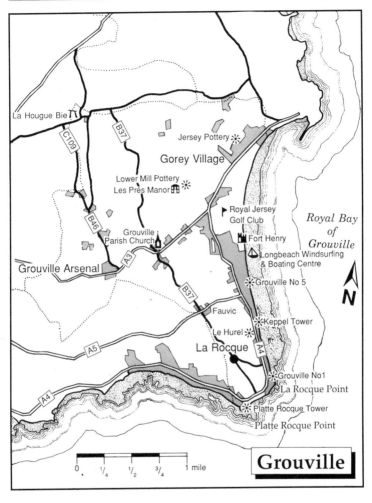

La Hougue Bie

Jersey Pottery

Gorey Village

Lower Mill Pottery
Les Prés Manor

Royal Jersey
Golf Club

Fort Henry

*Royal Bay
of
Grouville*

Grouville
Parish Church

Longbeach Windsurfing
& Boating Centre

Grouville Arsenal

Grouville No 5

N

Fauvic

Keppel Tower

Le Hurel

La Rocque

Grouville No1

La Rocque Point

Platte Rocque Tower

Platte Rocque Point

0   ¼   ½   ¾   1 mile

Grouville

spoke in his sleep and revealed himself as his master's traitorous
murderer. Immediately the Dame of Hambye had Francis hung for his
heinous crime and gave orders for the body of her first husband left
behind in Jersey to be covered by a mound so high that she could see
it from where she lived in Normandy.

In order that there could be masses said for the soul of her murdered
husband, she also had built, on the very top of the mound, a chapel
which was dedicated to Notre Dame de la Clarté — Our Lady of the

Dawn. It could be that from this lady's faithfulness to her husband comes the name of the mound by which it is known today, La Hougue Bie — from La Hougue Hambye. Certainly both the mound, covered with wild daffodils and primroses in the spring, and the tiny chapel are still there, over the site of the prehistoric grave.

There is though, a second chapel on the top of the mound, which also has a story attached to it. Several centuries after the murder of Seigneur de Hambye, in 1509, Richard Mabon was appointed Dean of Jersey. He immediately had the Hambye Chapel restored as a thanksgiving for his safe return from a pilgrimage to Jerusalem. Then, that same year, he started to build a second chapel beside the first with later, below it, a crypt as nearly resembling the Holy Sepulchre as he could remember it. The chapel came to be known as the **Jerusalem Chapel** and all three places of worship on the mound started to attract numbers of pilgrims. It is said by later Protestant writers that the Catholic Dean Mabon made quite a thriving business from them by fraudulent tricks.

In the Jerusalem Chapel, it is said, 'He hid in the wick of candles a very thin wire, which he fastened to the roof of the Chapel. The smoke from the flame made the wire invisible, and the candles seemed to float in mid-air, and people believed that they were held by the virtues of Our Lady'. Another so-called 'miracle' occurred in the crypt. The statue of Our Lady was placed in an alcove with her hand outstretched for alms. When the coins were placed on her hand they fell through it, touching a spring, which made it look as if her hand was moving in gratitude for the money given.

The name Prince's Tower Road which leads to La Hougue Bie is the only relic of the time in the eighteenth century when a certain James Dauvergne built a tower over the two chapels from the top of which could be seen Gorey Castle. When Philippe Dauvergne, who also had the title 'Prince de Bouillon', inherited the tower from his uncle James, it came to be known as the Prince's Tower. It was only demolished in the 1920s, when the two chapels were restored to their original state and function.

La Hougue Bie, with its Neolithic grave, its two chapels and crypt are now cared for by La Société Jersiaise and further attractions for visitors have been added to in the grounds which extend between Prince's Tower Road (B28) and La Rue des Pigneaux (B46). There is a clear plan at the entrance to show exactly where all the different museum sections are in relation to La Hougue Bie itself. To the left of the entrance is the **Archaeological Museum**, which has among its many fascinating exhibits, a few coins from the hoard of 2,500 dating back to 56BC, which were discovered by a Grouville farmer on his land at the end of the 1950s. Archaeological finds in the island from most periods are represented here: the mammoth tusk and tooth from La Cotte de St Brelade from prehistoric times, and on the wall the carved corbels that come from the ruined Grosnez Castle in St Ouen which dates back to about the fourteenth century.

The Geology Gallery which is in the basement of the Archaeological Museum is clearly displayed and explained. It shows Jersey's geological setting in the Armorican area of which it is a part.

One attraction did not have to be added at La Hougue Bie, because it was already there — the **German Command Bunker** which was sited at the foot of La Hougue Bie at the time of the German Occupation of Jersey 1940-5. At the entrance to the bunker is the actual boat used by the only Jerseyman who managed in 1941 to escape from the island, by rowing all the way to England. In the communications room there is a life-like model of a German operator; on the wall in the Gestapo office is a picture of Hitler; while proclamations from him concerning the government of the Channel Islands are hung up in the corridors. At the very end of the bunker is a salutary reminder of how the Occupation ended — it shows the thousands of German troops after Liberation Day waiting to be taken off the island as prisoners of war.

The complex at La Hougue Bie includes a museum shop where posters, books and postcards and light snacks such as coke and crisps or a hot drink can be bought. There are also toilet facilities in the grounds and room for parking. Only part of the site is accessible for disabled visitors. To reach La Hougue Bie, follow the A6 or A7 from St Helier to the Five Oaks roundabout, then bear right on to the B28 and continue for approximately 1 mile.

La Rocque

La Rocque harbour (*Bus 1*) on the south-east corner of Grouville will retain its fame as the place where in 1781 French troops got ashore unchallenged — the last French invasion the island had to suffer. Just before midnight on Friday, 5 January, 1781, thirty small boats cautiously approached La Platte Rocque. They were being skilfully piloted through the hazards of that treacherous coastline by a renegade parishioner from Grouville. Yet everyone else on board was French and under the command of Baron de Rullecourt, who wanted to conquer Jersey for Louis XVI of France.

The 4-hour-long disembarkation took place on the sands at low tide and went unchallenged because the Chef de Garde had been so busy celebrating the eve of Twelfth Night that he had forgotten to post a sentry at La Rocque battery or to send out patrols along that part of the coast. Before all could be got ashore, however, the fast incoming tide prevented the landing of not only the drummers, but, more importantly, the gunners. So de Rullecourt without meeting any resistance, left a small force at La Rocque to cover his retreat and led less than a thousand men through the deserted country lanes to St Helier.

By about 5.30 that morning the French invaders had got as far as Colomberie without even the night watchman apprehending them. In fact, the first casualities of the invasion were innocent victims in St Helier who happened to look out of their houses at the sound of marching feet. Once at Hill Street, de Rullecourt divided his troops to form an attack on the Royal Square from two sides and by 6.40am the French invaders had captured the centre of St Helier without meeting any military resistance whatsoever.

De Rullecourt then ordered the Lieutenant-Governor, Moses Corbet, who was still in bed, to meet him at what is now the Royal Court in the Royal Square. At the meeting, the French commander demanded the surrender of the rest of the island, threatening that the alternative was wholesale slaughter and pillage by the 4,000 troops he had at his command. Falling for this bluff, Moses Corbet surrendered.

However, while de Rullecourt was proclaiming himself the new Governor of Jersey and planning a celebration dinner at Government House, rebellious forces at Elizabeth Castle and Westmount were refusing to lay down their arms. By 11.30am, the 3,000 troops on Westmount were being organised by the young English Major Peirson, to swoop down on the Royal Square, where the invaders were now cooped up. By mid-day the Battle of Jersey had begun in the Royal Square, but, just at the point of victory, the gallant Major Peirson was mortally wounded and did not live to see the complete rout of de Rullecourt and his forces. De Rullecourt also died that same day, just 24 hours after he had landed so confidently at La Rocque.

Meanwhile, back in Grouville, the invasion remained undetected for several hours until the officer in charge of Fort Conway (now Fort Henry) received a message from St Helier. Urged on by the rector of St Martin, Captain Campbell sent a troop of 120 grenadiers to attack the French troops left behind at La Rocque. A platoon of forty men led by Lieutenant Robertson were the first to arrive on the coast and immediately started to attack the enemy, despite being outnumbered by them. Though the battle was small, heavy casualities were sustained, with loss of life on both sides. A memorial to the seven men in Robertson's platoon who died can be seen to the right of the west door in the churchyard of Grouville parish church. A plaque at La Rocque commemorates the invasion.

La Rocque is a typical fisherman's harbour with its sea walls — the oldest on the island — and its nineteenth-century granite pier. The beach which faces south is a sandy one with safe bathing at high tide and at low tide a 2-mile stretch of beach is left exposed for rock clambering and exploring. Visitors should, however, be extremely careful not to get stranded on the rocks by the swift inrush of the sea, especially at the time of the spring tides which occur every month shortly after the new and the full moon. There is limited parking at La Rocque, a kiosk and toilet facilities. An added attraction is to watch the fishermen bringing back their catches.

Although unsuccessful, this French invasion made the islanders determined to fortify this vulnerable east coast against any further attacks. Thus it is that so many towers can still be seen in Grouville. **Seymour Tower** was completed the following year, in 1782, on L'Avaraison islet about 1½ miles off La Rocque Point. It replaced an earlier tower which probably accounts for the fact that it is square — unique among Jersey's coastal towers. It stands in lonely isolation on the horizon and is accessible at low tide but visitors should take extreme care not to be trapped there by the rapidly returning tide. This happened in 1987 to two riders and their horses and their dangerous plight in having to stay overnight in the tower until low tide the following day was reported not just locally but by the UK news media as well.

Other towers which were hastily built to defend the Grouville coastline were Platte Rocque Tower, Grouville No 1, Keppel Tower, Le Hurel, Fauvic and Grouville No 5. These were all put up by the States before 1794 but are now in private ownership, so visitors should take care not to invade the privacy of the present occupiers of these towers.

The Royal Bay of Grouville

Queen Victoria was so impressed by Grouville's east-facing coast, when she visited Jersey in 1859, that she sent a message to the Bailiff on her return to England that she would like it to be known in future as the Royal Bay of Grouville (*Bus 1, 1a, 2c*). And what a great deal of natural beauty there still is today — not just the sea and the sand but also the common.

The bay offers nearly 5 miles of sandy beach — plenty of space for beach games and family picnics as well as safe bathing. The stretch of sand is also ideal for walking from Le Hurel slip, on the A4 in the south, to Gorey, or for the more energetic to jog along. The distance is about 4 miles and the return journey can be made by walking (or jogging) up Beach Road to the Gorey coast road, turning left and coming along the A4 road which runs through the common and through the woods back to Le Hurel.

Any winter walker will be delighted by the sight of numerous wading birds on the shore over wintering here, such as brent geese, curlew, redshank and plover: summer walkers can spot the common and sandwich tern as well as the oyster catcher which breed here during the warmer months.

In the centre of the bay, for watersport enthusiasts, there is the **Gorey Watersports Centre**. The craft on hire include sailing dinghies, windsurfing boards, Hobie Cats and fun canoes, together with all the necessary equipment. For the novice or the sailor who wants to learn more, tuition is given in both sailing and windsurfing. Grouville Bay is certainly the ideal sailing bay of the island, for it stretches along for about 5 miles and, except for its southern tip, is free of rocks and treacherous currents. Nevertheless the Gorey Centre has a guardboat in case anyone experiences any difficulty. This is certainly a beautiful setting, with Gorey Castle as a backdrop.

Grouville Bay is just the right sheltered spot when the wind is from the south-west or north and, for those who do not like sand in their sandwiches, there is the alternative of the common which runs along the length of most of the beach for picnicking. To the left from the beach and the common the rugged splendour of Mont Orgueil can be seen, together with Gorey's picturesque quay and waterfront — an ideal subject for photographs. There is ample parking space and there are cafés and kiosks along the beach. Toilets are sited at the coast end of Beach Road, just past Fort William.

The Germans, during the Occupation, made extensive use of Grouville Bay. They realised that the texture of its sand was ideal for making the concrete needed to turn Jersey into an impregnable fortress. To facilitate the moving of the sand, the Germans built a railway from Gorey to St Helier. By the end of the Occupation over a million tons of Grouville beach had been used in the miles of concrete defences the Germans built over the island.

The 71 acres of common land which flank the beach have been popular with islanders over the centuries for several different reasons. In the eighteenth century **Grouville Common** (*Bus 1, 1a*) was the favourite spot for duels. In 1843 the horse races which were first run on St Aubin's sands and then at Grève d'Azette were moved to Grouville Common. So successful was the move that for 60 years all horse racing took place here, together with a splendid carnival complete with side shows and stalls. The Jersey painter, Ouless, in 1849, captured the feeling of it in his famous painting *The Jersey Races*. This now hangs in the Jersey Museum, where postcard reproductions of the colourful scene are also available.

An important part of Grouville today as far as conservationists are concerned, is the flat, fresh water marsh behind Gorey Common, known as **Grouville Marsh**. Though much reduced in size from what it once was, it still retains throughout the spring a good amount of fresh water, so providing the perfect habitat for wintering ducks, such as teal and shoveler as well as grey heron and common snipe. It is also visited in both spring and autumn by many migrating birds, including the reed, garden and willow warbler. It is also a breeding site for the great and lesser spotted woodpecker as well as the yellow wagtail. It is thought to be the best ornithological site on the island and a good viewing point is from La Cache des Prés off the A3. The flora is typical of a wetland area, featuring both reed and iris beds.

Another part of the common is the course which belongs to the **Royal Jersey Golf Club** (*Bus 1, 1a, 2c*). Many golfers might be familiar with the name Harry Varden — the champion golfer who won the British Open Championship five times — but few may realise his connection with this course at Grouville. Harry Varden had his early training at the Royal Jersey Golf Club, which had been established in the island as early as 1878, under the name of the Grouville Golf Club. Other players who began here include Ted Ray and the Ryder Cup Player Tommy Horton, now the club's resident professional.

Visitors are welcome to the 18-hole Royal Jersey Golf Club but are subject to starting times which are in force when they play. They must also be members of a recognised golf club and should contact the club early in their holiday if they want a game, as the sport is very popular.

Gorey Village

The tiny shopping centre of the parish is Gorey Village (*Bus 1, 1a, 1b*) across the road from the common. Here, as well as Jersey Pottery, there are several small shops including a newsagent, a grocer, a chemist and a post office. The village has an old world charm and is best explored on foot to take in the architectural details that are particularly 'Jersey', such as the dormer windows with their glazed sides and decorated bargeboards or gables. This is certainly the appropriate place to buy tomatoes, as the parish is famous for growing them.

The famous novelist Mary Ann Evans, better known as George Eliot, who came to Jersey in 1857 for a 3-months' holiday, stayed in Gorey Village. After she and her companion had checked into the Union Hotel in the Royal Square as Mr and Mrs George Lewis, the couple later took lodgings in the house in the main road, now known as 'Villa Rosa'.

George Eliot wrote of the time they spent at Rosa Cottage, as it was then called, as 'a sweet, peaceful life'. In the evenings she and Lewis strolled by the sea, preferring the common to the beach itself as 'you can have the quietest, easiest walking'. They also watched the races and saw there, as the novelist puts it, 'a little of Jersey human nature'. Here, at Rosa Cottage, Eliot wrote 'Janet's Repentance', the third of her *Scenes of Clerical Life* short stories.

By mid-July George Eliot was finding the heat too much for her and so they decided to return to England. Though they had both found

Jersey 'disappointingly English in habits and prices', Eliot summed up their impressions of 'such grassy valleys in this delicious island' as 'a sweet spot in our memories'.

The largest pottery in the Channel Islands, **Jersey Pottery** (*Bus 1, 1a, 1b*) is in the main road, Gorey Village and with its Egon Ronay recommended restaurant and over 3 acres of attractively laid-out gardens it is definitely a place to visit.

There are two different methods of making the pottery and the open-plan layout, together with the clear explanations of the different stages on the walls, make it easy to follow exactly what happens from the raw clay stage to the finished product. The casting method begins in the mould-making studio, where plaster of Paris moulds are made of the item required. The next stage is for semi-porcelain to be poured into the mould and left to dry. Any decoration is then hand-painted onto the shape before it is glazed and put into the kiln for firing.

The throwing method of making pottery uses a heavier clay, which is fashioned into objects on a wheel — an intriguing process to watch. Then come the decorating and firing of the piece.

The climax of this family-owned complex is the showroom, where nearly 200 different lines of pottery, which are made on the premises in their various colour combinations, are put on display. There is everything here from tiny candlesticks to large lamp stands. Popular items with visitors are the traditional Jersey items such as the bean crock, the milking can and anything featuring the gentle Jersey cow. Those objects which cannot be carried home, can be carefully packed and posted by the Pottery. Jersey Pottery can only be bought in the Channel Islands and, as well as being on sale at the Pottery itself, can only otherwise be bought in their shop in Bond Street, St Helier or in Guernsey.

Jersey Pottery is also a place to eat and somewhere to relax, for it has a first class restaurant where meals can be eaten inside or out, plus attractive gardens laid out round patios, pools and a fountain, with seating in the shade and in the sun. The Pottery is clearly signposted on the main St Helier-Gorey road going east, with plenty of space for cars at the back of the complex. Disabled visitors will find that ramps and special facilities have been provided for them. Visitors could easily spend half a day here, there is so much to see and enjoy.

Inland Grouville

The parish of Grouville is not just eastern and southern coastlines, impressive though those may be. It has always been noted for its agriculture and its inland pathway. Going back to an old agricultural practice, when Jersey's grain was ground by either wind- or watermill, in this parish is the island's oldest windmill, whose history can be traced as far back as 1331. Now sail-less, it is still preserved, to the west of the B37, as a landmark to help ships navigate the reef-strewn waters over which it looks.

Once the site of three working watermills and now turned into the island's third reservoir is **Queen's Valley** (*Bus 3a*). It lies behind Jersey Pottery and one of its watermills has quite a different use than originally intended. Moulin de Bas is now the Lower Mill Pottery where visitors are welcome to see the unusual work of Robert Boissière. Also on display are paintings by local artists of the valley before it was flooded for the reservoir.

With the construction of the Queen's Valley Reservoir, the island now has an extra storage capacity, holding about 260 million gallons of water. This will finally, from its own catchment area together with surplus water pumped from other areas, yield 450 million gallons a year, an increase in the total reservoir storage of a further 80 per cent.

A bonus to the walker is that the reservoir has not only been carefully planned to preserve as much of the natural environment as possible, but that a walk has been laid around it too. This walk follows the natural contours of the land and has several seats sited at scenic spots along its route. Certainly the extensive planting of trees and shrubs, together with the use of local granite to clad the concrete structures within the boundary of the reservoir, have done much to retain the rural charm of the valley.

Visitors keen on fishing will be interested to know that this sport is actively encouraged by the waterworks company, as the reservoir is stocked with trout as a means of monitoring the quality of the water being stored. For further information on fishing contact PJN Fishing Tackle ☎ 74875.

Both walkers and fishermen coming to the valley by car will find parking areas at either end of the reservoir. Unfortunately, though, parts of the 2 mile walk are not suitable for visitors in wheelchairs.

On the way to Queen's Valley Reservoir from Chemin des Maltières is the manor farm once known as La Maletière, as it belonged from 1170 to the Malet family. It has one of the best examples on the island of a spiral stone staircase and, incredibly, in its 800-year-old history, it has only been sold twice. The manor, now known as **Les Prés Manor**, has been in the present owner's family since 1841 and the grounds are open to the public on such occasions as the annual church garden party in July.

Having established Grouville's claims to fame then and now, it is interesting to speculate how it got its name, because it is the only parish whose name does not have a religious association. The old form of Grouville was Grosville. This would suggest that, as ville or villa merely meant a farm with the land attached to it, someone on the south-east of the island had a particularly large (*gros*) farm which eventually gave its name to the whole district.

Although **Grouville parish church** is always spoken of as Grouville, its full title is the parish church of St Martin de Grouville. So St Martin of Tours is the patron saint of both Grouville's and St Martin's parish church, though the latter is the older dedication of the two. The saint's story is depicted in the east window of the north chapel, with the first panel showing the well known incident of St Martin sharing his cloak with a beggar. Again, unusually for Jersey, although the oldest part of most island churches is the chancel, with Grouville it is the nave, which is thought to be over 1,000 years old. Its antiquity can be judged from the stones obviously brought up from the beach which makes its walls.

Items worthy of note inside the church are the church plate, which includes the work of local silversmiths dating back to the seventeenth century, the font and the *bénitier*. The eight-sided font has a curious design as well as a strange history. Made of Chausey granite sometime in the Middle Ages it has a double bowl, the smaller bowl perhaps intended to catch the water from the baby's head as it was baptised, so that it would not contaminate the holy water in the larger bowl.

At the time of the Reformation it was thrown out of the church and was discovered in 1650, with another font, being used in a farmyard as a pig trough. Both fonts were brought to the town church to be placed there but the strict Calvinist congregation refused to let them in what they called their 'temple'. The double-bowled font was then lost sight of for nearly 200 years, when it unexpectedly appeared, in a painting of about 1830, lying abandoned in the grounds of La Hougue Bie. When La Hougue Bie was bought by La Société Jersiaise, it gave the font back to its rightful owner, Grouville church. Only the bowl, whose rim has had to be restored, is original, the plinth on which it stands is modern.

Next to the lectern is what is generally believed to be a holy water stoup, or *bénitier*. It has a stone bowl with a heart-shaped outlet and the letters 'IHS' carved on the side, the Greek initials for the name of Jesus.

Outside the church, as well as the monument to the grenadiers killed attacking the rear-guard of the French invasion forces at La Rocque, are marks which indicate the uses to which an island parish church was put until this century. The west door has been made extra wide for wheeling out the parish cannon and there are also stones marking where the upper school door used to be. Booklets at the back of the church, though written for visiting children, reveal fascinating detail about the church to any visitor.

PLACES OF INTEREST
IN THE PARISH OF GROUVILLE

La Hougue Bie
On B28 and B46
Cruciform passage grave from about 3100BC. One of the finest in Europe. Surmounted by Hambye Chapel and the Jerusalem Chapel and crypt. Site also of several museums and German Command Bunker. Shop.

Gorey Watersports Centre
Royal Bay of Grouville
Boats for hire, windsurfing boards etc. Tuition given.

Royal Jersey Golf Club
Grouville Common
Eighteen-hole course.

Jersey Pottery
Gorey Village
Whole process of making pottery, plus gardens and restaurant.

Les Prés Manor
La Cache des Prés
Grounds occasionally open to public.

Lower Mill Pottery
Queen's Valley
See the work of Robert Boissière. Paintings of Queen's Valley before the reservoir.

Parish Church
La Rue à Don
Eleventh century. Seventeenth-century church plate.

Beaches
La Rocque
Grouville Bay

Activities
Inland walk round Queen's Valley Reservoir
Coastal walk from Le Hurel slipway north to Beach Road
Sailing and windsurfing in Grouville Bay
Golf at Royal Jersey Golf Club

'THE MINKIES'

There is still an unusual part of Grouville parish which has not been discussed. This is a rocky reef called **Les Minquiers**, spoken of locally as 'The Minkies'. At low tide the part of this reef which becomes uncovered is larger than Jersey, but at high tide only Maîtresse Ile remains sufficiently above sea level to be habitable. This group of tiny islands, about 16 miles south of Grouville which showed signs of being visited by seal hunters in prehistoric times, is administered by the parish.

Up to the nineteenth century, granite was quarried from Maîtresse Ile, some of it used to build Fort Regent, but more importantly the islet was used as a base for Jersey fishermen. In the eighteenth century, twenty granite huts were built there to give the fishermen more permanent shelter during the fishing season.

About a hundred years ago, however, the French began to question the right of Jersey fishermen to have sovereignty of a reef around which teemed so many fish. Frequent brawls broke out between the two groups, and French fishermen tried to sabotage the islanders' fishing by interfering with their nets and taking away their lobster pots.

Matters came to a head in 1952 when the question of who owned 'The Minkies' was brought before the International Court of Justice at The Hague. A year later the court decided that they belonged to Jersey. So now the Jersey authorities pay a regular visit to 'The Minkies' and the Union Jack is hoisted on Flagstaffe Hill, at the northern end of Maîtresse Ile, just in case anyone is in any doubt as to whose it is!

Any visitor who sees 'The Minkies' show up on the horizon to the south-east of Elizabeth Castle should immediately reach for their umbrella — seeing 'The Minkies' is a sure sign of rain to any Jersey fisherman. But anyone keen for a trip there to see Maîtresse Ile and the rest of the reef for themselves should try to get a friendly fisherman to take them there.

5 ST SAVIOUR

Around the Parish

(*Bus 1, 1a, 1b, 3, 3a, 3b, 20, 21, 23*)

Once a predominantly agricultural parish, the western tip of St Saviour has become increasingly built up, serving as a kind of suburb to St Helier. The heart of this long narrow parish to the north-east of town is round the church, with the Parish Hall, built in 1890, opposite and the lane running south by the side of it leading to Government House. This spot is also the focal point for tourists visiting the parish, as it was in St Saviour's Rectory that the famous Edwardian beauty Lillie Langtry was born; in St Saviour's church that she was twice married; and in its graveyard that she was buried.

The full name of one of the four chapels which eventually became **St Saviour's church** (*Bus 3b*) — St Saviour of the Thorn — tells of an old Christian belief. During the time when the whole of Europe was Catholic, no altar could be consecrated unless it contained a holy relic. So it is thought that the owner of the original small thatched chapel had in it either a thorn from Christ's crown of thorns, or a thorn from the sacred Glastonbury thorn planted by Joseph of Arimathea. This thorn is still remembered in the parish crest of three nails surrounded by a crown of thorns.

The church that eventually sprang in the twelfth century from this St Sauveur de l'Epine, together with the three other private chapels, is well worth a visit and not just because Lillie Langtry was married and buried there. Outside the church there are three items of note: on the south-west corner, set into a buttress, is a scallop shell, probably commemorating a pilgrimage from St Saviour to the shrine of St James in Compostela; there are several medieval windows, including two with flamboyant tracery on the eastern wall; at this eastern end are two megalithic blocks which could have come from an earlier church, or even a pagan place of worship.

Inside, the church, with its two chancels and two naves side by side, is rather dark because of the stained glass in every window, but there are time switches for the visitor to use. With the lights on, the glory of the chancel window, dating back to the 1440s, with the dignity of its simple lines, and the more modern colours of the fine pre-Raphaelite stained glass can be enjoyed to the full. On the south wall of the south nave is a memorial to Canon Cohu, who acted as the rector of the parish during the Occupation. He was imprisoned by the Germans for spreading British news from the BBC heard on a hidden wireless. He was later sent away to a concentration camp in Germany, where he died.

On the north wall are memorials to the relations of Lillie Langtry — the Le Breton family. The impressive oak carving in the church and the painting of the reredos panel was by Jerseymen.

In that part of the cemetery known as Le Clos de l'Hotel Dieu is the grave, clearly signposted, that everyone comes to see — where the Jersey lily, Lillie Langtry was buried. The purity and delicacy of her monument — just a few feet away from a widespreading beech — is in striking contrast to the heavy granite memorials in the rest of the churchyard. The two small oaks which stand either side of the lychgate were, incredibly, planted from acorns found in a joint of venison sent to a rector of St Saviour at the end of the last century!

 Government House to the south of the church is the official residence of the Queen's representative in the island, the Lieutenant-Governor. The main drive to what was originally an early nineteenth-century merchant's house, built in the French 'pavilion' style, is to the left up the steep hill, overhung with trees, from St Helier to Five Oaks — St Saviour's Hill. Every year an invitation is extended to the people of Jersey to attend the garden party held at Government House on the Queen's official birthday in June, otherwise the house is not open to the public, though the lodge and glimpses of the house can be seen from the road.

It was in Government House in 1876 that two Edwardian beauties, both born in Jersey, had an unusual meeting. They were the novelist Elinor Glyn and the society beauty Lillie Langtry.

Elinor Glyn (1864-1943) was born Nellie Sutherland and after an absence of 7 years returned with her mother and stepfather to live in a rented house, 'Richelieu', in St Saviour. The future novelist's reading was only from the shelves in the library that she could reach, so it included such diverse titles as *Don Quixote* in eighteenth-century French, the *Illustrated History of England* and Kingsley's *Heroes*.

Her impressions of the seas round Jersey were lasting. Of a high spring tide she had witnessed at La Collette, westwards along the coast from the Dicq, she wrote in 1936, 'the awful mountains of water hurling themselves against the jagged rocks there ... the vision of them comes back to me in my nightmares even now.'

When she left Jersey she became the beautiful and intelligent companion of men like Lord Curzon; the author of the banned *Three Weeks*; and had written about her the famous lines:

Would you like to sin
with Elinor Glyn
On a tiger skin?

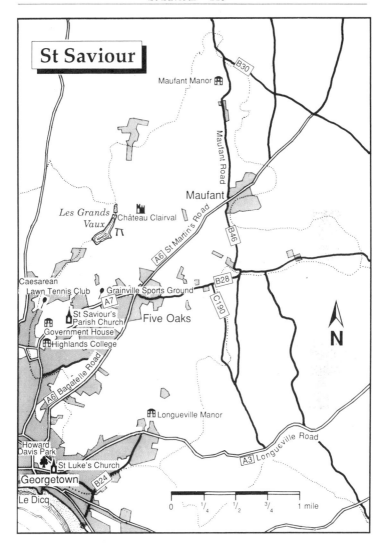

Or would you prefer
To err
With her on some other fur?

And the meeting between Elinor Glyn and Lillie Langtry took place when Elinor was only 12 and she and her sister and the Lieutenant-

Governor's daughter hid under a dressing table in Government House to get a glimpse of the Jersey lily as she took off her cloak. When a fit of the giggles gave them away, Mrs Langtry promised not to tell on them and even had some supper sent up for them in the nursery.

Emilie Charlotte Le Breton was born in St Saviour's Rectory, just behind the church, the daughter of the Dean of Jersey, on 13 October, 1853. Both her parents were known for their good looks and she obviously inherited her beauty from them. However, as a girl she was a tomboy, always hoping to be included in the escapades of her elder brothers. These involved stealing door knockers from houses hearby; scaring parishioners as they walked through the adjacent churchyard and being dared to run down the lane with nothing on!

She was only 14 when she received her first offer of marriage, but was 20 when she met the man who was to take her from Jersey and introduce her to London society. He was Edward Langtry, a rich Belfast widower who was in Jersey as a guest at Lillie's brother's wedding. One of the wedding festivities was a dance given on his 200 ton yacht, *Red Gauntlet*, and it was there that Edward and Lillie met. They were engaged 6 weeks later and were married in St Saviour's church on 9 March 1874.

Lillie caused her first major sensation when she accompanied her husband, 2 years later, to a reception given by a well known London hostess of that time, Lady Sebright, in Lowndes Square. All the other women present were wearing colourful, elaborate and restricting clothes: Lillie appeared in a plain black, square cut dress, made by a St Helier dressmaker. She had no jewellery and her auburn hair was twisted carelessly into a knot at the nape of her neck. As if her simple style were not enough, those at Lowndes Square that day were also impressed by her beauty and her vivacity.

Lillie was painted in that same black dress by Sir John Millais, who also came from Jersey, when they were both in London. The flower she holds in her hand is meant to be a Jersey lily — hence the double meaning of the title *Jersey Lily* for the title of the portrait — but, as they could not find one in London, they had to make do with a lily from Guernsey! The painting, which caused a sensation when it was exhibited at the Royal Academy in 1878, can be seen in the Barreau-Le Maistre Art Gallery in the Jersey Museum, together with Sir Edward Poynter's *Mrs Langtry*.

Soon after her success at Lady Sebright's, Lillie Langtry was introduced to the Prince of Wales. From that moment her life became an endless whirl of socialising — often in the company of the Prince of Wales. Her husband preferred to go off by himself to a life of fishing and drinking.

For several seasons Lillie's triumph as the Prince of Wales' acknowledged mistress was unallayed, but then society, as suddenly as it had taken her up, dropped her. She remained a friend of the Prince of Wales and his wife to the end, but when she was found to be no longer the pet of society, tradesmen began to press for the payment of the huge bills she had run up. Bailiffs eventually took possession of her London house and Lillie fled back to Jersey.

When she returned to London it was as an actress. She appeared as Kate Hardcastle in *She Stoops to Conquer* at the Haymarket theatre and in other plays. Later there followed a tour of the United States. During her 5-year stay in America several things happened: Lillie begged a divorce from Edward but he refused; she became a naturalised American citizen; and a town in Texas was renamed Langtry in her honour.

On Lillie's return to England she was determined to fight her way back to society — through racing. She started up a racing stable of her own and in 1897 won the Caesarewich with her horse Merman. The Prince of Wales himself publicly escorted her into the Jockey Club enclosure. Forty-eight hours after Merman's victory, which brought her £39,000 she learned of the death of her husband Edward, in Chester Asylum.

Two years later, when she was already 46, Lillie married Sir Hugo Gerald de Bathe, a young guardsman of 28. They were married, as she and Edward had been, in St Saviour's church. Then they bought a small cottage in Beaumont in St Peter, which Lillie insisted should be called 'Merman'.

Lillie's stay in Jersey was not a long one — she felt the call of both London and the stage. Once back there she bought the dilapidated Imperial Theatre in Westminster and spent over £50,000 in restoring it. Her venture was not a success and after World War I she retired from the stage and London and built a villa in Monte Carlo. Lillie died there in 1929 but, as she had specifically requested, her body was brought back to Jersey to be buried in St Saviour's churchyard near the church where she had been baptised and twice married.

Each October there is a special event linking Jersey and Bournemouth, through their association with Lillie Langtry. For it was in Bournemouth that Bertie, the Prince of Wales, built in 1877 a house for his Jersey lily, where they could enjoy their close relationship out of public sight. It was called The Red House and still stands today, a fine building in its own grounds. Now, though, it is a hotel called The Langtry Manor and it is the Bournemouth centre for the double celebration of Lillie Langtry's fame and beauty.

Though the area round the church may be regarded as the centre of the parish for tourists because of its Lillie Langtry associations, the shopping centres are to be found at the top and bottom of the parish. Continuing up St Saviour's Hill after the church is Five Oaks. Here, where St Saviour's Hill, Bagatelle Road, Prince's Tower Road and La Grande Route de St Martin meet, are several shops, including banks (*Bus 3, 3a, 3b, 20, 23*).

Down in the south of the parish, in Georgetown, there are more shops, a post office, banks and a supermarket (*Bus 1, 1a, 1b*). Further to the east on the Longueville Road is another parade of shops, which also includes a bank (*Bus 1b*).

Jersey's largest trading estate is also on the Longueville Road where 50 *vergées* were allocated in 1970 for the use of light industry and activities which are better sited out of St Helier.

Opposite La Rue des Prés Trading Estate is **Longueville Nursery and Garden Centre** (*Bus 1b*). This clearly laid-out gardener's paradise is becoming increasingly popular with visitors, because here they can often buy plants they can not find in the UK. More than that, visitors are appreciative of the fact that the assistants have the time to give tips on the best way to grow the plants they buy. There is a large car park and the garden centre is clearly signposted along the Longueville Road, in both directions.

The obvious centre of sporting activities in this parish is the **Grainville Sports Ground** (*Bus 3b, 20*) at the top of St Saviour's Hill to the left, on the way up to Five Oaks. League Cricket is played here every evening during the season and first class matches with visiting teams at weekends. There is ample room for spectators — who can enjoy between overs the view across to the sea or below to the cows grazing in the fields — as they settle themselves comfortably in sun or shade on the banks around the pitch. Charity cricket matches are also held here and attract a great deal of local support.

St Saviour's Bowls Club has its headquarters here, but any visitor who wishes to play must be a member of a bowls club back home. Although there are tennis courts beyond the bowling green, these are usually fully booked by schools or clubs. Anyone wishing to book a court should ring the Education Office on 509460, as early as possible before playing.

During the winter, the spectator sports are football and hockey. Also part of the complex is a new indoor bowls stadium. There is a sports pavilion with full changing and shower facilities for anyone taking part in any of the sports facilities provided at Grainville and plenty of space for parking.

A long established tennis club, the **Caesarean Tennis Club** (*Bus 20, 21, 23*) can be found on Les Grands Vaux, on the left going north towards Grands Vaux Reservoir. Here there are eight all-weather courts, two of which can be floodlit, plus full club facilities, which include a bar and a snooker room. Visitors are welcome to come and play or to watch the various tournaments which are put on during the season. The airdrome courts are for members only.

In the leisure complex of the Hotel de France, the **Lido de France** (*Bus 3b, 20, 21*) in St Saviour's Road, visitors are welcome to join in the weight training, aerobics and squash and other activities, which are available there.

There is a grisly legend connecting St Saviour's only surviving manor, **Longueville Manor** (*Bus 1b*) and the field which lies next to it. The field was called Le Pré d'Anthoine and the sixteenth-century Seigneur, or Lord of the Manor, Hostes Nicolle, wanted to add this sole possession of a poor butcher to the many vergees of land he already owned. Despite being Bailiff of Jersey, Nicolle could think of no legal way of getting Anthoine's property and land for himself, so he got it by trickery, with terrible consequences.

He told two of his servants to kill two of his best sheep and hide them in Anthoine's house. Next day he told the Constable that two of his sheep were missing and the Constable eventually found them — hanging dead in the butcher's stable. Anthoine was arrested, tried, found guilty and sentenced to death. As the hangman put the noose round his neck, the innocent butcher turned towards Nicolle and said 'I summon you to appear within forty days before the just judge of all to answer for this injustice!' On the thirty-ninth day after Anthoine's execution, Hostes Nicolle fell dead. From that time a curse was put on all the Seigneurs of Longueville Manor that they would never have a male heir and that, when their time came to die, clattering hooves of phantom horses would be heard in the courtyard.

Perhaps the curse has come true because today there is no Seigneur of Longueville, though the coat of arms of the wicked Hostes Nicolle can still be seen on top of the fine stone arch round the front door of his manor. The *colombier* built by a later Seigneur of Longueville — a prestigious status symbol as well as the source of plentiful pigeon pie — still stands to the north of the manor. Access to it is up La Rue St Thomas and through a gate on the left. The circular *colombier*, or dovecote, is on the right of the path leading from the gate.

The manor is now a five-star hotel, where both locals and visitors like to take advantage of its reputation for good food. Longueville Manor Hotel is on the Longueville Road (*Bus 1b*).

The **Rocher des Proscrits** makes St Saviour's only stretch of coast, near the Dicq (*Bus 18*) in St Clement's Bay, famous. It was here that Victor Hugo and other political refugees from Europe would discuss their revolutionary plans to put the world to rights. It has a plaque to mark it and is near the the Dicq slipway. From the Dicq there is Havre des Pas to the west to explore, with its swimming pool and beaches, in the parish of St Helier and the long sandy stretch of Grève d'Azette to the east, in the parish of St Clement.

The island's only further education college, **Highland's College** (*Bus 3b, 20, 21 Hôtel de France*), whose entrance for car drivers is along Bon Air Lane, runs one way from Wellington Road to St Saviour's Hill. Pedestrians should walk up Highland Lane, the first turning to the right after Hôtel de France. The original house, which probably dated back to 1800, was bought by the English branch of the Jesuits in 1894, to extend it and turn it into a French naval preparatory school. This school later returned to France and a French secondary school took its place until after World War I. The last religious order to run Highlands were the French Brothers of Christian Education who sold the property to the States of Jersey in 1972. The Brothers stayed at Highlands throughout the Occupation, despite the German Army requisitioning part of the building, and reported that the Germans respected both them and their work, as well as their three chapels.

Anyone who wants to learn about the generous benefactions given to the island in memory of the young Howard Davis who fell in World War I, should go to the memorial hall in **Howard Davis Park** to the left of the main gate on the corner of Don Road. Here in the tranquil room is the story of young Howard told in words and photographs until his untimely death in action near Boulogne in 1916. Outside are the ornamental gardens which his grieving father had laid out as a perpetual memorial to him and which were officially opened in 1939.

Since then, many locals and visitors have looked on this as their favourite park. Immediately in front of the main gate is the statue of George V and behind it the flagstaff which was originally from one of the wealthy Mr Davis' yachts. The beds near the statue depict in hundreds of tiny plants the logos of any organisation celebrating a special anniversary that year.

Further into the park, there is the sweep of a wide and carefully tended lawn, where holidaymakers can lie in the sun or listen to one of the visiting bands and children can dance to the music. To the left of this long lawn are heather beds, a rockery and the peaceful, walled rose garden where over a thousand roses, all clearly labelled and carefully tended, bloom throughout the summer. These 10 acres of park with their beds of colourful flowers and shrubs are a must for all garden lovers.

The church at the south end of the park also has a strong connection with Mr T. B. Davis, the park's creator. St Luke's church was his family's

PLACES OF INTEREST
IN THE PARISH OF ST SAVIOUR

St Saviour's Parish Church
St Saviour's Hill
Twelfth century, fifteenth-century
stained glass, burial place of Lillie
Langtry.

Government House
St Saviour's Hill
Lieutenant-Governor's official
residence, not open to the public.

**Longueville Nursery and Garden
Centre**
Opposite La Rue des Prés Trading
Estate.
The opportunity to buy plants not
available in the UK.

Grainville Sports Ground
St Saviour's Hill
Facilities for league cricket, bowls,
football, tennis, hockey etc.

Caesarean Tennis Club
Les Grands Vaux
Courts available to visitors at
weekends. Snooker room.

Lido de France
St Saviour's Road
Weight training, aerobics and
squash.

Longueville Manor Hotel
Longueville Road
Some features date back to
seventeenth century. *Colombier* in
grounds.

Le Rocher des Proscrits
Meeting place at the Dicq of Victor
Hugo and other political refugees.

Highlands College
Bon Air Lane
Island's College of Further
Education.

Howard Davis Park
East end of Çolomberie, Don Road
Island's finest park.

War Cemetery
South end of Howard Davis Park,
near St Luke's church.

Activities

Walk from Parish Hall to Les
  Grands Vaux Reservoir

Circular walk from La Fosse à
  l'Ecrivain

Grainville Sports Ground and
  Bowling Club

Caesarean Tennis Club

church, where he himself sang in the choir and it was here he attended,
quite by chance, his own memorial service! Running away to sea at 14,
Tom Davis was shipwrecked off Norfolk, drifted 36 hours by himself in
a small boat in the North Sea, and was finally rescued by a passing boat
and brought back to Jersey. When he landed, as it was a Sunday, he
went straight to St Luke's church, only to find the vicar holding a
memorial service for him!

Davis was soon back at sea, however, and made himself a millionaire, organising coastal traffic along the shores of Africa. After his son Howard had been killed, he set aside part of his great wealth to benefit islanders in his memory. So as well as Howard Davis Park, there is also the theatre at Victoria College, and an experimental farm, as well as various scholarships, bearing his son's name.

To the west of St Luke's church is the **War Cemetery** which was dedicated in 1943 as the last resting place for Allied airmen or sailors who lost their lives while fighting over or around Jersey. On 16 November 1943, for example, many bodies were washed ashore, especially in the west of the island. They were members of the crews of the British ships *Charybdis* and *Limbourne*, who had lost their lives in a naval engagement with the Germans in the Gulf of St Malo on 22 October. To begin with, the twenty bodies were all buried with full naval honours in a common grave at Mont à l'Abbé, but were later reburied in this special cemetery. All the graves are marked by a simple wooden cross and are always part of the island's Remembrance Day services.

Walks in St Saviour

Before describing some of the walks St Saviour has to offer, a look at two of the road names involved might be of interest. First there is La Rue à la Dame, the narrow hill — with typical Jersey cottages dotted along its sides — that winds down from Five Oaks to the reservoir at Les Grands Vaux. It is called La Rue à la Dame, after the 'Dame' or fairy that was once supposed to live in the prehistoric remains at the bottom of the hill. This road has a reputation for being haunted to this day.

The second is La Fosse à l'Ecrivain, which goes west from La Grande Route de St Martin to the football pitch on the way to Trinity. The name of this road means lawyer's grave and legend says that the lawyer had been visiting friends in one of the country parishes and on his way back to St Helier was thrown by his horse into a ditch. His injuries were so severe that he died there. Shortly afterwards, a violent rainstorm broke the sides of the ditch so that they fell in on the body and it was not discovered until some time later.

Walking down La Rue de Deloraine, or going down La Rue à la Dame from St Saviour's Hill, one comes to Les Grands Vaux, once the site of three watermills where now a dam and reservoir have been constructed. It is not possible to walk round the reservoir, but its tranquil stretch of water with its resident mallard, shoveler, teal and tufted duck can be viewed from a small parking area, alongside an inner pond, directly to the left of the steep hill, Paul Mill. An interesting walk to the reservoir could start from the Parish Hall where there is ample car parking space.

Cross the road into Rectory Lane and at the end of the lane, cross the road again into Swan Farm Lane. This leads on to the footpath to Les Grands Vaux. At the end of the path, turn right on to the road with

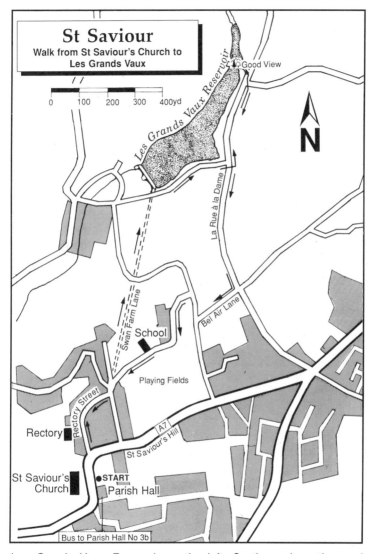

St Saviour
Walk from St Saviour's Church to
Les Grands Vaux

0   100   200   300   400yd

Les Grands Vaux Reservoir

Good View

La Rue à la Dame

Swan Farm Lane

School

Bel Air Lane

Playing Fields

Rectory Street

Rectory

A7

St Saviour's Hill

St Saviour's
Church

●START
Parish Hall

Bus to Parish Hall No 3b

Les Grands Vaux Reservoir on the left. Continue along the road
towards Victoria Village for a quarter of a mile. Then turn left on to land
at the head of the reservoir to have the view of the water on either side.
Retrace the route for a quarter of a mile, then turn left into La Rue à la
Dame. Next take the right turning into Bel Air Lane. At the end of the

lane, cross La Rue de Deloraine and enter the Education Committee car park. Cross the car park towards the school buildings where there are steps to the pathway. Then turn left, passing FCJ convent school on the right, and on to Rectory Lane, which leads back to St Saviour's church and the Parish Hall opposite. One-and-a-half hours of easy walking with only one slight climb up La Rue à la Dame.

 A second walk starts from La Fosse à l'Ecrivain, the third turning to the left going north after the Five Oaks roundabout, along which car drivers could park their car. Walkers should then return to La Grande Route de St Martin and walk north up it until the lane on the left, La Ruette du Ponterrin. Along this lane is Le Ponterrin, a house of great antiquity fronted by a magnificent arch which Philippe Falle had built in 1641 and which still bears his initials.

After passing the house, turn left at the crossroads into La Rue du Vieux Ménage, which wanders through the area known as Maufant (a muddy place), and leads to La Rue du Pont. Take a left turn at this 'T' junction and walk as far as the boundary stone between St Saviour and Trinity at the beginning of the first turning on the right, La Rue de Delament.

Walking north up La Rue de Delament, take the first turning on the left to start the circular trip back to La Fosse à l'Ecrivain again. This entails going down La Rue des Boulées until La Rue de la Guilleaumerie, which makes a 'T' junction to it. Walk to the right along it and then turn first left into La Rue de la Boucterie, which passes by the modern housing development known as Victoria Village. Take the first turning to the left off La Rue de la Boucterie into La Rue de Ponterrin and then right into La Rue du Château Clairval. The *château* itself is typically mid-nineteenth century. La Fosse à l'Ecrivain, where car drivers left their cars, is the road opposite the football pitch.

6 TRINITY

(*Bus 3a, 3b, 4, 21*)

This north-eastern parish, which lies between Rozel Bay and Havre Giffard and whose southern tip is only 2 miles from the Royal Square, is large and has a great fund of stories to match. The earliest have an element of magic and were all associated with the prehistoric remains that can be found along the northern coast of the parish.

Around the Parish

Starting on the north coast, on a rocky ledge overlooking Vicard Point, south of Petit Port, is a huge stone 15 by 13ft. This fallen menhir is known as **La Pierre de la Fételle**, the fairystone, as it seemed obvious to the descendants of prehistoric man that such a heavy object could only have got to its present position by magic! Vicard Point is on the coastal walk between Bouley Bay (*Bus 21*) and Bonne Nuit (*Bus 4*) and is clearly signposted.

Further west is the headland of **La Belle Hougue.** Two caves have been discovered here and are important archaeologically because of the fossil animal bones found in them, belonging most probably to the period just before the last Ice Age. Some of the remains belong to a special type of red deer and they can all be viewed at La Hougue Bie Museum in Grouville. The magic stories, though, are reserved for the mineral spring which can be found on the promontory itself. This is known as **La Fontaine ès Mittes**, the Naiads' Fountain, and was believed until this century to have magical properties, capable of bringing back sight to the blind and the power of speech to the dumb.

Inland from La Belle Hougue, to the highest point of the island, over 400ft above sea level, is **La Hougue des Platons**. Just north of the BBC transmitter and mast is a low prehistoric burial mound (3ft high, 36yd in circumference) under which was discovered a cist in which were two urns. In one of these were the charred remains of a woman and a child. La Hougue des Platons can be reached by going west along La Rue des Platons, and turning right, after La Rue d'Egypte, along a footpath across the common.

To walk to La Fontaine ès Mittes and La Hougue des Platons (see map page 133) take the footpath signposted to Bouley Bay. The path leads to the rocky promontory, La Belle Hougue, from where there are fine views of Guernsey, Sark, the French coast and Bonne Nuit Bay. Follow the path around the back and down the steps, where there is a signpost pointing to the right and the main road. Take the path to the left and walk straight on for 60yd and there on the left, behind the bracken and bushes is La Fontaine ès Mittes with its healing waters. Incidentally, the temperature of the water remains constant throughout the year.

Retrace the path to the sign to the main road and follow this grassy path which continues between hedges and banks. This path leads on to the lane Rue d'Egypte. Continue up Rue d'Egypte, turning right on to the grassy path, immediately after the entrance to 'Springfield'. Walk up this path for 100yd, then turn right, continuing over tussocky grass. Fifty yards in front is the tumulus, La Hougue des Platons. On the north side of this walled grassy mound is the pink granite reference stone.

To return to the car park, retrace the path to Route d'Egypte, to avoid trespassing on private property. After a short distance turn left, towards the sea, taking the path to the rocky promontory. From this point the cliff path can be seen below, so take either of the paths leading down to it. The walk back to the car park along the cliff path should take approximately 10 minutes. The whole walk should take about $1^1/_2$ hours, is quite hilly and it is worth taking binoculars.

That this stretch of the north coast was held in superstitious awe is further confirmed by the fact that witches covens on this part of the island were supposed to have their ritual meeting place at Le Becquet ès Chats. This 'witches playground' is just to the west of the View Point on La Rue des Platons where it makes a 'T' junction with La Rue du Betchet ès Cats (another spelling) a continuation of La Grande Route de St Jean.

The next fund of stories concerns **Trinity church** (*Bus 4*) and one of the most picturesque ways to approach it is to come up from the south of the island along La Route de la Trinité. This is lined in part with silver birches and, just before the church, by a fine beech hedge, Jersey cows can often be seen grazing in the water meadows to the right. Then the church itself comes into view, rather spoiled for some by the modern cement shell preserving its oddly proportioned spire.

In fact, the only parts of the church which date back to the twelfth century are the spire and tower. The chancel was rebuilt a hundred years later and the nave, on the old medieval foundations, as recently as the middle of the last century. Two relics of when Catholic services were held in the church are the silver chalice — the oldest in the island — and the wooden pews or misericords in the chancel, with their carved undersides which could be raised for the priests to lean against during long periods of standing in the lengthy services. The pews in the nave are of a Victorian type.

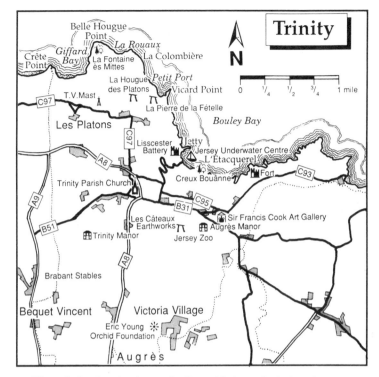

The whole church gives a feeling of light and air, but the seventeenth-century memorial to one of the important members of the de Carteret family, though probably the finest mural monument in the island, does seem rather too large for the dimensions of the fifteenth-century Lady Chapel.

Three unusual features of the church are that it only has one aisle; that its organ loft and choir are over the west door; and that it is the only island church not to be named after a saint. The belief in the Three in One nature of God — Father, Son and Holy Spirit — La Sainte Trinité to whom the church is dedicated, is the origin of the parish crest. The initials PFSD stand for *Pater, Filius, Spiritus Sanctus* and *Deus*.

The three stories connected with Trinity church are also unusual. Twice the church was used for a sitting of the States of Jersey. In 1541 the States Members met there to hear an angry letter from the Governor about the refusal by certain Jerseymen to pay taxes for the defence of their island. In 1643, when the island had been invaded by Parliamentarians, the Royalist George Carteret thought it safer to be sworn in as Bailiff and Governor in Trinity than in mainly anti-royalist St Helier.

Trinity spire is the subject of the next tale. It was struck by lightning no fewer than three times in the 19 years between 1629 and 1648 — all signs of the wrath of God, thought the terrified parishioners, aimed, particularly the first time, at 'the pontifical grandeur' of the island's Dean. Despite these disasters to the spire, the parish waited 300 years before installing a lightning conductor!

The last story concerns a strange funeral by torchlight — a funeral which should have taken place in St Ouen. It concerns Sir Edouard de Carteret — Usher of the Black Rod to Charles II — who died while on a visit to St Ouen's Manor. Plans were therefore made to bury him in St Ouen. However, just as the funeral procession was about to start, there was a sudden clap of thunder. The six horses who were pulling the hearse were so startled by this that they bolted, still pulling the hearse behind them, and did not stop until they reached Trinity church. Once there, the mourners — who had been forced to follow this wild cross-country funeral procession — decided that the thunderclap and the bolting horses had been a sign from the dead — Sir Edouard wanted to be buried in his own parish. So they hastily dug a grave and held a funeral service for this loyal Trinity parishioner by torchlight. It is Sir Edouard's huge memorial that still dominates the Lady Chapel.

A modern link between the parish church and its manor is the tomb of Athelstan Riley, just to the left of the west door. Athelstan Riley, writer of such well known hymns as 'Ye Watchers and Ye Holy Ones', as Seigneur of Trinity also provided the impetus to rebuild **Trinity Manor** (*Bus 4*). He was just one in a long line of colourful characters who have held the fief and have been its Seigneur.

The first recorded holders of the fief were the land-grasping de St Martin family who, in the thirteenth century, seized hold of land in both Guernsey and Jersey without paying for it. In the seventeenth century Amice de Carteret, as he lay dying in France, asked for his heart to be embalmed and sent back to be buried in his manor grounds. One of his descendants in the next century, Rear Admiral Philip de Carteret, in his sloop, *Swallow*, sailed round the world. Discovering on his way a group of islands in the South Seas which he called Queen Charlotte Islands, as a patriotic Channel Islander he gave to four of the islands in the group the names of Sark, Alderney, Guernsey and, of course, New Jersey.

Perhaps the most famous and romantic Trinity Manor story centres round its most eminent visitor — Charles II. As Prince of Wales, on the run from the Roundheads, he fled in 1646 to Jersey. During his 10 weeks here he was said to have behaved cavalierly towards Marguerite, the sister of Trinity's Seigneur, another Amice de Carteret.

From this dalliance was supposed to have sprung a certain Jacques La Cloche — with a page torn from Trinity parish register to conceal the illegitimate royal birth. Certainly a Jacques La Cloche showed Jesuits in Rome, 22 years later, a letter in which Charles acknowledged the

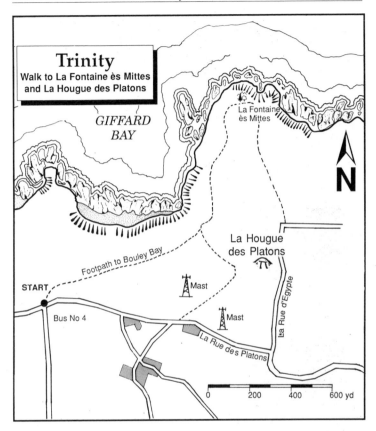

Trinity
Walk to La Fontaine ès Mittes
and La Hougue des Platons

GIFFARD BAY

La Fontaine ès Mittes

N

La Hougue des Platons

Footpath to Bouley Bay

START

Bus No 4

Mast

Mast

La Rue d'Egypte

La Rue des Platons

0   200   400   600 yd

young Jerseyman as, 'born to us, more through the frailty of early youth than of deliberate wickedness, of a young lady of one of the leading families in our kingdom.'

Sadly for writers of historical novels, some of whom even suggest that Jacques La Cloche was the 'Man in the Iron Mask', the page torn from the parish register was for 1648, not 1646 when the Prince was in Jersey. Secondly, the letters which Jacques La Cloche carried to Rome were found to be forgeries. Yet the Prince did visit Trinity Manor and, when he became Charles II, presented his erstwhile host with a portrait of himself by Lely. This still hangs in what is known as La Chambre du Roi — the King's Room. From the window can be seen a later replacement of the great Turkey Oak under which Charles was meant to have sat, as well as the large stone table on which he was supposed to have feasted. The façade of the manor, however, is quite changed

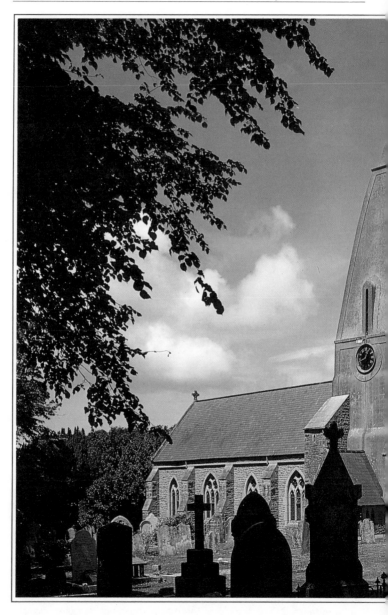

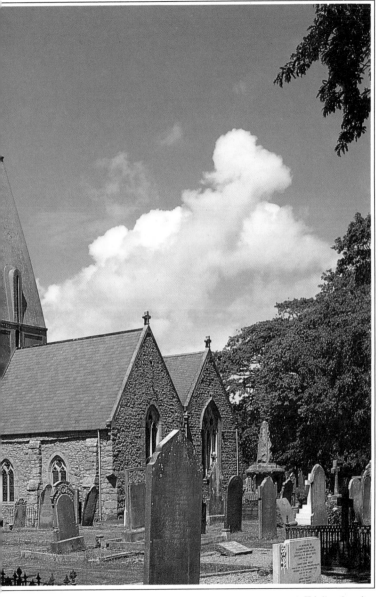

Trinity church

from how it must have looked in the seventeenth century, as Athelstan Riley noted during its final restoration, in 1913, on the model of a small French *château*. The main door on the south front is the entrance to the original sixteenth-century house; the second front door, on the north side, is the entrance to the nineteenth-century rebuilding, in which the manor was exactly doubled in size.

The manor now has a dairy farm on part of its 100 acres and kennels for the island's Drag Hunt and Chase Club, of whom the present Seigneur of Trinity is the President. It is a most picturesque sight to see the huntsmen and women in their hunting outfits gather at Trinity for a hunt in which the quarry is not an animal, only the scent of one.

In this century the Seigneur's only remaining duty to his visiting sovereign is to offer the monarch a pair of mallard ducks — for which purpose ducks are always supposed to be reared in readiness on the manorial ponds. Unfortunately, for the Queen's visit in 1976, the Seigneur's own ducks' plumage did not look sufficiently colourful, so he had to borrow two from Gerald Durrell's zoo!

The manor grounds are quite often open to the public on such occasions as charity fêtes, and anyone going to them should visit the Seigneural Chapel and in spring notice the tulips for which the gardens have been famed since their introduction in the seventeenth century. The manor itself is open on special occasions, such as art exhibitions, so attention should be given to 'What's On' in the media.

There are not many facilities for shoping in this northern parish and there are no banks. The only post office, which is also a general store, is near Trinity church. Two other general stores can be found in Victoria Village and at Les Hautes Croix, where La Grande Route de St Jean meets La Rue Militaire and Le Chemin des Hautes Croix. While in the Le Chemin des Hautes Croix area, visitors can watch a forge in action, on Route d'Ebenezer. The forge, which specialises in wrought-iron work, is on a dangerous corner so visitors should park down the nearby side road, but not in front of the forge or the garage next door. Find Rue de Bechet (off A8 and A9) and explore the Steam Museum, open Monday-Saturday, which has rides in Victorian railway carriages three days a week.

Bouley Bay

Bouley Bay is a good starting point to explore Trinity's northern coastline and is reached by a steeply winding road down from La Rue de la Petite Falaise. The bay is named after the birch tree (*bouleau*) and is 2 miles across. To the east of it are hills over 400ft high and to the west the headland of La Belle Hougue. Such an ideal landing point for would-be invaders of the north of the island had to be defended and the fort at L'Etacquerel to the east and the Lisscester Battery (named after Elizabeth I's Earl of Leicester) to the west still remain as part of that defence.

Some invaders over the centuries, nevertheless, did get through this line of defence and one was a French raiding party in 1549. Fortunately, once the invaders had got as far as Le Jardin d'Olivet, just above the bay, they were defeated with a great number of French casualties. In 1643 the invading soldiers were English, sent by Cromwell to round up any Royalists who had not taken refuge in either Mont Orgueil or Elizabeth Castle.

Today Bouley Bay can be enjoyed either on its cliff tops or on its shingle beach, where the gorse- and bracken-covered hills come right down to the sea. The cliff path starts in Rozel and follows the cliffs past the disused L'Etacquerel Fort into Bouley Bay itself. This path can be joined on La Route de Rozel either to the east or west of the Côtes du Nord Hotel or from the car park at Le Jardin d'Olivet.

The beach at Bouley Bay faces north-east and so is at its best before noon. It offers safe bathing in the harbour area but families with small children should take care as the shore shelves quickly into deep water. Access to the beach is either down some steps or along the path by the beach café which links in with the coastal path from Rozel. There is also a small rocky beach to the left of the pier which would be ideal for a picnic when the tide is out. The pier itself was built in 1828, primarily for the oyster industry but for also defence. The initials of F. de la Mare, who was responsible for constructing it, can still be seen on the side of the harbour wall.

The pier is now a favourite spot for locals to fish, with conger in good supply in the summer nights and turbot and brill in the shorter days of autumn. Bouley Bay is also the place for discovering the sun-basking wall lizard.

The island's **Underwater Centre** is based at Bouley Bay, so any sub aqua enthusiasts should make their way to this quiet and ideal spot. Here there are skin diving, boat dives and the possibility of hiring gear. Bottle filling facilities are also available. For swimmers, picnickers and divers there are toilet facilities, a café and limited parking.

There are two legends connected with Bouley Bay — Le Chien de Bouley and Le Cri des Tombelènes. The first concerns a monstrous black dog with huge saucer eyes that was said to roam the lanes round Bouley Bay. Did it really exist, or was it just a tale invented by the smugglers of Trinity to keep the islanders at home while they brought their booty ashore? Whatever the explanation, if any visitor should catch sight of Le Tchan du Bouôlé, as the dog is known in Jersey Norman-French, there is definitely going to be a storm!

The second legend tells of the time in the fifteenth century, when Jersey was occupied by the French, and the story was confessed on his death bed by one of the invaders who witnessed the terrible deed. A

Bouley Bay

young Jerseyman, Raulin, was taken prisoner by a band of French brigands and taken by his captors to a cave just close to L'Islet, the rocky outcrop to the right of the bay. There he was to be hung. His dog, however, had escaped the ambush and had raced back to the farm where the Jerseyman's fiancée, Jeanne, lived. Just as Raulin was about to have the rope put around his neck, the dog and the young girl reached the cave. Jeanne rushed to her lover and begged the brigand to kill her too. Suddenly, as two of the Frenchmen came towards her, Jeanne seized one of their daggers, while the dog leapt at the throat of the other. In the confusion the girl then cut Raulin's bonds but, when instead of escaping he tried to defend her, the chief of the brigands plunged his dagger into Raulin's heart.

Without a sound Raulin fell dead, but Jeanne's shriek of horror echoed and re-echoed in the cave, until in her madness of grief she plunged her dagger into the throat of the brigand chief and rushed across the beach to L'Islet. There she stood on its very summit until a huge wave covered her and as she sank beneath it, again that eerie cry — Le Cri des Tombelènes. It is said that Jeanne's cry can still be heard near the cave — now called Creux Bouânne, the Accursed Cave — whenever there is a storm.

Any cries heard round Bouley Bay in the summer are likely to be the excited cheers of spectators as they line the road up from Bouley Bay for the three popular races known as the Bouley Bay Hill Climbs. The first is at Easter, the second on the Spring Bank Holiday, the third in July and all are organised by the Jersey Motor Cycle and Light Car Club. The summer meeting is the most important of all, as it is the British Hill Climb Championship. The classes included in the various hill climbs are motor bikes, saloon cars, racing cars and sports cars. Even events for cycles and karts are held. These races are the only time when the essential tranquility of this northern bay is broken and they certainly make for thrilling viewing.

Bouley Bay affords a further walk to the west, to Belle Hougue Point and then round to Giffard Bay, the parish's western boundary. The keen walker can continue the 4 miles to Bonne Nuit in St John's parish or complete the north coastal walk to Grosnez in St Ouen. However far one walks, the views from the cliff tops are breathtaking: at Vicard Point there is the view back across to Bouley Bay; on the cliffs above Giffard Bay there is the long rock down below to the right which looks like the body of a man giving the bay its nickname of Dead Man's Bay.

The headland of La Belle Hougue, certainly lives up to its name of 'beautiful' with the sea on both sides, strange shapes of rocks at its peak and an atmosphere on a sunny day of tranquility and changelessness. The views from here extend across St John's Bay to the west and eastward back beyond Bouley Bay to Rozel. La Belle Hougue offers plenty of natural picnic sites on rock or grass and there are seats all along the coastal walk for those who like frequent rests. In the spring there is the added bonus of the slopes down to the sea being carpeted with daffodils, known locally as lent-lilies. Later come the green fronds of the bracken with their distinctive scent. The paths around the headland pass by the spring La Fontaine ès Mittes, at the end of the path known as Le Chemin de la Belle Hougue, and above the caves which have already been mentioned. Only experienced climbers, by the way, with the correct equipment including ropes and torches, should attempt to visit the two caves.

Augrès

Augrès (*Bus 4*) is one of the ancient fiefs into which Trinity is divided and is to the west of La Route de la Trinité (Trinity Road). On the way up to it is the Sir Francis Cook Art Gallery and in the grounds of Augrès Manor is Jersey's world renowned zoo, founded by the author and naturalist Gerald Durrell. Just past the zoo, to the west along La Rue des Câteaux, is an ancient earthwork.

Les Câteaux earthwork, also known as Le Chastel Sedement, once showed what stern stuff Jerseymen were made of. This high embankment, then surrounded by a moat and enclosing about 20 acres of land, was looked on by islanders as a safe refuge when the island was invaded by marauders. It was here that men, women and children fled in 1406 when a Breton and a Castilian had successfully invaded Jersey from the south. When an envoy from the Castilian Nino marched north to confront them, he was met by Jersey envoys who told him that the entrenched camp or '*ville*' as they called it had never been entered by the French or English 'and we are sworn in no wise to yield it either to friend or foe while a single one of us is alive'. Faced with such determination, Nino and his troops decided to accept a ransom of 10,000 gold crowns and left the island. The earthwork is now part of Le Câtel Farm.

Coming back to our own time, art lovers will be interested to learn about the **Sir Francis Cook Art Gallery** (*Bus 4*) which is at the top of Trinity Hill on La Route de la Trinité right next door to the Oaklands Lodge Hotel. There is a large car park behind the gallery, which was a former Methodist chapel and schoolroom, converted by Jersey resident and artist Sir Francis Cook and generously donated to The Jersey Heritage Trust by his widow in 1984.

Although there is no permanent exhibition housed at the gallery, there are a number of temporary exhibitions planned throughout the year, details of which will be found on the list of 'What's On' put out by the media. When these exhibitions are on, it is possible to view a selection of Sir Francis Cook's own paintings in two adjoining rooms.

Sports diving

selection of Sir Francis Cook's own paintings in two adjoining rooms.

The obvious focal point in this area — though actually in the *vingtaine* of Rozel — to which thousands of visitors flock every year, is Augrès Manor, the home of author and naturalist Gerald Durrell. It is also the headquarters of the Jersey Wildlife Preservation Trust, widely known as the **Jersey Zoo** (*Bus 3a, 3b, 21, 23*). It is on the corner of La Profonde Rue (B1) and La Rue de Diélament, after Trinity church travelling east.

Coming to **Augrès Manor** is a double treat, because there are the interesting architectural details to enjoy as well as the fascinating animals to watch. The first double stone arch through which one passes has the Dumaresq (pronounced Dumarick) arms, plus supporters, helmet and plumes on the smaller arch, with a date stone, 1741, divided by the Payne family trefoils, with the initials below of EDM and EDC separated by a heart. The initials are of Elie Dumaresq who married the heiress Elizabeth de Carteret, whose granddaughter inherited the Seigneurie of St Ouen and who is, therefore, an ancestor of the present Seigneur of St Ouen. The main part of the manor itself also dates back to the eighteenth century, as can be seen by its balanced proportions and the gable stone with a carved face dated 1795. The east-facing wing, with its arch and several blocked windows, could be all that remains of the front of an earlier manor house.

The manor is set in 25 acres of parkland and here in their family groups are to be seen over 1,200 of the world's rarest animals. They do not make up just another 'zoo' but are part of a unique sanctuary where colonies of threatened species have been established and built up into reservoirs against extinction. As the breeding groups have grown since the setting up of the Wildlife Preservation Trust in 1963, some have been returned to their original habitat, such as the pink pigeons hatched in captivity and set free in their native Mauritius. Others have been sent to similarly conservation-minded zoos to help with an overall breeding plan for endangered species.

The trust also has an International Centre for Conservation and Captive Breeding which was opened by the trust's patron, Princess Anne, in 1984. Here students from all over the world study the techniques necessary not just to breed animals in captivity but also to conserve species in their own native environment. The trust's symbol of the dodo, a species already lost to the world, enshrines Gerald Durrell's determination to ensure that no more endangered species should suffer the same fate. Anyone visiting the zoo can see the results of that determination.

On a later visit, in 1990, the Princess opened the pavilion which provides visitors a greater awareness of the trust's work around the world. Here in the theatre, there is the audio-visual experience 'Before Another Song Ends' and the pavilion is also used as an activity centre with exhibitions and activities for both adults and children. Favourite are the so-called 'Keeper Talks', when the secret lives of the animals in the collection are shared with the audience.

Among the birds most popular with visitors are the talkative mynahs and parrots, the showy Palawan peacock pheasants, and the elegant, pink-tinted Chilean flamingoes. Most of the larger birds have their own special areas where they are free to live as they would in the wild, such as the serious-looking white-naped cranes who dig in the turf for root tubers and seeds in one of the marshier parts of the manor grounds.

Wandering round the park, one can see unusual members of the horse and cat families, such as the Przewalski horses and the snow leopard and the serval cats. Then there are the strange-looking fruit bats, the appealing lemurs, including the ringtailed and the black-and-white ruffled varieties, the ayes-ayes which can only be seen in Jersey Zoo, or the different types of monkeys, from the cotton-topped tamarin to the larger, sad faced ursine black-and-white Colobus monkey. Gerald Durrell's expedition to Sierra Leone in 1965 to bring back Colobus monkeys is vividly told in his *Catch Me a Colobus*.

The larger primates, such as the apes, orang utans and the gorillas all have their special and separate breeding and play areas where they can be seen with their families without any danger to the public. Listening posts are provided for those who want to know more about these distant relatives of man.

Perhaps the animals that most visitors want to watch and photograph are the gorillas in their half-acre complex. Many remember the gentle giant Jambo, the first male gorilla to be born in captivity. It was he who showed such concern for a young boy who fell into the gorilla enclosure, that he kept the other gorillas away. Now there is the Australian-bred Ya Kwanza to take his place.

There is an admission charge to the zoo, but there is a shop before the entrance where visitors are free to browse round the enormous range of items for sale, from animal prints, ornaments and fluffy toys to jigsaw puzzles, stationery and books, including all the well loved titles by Gerald Durrell, including *My Family and Other Animals*. There is a guide to the zoo on sale at the entrance, for those who want more background information about the reptiles, birds and animals on show.

Jersey Zoo is an ideal place for the whole family to visit, for not only is there a special playground for the children, where they can imitate the athletic antics of the gorillas nearby, but also the Café Dodo where everyone can relax over a cup of tea or light refreshments. As the grounds are so vast, you can see just as little or as much as you want to in newly wooded parkland in a beautiful part of the island. Disabled visitors are welcome and anyone wishing to further the work of the Jersey Wildlife Preservation Trust, which is registered as a charity in both Jersey and the UK, can become a member.

Other Places of Interest in Trinity

Trinity has benefited not just from the abiding passion of one of its residents but two. So just as Gerald Durrell's youthful enthusiasm for all living creatures has led to Jersey Zoo, so the late Eric Young's enthusiasm for orchids has led to the setting up of **The Eric Young** **Orchid Foundation** (*Bus 21 to Victoria Village*).

Eric Young was born in 1911 in Derbyshire and his passion for orchids began in his early teens when he was shown two orchid plants by the family gardener. When he arrived in Jersey after World War II, Eric Young bought a rundown market garden in Mont Millais, St Helier, and stocked it with the plants from an old orchid nursery in England that was closing down — so came about the nucleus of the superb collection that has been growing in quality and renown ever since.

During the 1970s, Eric Young's work with orchids gained him such prestigious positions as Chairman of the World Orchid Conference Committee and membership of the Research Committee of the American Orchid Society, of which he was also appointed an Honorary Judge. In 1982, in the RHS British Orchid Growers' Association Show, his exhibition was awarded a Gold Medal for its quality of plants and standard of cultivation.

There was still a dream to be fulfilled, however. Eric Young wanted to set up a foundation to maintain the collection and continue his work in perpetuity. A suitable place was eventually found — on the site of a derelict tomato nursery in Victoria Village, Trinity. Sadly Eric Young died before his dream could be fully realised. The results, though, of his life-long passion for orchids are now on show for the general public to enjoy and appreciate on Thursday, Friday and Saturday only all year.

To get to the Orchid Foundation from St Helier, take the Trinity Road to the Town Mills and then follow the road through Les Grands Vaux, with the reservoir on the left. Continue up Le Mont de la Rosière and on through Victoria Village, turning left at the sign for the Orchid Foundation. Coming from any other part of the island make for Victoria Village and turn down the road on the south side of Victoria Stores, La Rue du Moulin du Ponterrin.

The whole environment of the Foundation complex is ideal — landscaped gardens in a typical part of rural Jersey at its best. There is also a large car park. Once inside the foyer, there is a wide range of literature on sale plus a list of UK nurserymen who would be able to supply the plants themselves, together with advice on their cultivation.

Then, on to the delights of the artistically laid out display area, with its soothing sound of running water, hundreds of orchids at every level and an exotic fragrance over all. The orchids have been displayed most imaginatively, sometimes on structures of Jersey granite, sometimes on branches of trees, and their cascades of blooms appear layer behind

The Trinity coastline

layer. The display is constantly being changed, but look for the white Sobralia from South America; the bright red spray of the Peruvian Cochlioda Noetzliana; the green flowers of the coolly elegant Lycaste Guinevere and the delicacy of the miniature Cymbidium, bred in Jersey and remembering in its name both an island beach and Eric Young's first nursery in St Helier — Cymbidium Petit Port 'Mont Millais'. The founder himself is commemorated in one of the Foundation's fine breeding lines, the mainly yellow Odontioda Eric Young.

The rest of the 28,000sq ft of glasshouse is subdivided into five growing houses branching off from the central display area. The southern sections at the far end contain the reserve collections and seedlings; the northern sections, which are occasionally open to the public, have the larger specimen plants which will eventually provide the central display. The excellent work done at this Jersey orchid centre and the superior quality of the plants it produces, is shown by the top awards it has been awarded at World Orchid Conferences.

Anyone who wishes to be associated with this work with orchids can

PLACES OF INTEREST
IN THE PARISH OF TRINITY

La Pierre de la Fételle
Fallen menhir at Vicard Point.

La Hougue des Platons
La Rue des Platons
Prehistoric burial ground.

Trinity Parish Church
La Grande Route
Twelfth-century tower and spire, oldest ecclesiastical silverware and finest mural memorial in the island.

Trinity Manor
Off the A8 Trinity Road
Nineteenth-century restoration in French *château*-style. Only occasionally open to the public. History connected with Charles II. Incorporates a dairy farm.

Forge
Route d'Ebenezer
Trinity
Watch the forge in action, specialises in wrought-iron.

Pallot Steam Museum
Rue de Bechet
Rides in Victorian railway carriages

Sir Francis Cook Art Gallery
La Route de la Trinité
Occasional exhibitions.

Jersey Underwater Centre
Bouley Bay
Diving gear for hire.

Jersey Wildlife Preservation Trust (Jersey Zoo)
Augrès Manor
Twenty-five acres of parkland, at home of Gerald Durrell, containing family groups of endangered species.

Eric Young Orchid Foundation
Victoria Village
One of the world's finest orchid collections.

Brabant Stables
A8 from St Helier
Specialises in novices, qualified instructors.

Beach
Bouley Bay

Activities

Cliff path walk from Rozel to Giffard Bay

Jersey Underwater Centre

Bouley Bay hill climb

Swimming, fishing, riding

become a member simply by filling in a form at the reception desk.

Finally, as Trinity is very much a country parish, why not explore it on horseback? Along the main A8 from St Helier there are the **Brabant Stables** (*Bus 4, ask for 'Les Ifs'*) — look out for the signpost. They specialise here in catering for novices, including children over six, and these are taken with a qualified instructor on a quiet ride. Those with more experience could be taken for a canter, also with a BHSAI instructor. Rides can include going along the north coast with its breathtaking scenery high above the Channel. What better way to enjoy Trinity?

7 ST JOHN

(Bus 4, 5)

As the parish of St John has probably one of the finest coastlines on the island, visitors will want to see it for themselves straight away. It extends from Giffard Bay, on the edge of Trinity, westwards to Mourier Valley, where the parish of St Mary begins, and from its headlands on a fine day the other Channel Islands and the Cotentin Peninsula can be seen.

The St John Coastline

Jersey's north coast is quite unlike any of the other island coastlines, perhaps more resembling Cornwall, with its sheer cliffs dropping to the tumultuous seas below. There are, though, several sheltered bays along its length, and in St John is the truly delightful **Bonne Nuit Bay** *(Bus 4)*, protected by the cliffs which reach round to La Crête to the east and Frémont Point to the west.

Les Nouvelles Charrières (C98) as it bends down to the bay gives glimpses of the sea through the trees before it comes to the tiny harbour of Bonne Nuit itself. The cliffs towering over 400ft above it are covered with purple heather in the summer, contrasting with, near where the few houses are perched, cascades of pink roses. The small beach extends at low tide to the end of the pier, revealing a long stretch of yellow sand, but swimmers should remember that when the tide is out, the beach shelves quite quickly into deep water. Otherwise bathing in the harbour area is quite safe.

The small pier was constructed in 1872 and the wooden huts on it are for the use of fishermen who can often be seen unloading their catch of lobsters and crabs. Early on a Saturday, local shoppers come here to buy their weekend sea food. The pier too affords a peaceful spot for angling.

Bonne Nuit is also the finishing point for the annual Sark to Jersey Rowing Race which is held in July. When the race was first rowed over 21 years ago, the time taken used to be anything from 4-7 hours to get all the competitors in. Now the first rowers are back in about 2½ hours. It is an exciting race to watch.

Bonne Nuit Bay

Right in the centre of Bonne Nuit Bay is a rock, Le Cheval Guillaume (William's horse), known today as the **Cheval Roc**. Both a legend and a tradition are attached to this rock. The legend concerns a kelpie (water sprite) and his efforts to secure one of the parish's beautiful young girls, Anne-Marie, as his wife. Disguised as her soldier lover William, the kelpie managed to drag her to the marriage bed he had prepared for her under the sea. Fortunately for the poor girl, as soon as the cock crew, the kelpie no longer had magic power to keep her and Anne-Marie floated up unconscious to the beach.

When William came home on leave, Anne-Marie told him all about being kidnapped by the kelpie but he told her that she had nothing more to fear with him by her side. He was puzzled, though, when he found that his stable now housed a splendid white stallion and could hardly wait to show off his riding prowess the next day, before he embarked for further duty overseas. That night, however, he had a bad dream, warning him of an unknown enemy against whom he could only be protected by a sprig of mistletoe.

Believing his dream, William got up before it was light and walked all the way to Rozel where he knew he could get his piece of mistletoe. With it safely in his button hole, and having bade Anne-Marie farewell, he got on his white horse and rode along the beach to join up with the rest of the troop. But the horse would not keep to the beach. It headed straight for the sea and with its beautiful white mane floating on the water, William suddenly realised with horror that this was no ordinary horse. He struck it on the head with the sprig of mistletoe and immediately it gave a terrifying yell. Then it began to stiffen and gradually turned into a rock. So the kelpie, for he it was who transformed himself into a horse to rid himself of Anne-Marie's sweetheart, stays forever in Bonne Nuit Bay petrified in the shape of William's horse.

From the Middle Ages the custom grew up on Midsummer's Day — the festival of St John the Baptist, the patron saint — to row round the rock for luck. So popular was this tradition that the largest fair on the island used to take place at Bonne Nuit Bay on this day, for islanders to enjoy before and after their lucky row. Though Cheval Roc is no longer the centre of their celebrations, parishioners of St John still have a Midsummer Fair on 24 June — the day when traditionally farmers paid the rent for their farms.

To the right of Bonne Nuit Bay is one of the fortifications put up by the British from 1736 to the mid-nineteenth century against a possible French attack. This fort, constructed at La Crête point in 1835, is now the weekend and holiday residence of the Lieutenant-Governor.

Earlier fortifications included a boulevard for two cannons, a guardhouse and a powder magazine. In the nineteenth century even a barracks was built. Yet for all the money the States poured into these defences at Bonne Nuit, the French never attempted to land here. What

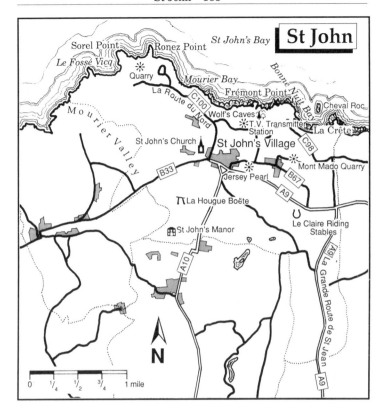

did take place, however, was a great deal of smuggling, of which this confession of the Eliza's captain is only one example:

'Instead of proceeding to St Germain, for which we had cleared, we went to Bonne Nuit, and took in 2½ tons of tobacco, spirits in casks, cigars, and snuff, which I agreed to take to Wales at the rate of £50 per ton. We proceeded to Fishguard, where we arrived on the fifth day, and, running in about eleven that evening, assisted in conveying the goods to a store close by. We then went to St Germain, took in 32 sheep, and returned to Jersey.'

To complete the picture of Bonne Nuit there is a harbourside café, decorated with hanging flower baskets, for souvenirs, beach requirements and light refreshments. It is open from 9am-5pm from March to November and has details of any fishing trips going from the harbour. Toilet facilities are just a few yards away along the road.

Bonne Nuit is certainly the spot to put visitors into a holiday mood.

Walkers, too, will be pleased to find it an excellent starting point for three different walks. To the east there is the 4-mile walk along the cliff path to Bouley Bay while to the west there is the shorter walk to La Saline. These cliff walks are quite strenuous and sensible shoes should be worn. The number 4 bus will take walkers back to Bonne Nuit or to St Helier. A shorter circular walk can be taken on National Trust property on the hillside overlooking the bay, on the south side of the C98.

A postscript to describing the charms of this bay is an explanation of why it came to be called 'Bonne Nuit' (Good Night), when the sea beyond the bay was always known as 'Maurepos' — Bad Repose. Perhaps the answer is that the haven of the bay guaranteed a good night's rest to anyone who had safely negotiated its approaches. In any event, the name Bonne Nuit was recorded as early as the twelfth century, so there is no truth in the story that Charles II gave it the name when he left this harbour for France, saying 'Bonne Nuit, Belle Jersey'.

Rounding Frémont Point and going west, the next place to visit is the **Wolf's Caves** complex. It can be reached by walking along the path from Bonne Nuit for 2 miles or by car along La Rue de Frémont. The huge 485ft IBA television transmitter just to the south of the caves is an unmistakable landmark!

On the cliff top above the caves is a large car park as well as a licensed restaurant and bar. The stuffed wolf in the bar lounge will suggest to some visitors the origin of the caves' name, but the truth is less dramatic. This part of the coast used to be famous for its sea perch and the French for sea perch is *loup de mer* (sea wolf). This, it is thought, could have given rise to the legend that in one of the caves a wolf once suckled its young.

The cave itself is 400ft down a steep and winding path of 307 steps. There is a warning at the top: first to check the tides and, secondly, that the steep climb back is not for the faint-hearted. For those who do go there is a cave 350ft long, 60ft high and at its widest 50ft wide. Anyone who manages the trek there and back can ask, for the price of a small donation to charity, for a signed diploma that certifies that they have 'achieved the distinction of an Honorary Membership to the Wolf's Caves Climbing Club'!

Those not fit enough to visit the cave can view photographs of it in the games room of the restaurant complex. These show intrepid Victorian tourists, despite their unsuitable clothing, going down to the cave in their droves, as well as a striking interior shot of the cave itself. In the grounds here are also fascinating examples of old machinery that was used on neighbouring farms in time past, and a children's play area. Every Monday evening (as well as Tuesday and Thursday in the season) there is live Country and Western music to enjoy here.

Continuing round the coast one is rather unpleasantly reminded that St John is the parish famous for its granite quarries. **Mont Mado quarry**,

St John's parish church

just north of the B63, was once the most famous. One of the uprights in Grouville's La Hougue Bie dolmen was brought from here; centuries later the States always demanded Mont Mado granite — renowned for its beautiful rose colour — for their official buildings, while the wealthiest families had their houses, if not entirely made of, at least faced with Mont Mado granite. Jersey's main quarry today, though, is **Ronez quarry**, on Ronez Point, looking eastwards over Mourier Bay and westwards over La Houle. It is an unwelcome intrusion, with its conveyor belts and noisy lorries, into the peace of the St John country-side but looking back from Sorel Point at its dusty quarried terraces, there is a certain fascination in watching Jersey's famous granite being hacked out of the ground.

Sorel Point, the next headland along the coast, is the island's most northerly spot. From here to the west can be seen the treacherous Paternoster reef and beyond that, Sark, while to the east can be seen the Normandy coast. At its tip is a lighthouse and inland to the left a cliff path leading to Grève de Lecq, past Mourier Valley and Devil's Hole, in the parish of St Mary. Sorel Point can be reached by joining the same cliff path at Bonne Nuit, or Wolf's Caves, or by driving west along La Route du Nord and looking for the turning on the right which is well signposted. There is a moto-cross track on the Sorel headland where about eight meetings are held between March and May, in September and the beginning of October. Anyone wishing for further details should see the local press.

Leaving the cliff tops for a moment, between Ronez and Sorel, when the tide is half way, it reveals in the cliffs, a rectangular hollow, 15ft deep which measures 25ft by 24ft. Such an unexpected shape at such an inaccessible spot obviously led islanders to speculate on its purpose. So they decided it was there for the fairy folk to bathe in and called it

 Lavoir des Dames!

The cliff path continues from Sorel Point into **Mourier Valley** (*no bus*), perhaps one of the most isolated spots in Jersey. At the sea end there are plenty of quiet spots among the rocks for a picnic and for a tranquil view of the St Mary coastline. There is also an inland path which leads to the waterwork's pumping station and eventually into the parish of St Mary. This is very much a get-away-from-it-all spot, ideal for the self-sufficient walker or rambler. Car drivers can continue west along La Rue de Sorel and Le Mont de la Barcelone and then turn right up Le Chemin des Hougues to reach the footpath into Mourier Valley.

The road which has made this coastal strip accessible to the public, La Route du Nord, was built — comparatively recently — during the German Occupation. Even before the war, islanders depended heavily on the tourist trade for their employment but once the Germans had landed in June 1940, tourist employees were immediately without a job, leaving the Labour Department the task of finding work for over 2,000 people. Then it was decided to use this redundant work force to build a road along the north coast, largely across private land, that would not help the German war effort, but would be of benefit to the island. La Saline was the starting point and the road makers managed to get as far as Sorel but then were prevented from getting to Les Mouriers, their original target, because the Germans designated the area between Sorel and Les Mouriers a military zone, to which no access by islanders was possible. After the Occupation, however, La Route du Nord was completed and the period of its first miles of construction are remembered in the dedication which can be seen in the car park off the road opposite Les Fontaines Tavern just before Ronez Quarry. 'This road is dedicated to the men and women of Jersey who suffered in the World War, 1939-1945'.

Walking the Coastline

 The main activity to be enjoyed in St John parish, is, of course, to walk that magnificent coastline. That there is this footpath network round the island's coasts is due to the hard work of those on the States' job

creation scheme, which operates during the winter for those who would otherwise be unemployed, together with the efforts of the National Trust and conservation volunteers, plus the co-operation of the many land-owners involved.

It should be remembered, however, that this is a cliff path and walkers would be well advised for both comfort and safety to wear a pair of stout shoes. It could also be dangerous or a question of trespassing on private property to leave the official footpath. Finally, as parts of this north coast path are strenuous, they may be too much for the elderly or unfit. For those who want a good walk, the starting point in this parish going west to Grosnez (8 miles) or east to Rozel (6 miles) is Bonne Nuit, on the number 4 bus route. At Bonne Nuit itself, on the hillside facing the bay is an easier, shorter and circular walk, well signposted.

The north coast is also ideal for all bird watchers and lovers of wild flowers. From the cliff paths, far out to sea, gannets from the nearby colony at Alderney can sometimes be seen feeding. Closer to shore are the puffins and razorbills and the best times to spot them are early morning or evening. On the rocky cliff ledges the herring gull, fulmar petrel and the glossy black shag lay their eggs, while those parts of the cliffs which are densely covered by gorse are ideal hiding places for the shy Dartford warbler. Often soaring overhead is the island's only resident falcon, the kestrel.

A joyful sight in spring is the wild daffodils, known as lent-lilies, pushing their way up through the dead brown bracken, on many a cliff slope. Other flowers to colour these cliff tops are yellow gorse, purple heather, pink foxgloves and campion, blue sheep's bit (rather like scabious) and white ox daisies.

Inland St John

As well as having such a spectacular stretch of coastline, St John also has within its boundaries, the stone which is meant to mark the island's centre. This is to be found on the left-hand side of La Rue des Servais, the road which branches to the left along La Grande Route de St Jean, just after the large Sion Methodist Church. The stone itself would not appear to be a local one but could have been part of the now lost dolmen at La Hougue Brune. In any event, the stone is prehistoric.

In this area of **Sion** (*Bus 5*), there are several places of interest. There is the **Methodist church** built to serve the growing band of Methodists in the country parishes. On the other side of the road, a little to the north and making the corner of La Grande Route de St Jean (A9) and Des Houguettes is another non-conformist landmark. This is **Macpéla cemetery**, which served as the burial place for non-Anglicans when in the early nineteenth century only Anglican clergymen were allowed to officiate at funerals in the parish church cemeteries. It was, therefore, much used by the refugee population who flocked to Jersey after the European upheavals in 1848. The man who often marched behind the red flag in the funeral procession and then delivered the funeral oration at the death of one of the exiles, during his own exile in Jersey, was Victor Hugo. Finally, there is also a useful general stores in this central part of the island and a large DIY centre to browse round, northwards up La Grande Route de St Jean.

ST JOHN'S VILLAGE AND THE SURROUNDING AREA
Leaving La Grande Route de St Jean, which has along its length so many pink granite walls and traditional arches, take the left turn at Hautes Croix, the continuation of the A9, for St John's Village (*Bus 5, 6*). Just beyond the intersection of the A9 and A10 are the four essentials of any village — the church, the school, the Parish Hall and a pub. A new housing estate, including a chemist, bank and general store, clusters discreetly round the north side of the church. There is also a children's playground, given to the parish by the holiday camp pioneer, Sir Billy Butlin, who retired to Jersey and lived in St John.

As with all Jersey churches, **St John's parish church** (*Bus 5*) has grown over the centuries. The chancel, with its high roof and rough stones, is in essence the original tiny church. As the population of the parish increased, the west wall of this early chapel was pulled down in order that the present nave could be built. At the end of the fifteenth century, the south aisle, the tower and the spire were added. The church has been the centre of parish worship for over 800 years and its list of known rectors goes back to the thirteenth century.

Relics of the island's past are still to be seen both outside and inside the church. Outside is the base of a wayside cross dating back to the fifteenth century; inside, the reredos of the Lady Chapel has the Ten Commandments, the Creed and the Lord's Prayer written in French, reminding today's worshippers that a French version of the Book of Common Prayer was used in all the parish churches right up until early this century. The chandeliers that hang from the roof of the church are the original oil burning lamps, wired for electricity as recently as 1935. The rose window, high in the west gable, is specially worthy of note for the vividness of its primary colours which convey the vital energy of the Holy Spirit's gifts — the subject depicted. Then there is St John's distinctive cross delicately engraved on the glass of the main doors.

A true story showing the determination of your genuine Jerseyman is connected with this church. Apparently in the 1820s there was a group of parishioners who always sat in the south aisle and objected to having their view of the rector, as he stood in the pulpit, blocked by a pillar. These anti-pillarites, as they were known, told the rector to ask the Ecclesiastical Court for permission to remove the pillar. The rector was

PLACES OF INTEREST
IN THE PARISH OF ST JOHN

Cheval Roc
Bonne Nuit Bay
Legends of magic associated with
this rock.

Wolf's Caves Complex
Near Frémont Point
Down 307 steep steps. Only for
the fit!

Macpéla Cemetery
Sion
Served as burial place for nine-
teenth-century non-Anglicans.

Jersey Carriage Driving Centre
Mont Mado
Drives, picnics, pony rides, tuition.

St John's Manor
Only open occasionally for charity.
'The Blenheim of the Channel
Islands'.

Parish Church
St John's village
Twelfth century. Ten Command-
ments in French.
Grave of Sir Billy Butlin.

Jersey Pearl
La Route des Issues
St John's village
Largest collection of pearls in
Channel Islands. Restaurant and
café.

**St John's Sports and Recreation
  Centre**
St John's village
Tennis, squash, badminton,
snooker, shooting, payground.

**Le Claire Riding and Livery
  Stables**
La Rue Militaire
Riding lessons and hacking.

Beaches
Bonne Nuit.

Activities

Cliff walk from Bonne Nuit to Sorel
Point

Children's playground in St John's
Recreation Centre

Recreation Centre

Fishing at Bonne Nuit

loathe to ask for the pillar's removal because he feared that if the pillar
went his whole church would collapse. Nevertheless, in 1831 the rector
did finally seek permission but the court turned it down. The anti-
pillarites tried to persuade the next rector to get the offending pillar
removed, but again, the answer was a firm 'no'. Then the determined
Jerseymen took the matter into their own hands. They waited for the
rector to go on holiday to France and then pulled down the pillar
themselves, dumping it in the rector's garden to welcome his return.
The church did not fall down and the pillar is in the rectory garden to this
day.

St John's *perquage*, the path by which criminals who had taken
sanctuary in the church were allowed to escape to the sea, is not a direct

one to the nearest harbour of Bonne Nuit as one would imagine. Instead the path crosses the whole of the island to St Aubin's Bay in the south, so that the criminal could have calmer waters when he sailed to his exile. After going through the garden of a house called Les Buttes, it then followed the course of the stream, until it met up with St Mary's *perquage* near Gigoulande Mill. From here it went down St Peter's Valley to Tesson Mill, where it joined St Lawrence's *perquage*. The last section of St John's *perquage* crossed Goose Green Marsh and came out on the shore between Beaumont and Bel Royal. A long last trek across his native island for any criminal about to be outlawed forever from it.

The ornate tomb of Sir Billy Butlin — the well known holiday camp millionaire and philanthropist who lived in St John — with its inscription containing 2,000 letters, can be seen in the cemetery 300yd west of the church along the main road.

For those keen on indoor sports the answer is **St John's Sports and Recreation Centre** (*Bus 5*) in St John's Village, whose latest extension, the Sir Billy Butlin Memorial Hall, was opened by the Duke of Edinburgh in 1983. Any visitor who wants to sample the sports on offer has to obtain a temporary membership card. Here there is indoor and outdoor tennis, squash, badminton, snooker and a shooting range. There is a bar overlooking the cricket pitch and football field.

A little to the east of the village centre is a new attraction which is proving very popular. It is on La Route des Issues, has a large car park and is called **Jersey Pearl** (*Bus 5*). Its showrooms hold the largest collection of pearl jewellery assembled in the island under one roof. Entrance is free and from the first moment inside Jersey Pearl the visitor will be aware of a feeling of luxury.

As well as the show cases filled with exquisite pearl jewellery which line the foyer, the skills of the girls who make the jewellery can be watched as they set rings or thread necklaces. Then there are the well stocked counters where jewellery with either cultured or simulated pearls can be bought — the range includes necklets and bracelets in single, double or triple rows, rings, earrings, pendants and brooches, in modern or traditional style. The price for an item can be as low as £3 or as much as thousands of pounds, all VAT free. This is certainly the ideal place to buy a piece of pearl jewellery as a holiday souvenir, to mark a special occasion.

To make a visit to Jersey Pearl even more pleasant, there is a licenced tea house, with an amazing pearl tree in the centre, serving fresh Jersey produce.

Not much of prehistoric times survives in the parish of St John but it does have one of the few inland dolmens. This is **La Hougue Boëte**, just north of St John's Manor. The mound shows what the monument looked like after it had been sealed. The remains that were found in the burial chamber show that at least one human and several horses were buried here. Though the closed chamber dating back to 3800-2000BC is on private land, it has an interesting link with more modern times. It was used as the meeting place for the seigneurial court of the fief in which the mound stood. There are several other instances in the island where a prehistoric site, because it has been hallowed by past centuries' worshippers, has been used in this way, thousands of years later.

La Hougue Boëte Manor, which is now known as **St John's Manor**, is architecturally one of the island's most impressive houses. It is not known, unfortunately, when it was transformed from the traditionally seventeenth-century Jersey house it once was to the fine classically proportioned one it now is. Nevertheless, it has been called 'The Blenheim of the Channel Islands', and, when it was sold in 1874, had in its grounds not only a cricket pitch but also a croquet lawn, an archery ground, a rifle range and a gravel pit. With the manor, in those pew paying days, went three pews in St John's church. The beautifully laid out gardens of St John's Manor are open to the public at least once a year in aid of charity, when visitors have an opportunity to admire the eighteenth-century façade of the manor as well. Any passer-by, though, can enjoy the colourful displays of flowers that mark both entrances to the manor.

A further activity to enjoy in St John's parish is horse riding. Le Claire Riding and Livery Stables is on La Rue Militaire (*Bus 4, 5, Hautes Croix*) and both riding lessons and hacking are available here. Any visitor who has come without the necessary gear but who fancies a ride through the leafy lanes of St John will be provided with a hat and wellingtons without extra charge. There are pony rides as well as carriage drives at the Jersey Carriage Driving Centre at Mont Mado.

8 ST LAWRENCE

(*Bus 7, 7b, 8a, 9, 12, 12a, 14, 15*)

T his central parish of St Lawrence is bounded by brooks and renowned for its water, its walks, the benefactions of Florence Boot, its Underground Hospital and the island's first woman Constable. On its southern side it has a mile or so of coastline along St Aubin's Bay from Millbrook to Beaumont. Its eastern boundary runs up along Waterworks Valley and its south-western limit starts at the brook just east of Beaumont. Its northern boundary is about a mile-and-a-half from St John's north coast. The prefix 'Coin' in the parish simply means 'district' and applies to four of the six vingtaines into which the parish is divided.

Waterworks Valley

The parish's chief glory is what used to be called St Lawrence Valley. This runs the whole length down Le Chemin des Moulins and today it is better known, rather prosaically, as Waterworks Valley (*Bus 7, 7b to St Lawrence's church*). Centrally positioned of Jersey's five pictur-esque valleys which run from north to south across the island, its swiftly flowing stream of 3 miles long once powered no fewer than six watermills — hence the stream's name, Mill Brooke. Right up until the mid-nineteenth century four of these watermills were part of Jersey's milling industry. The wheat was bought in Russia, carried to the island tax free in Jersey boats, ground here into flour and then exported, mostly to the colonies. This lucrative trade only came to an end with the introduction of the faster and more powerful steam flour mills. The other two mills in St Lawrence Valley were used for paper making and crushing sugar cane.

That the watermills were no longer needed did not mean an end to the harnessing of the plentiful supply of water in St Lawrence Valley. With the large increase in population of St Helier in the 1880s, supplying the town with fresh water was a problem for which the system of street pumps which already existed proved quite inadequate. So, in 1863, a waterworks company was formed which decided to utilise the water in St Lawrence.

The venture, excellent though it was in principal, in practice proved

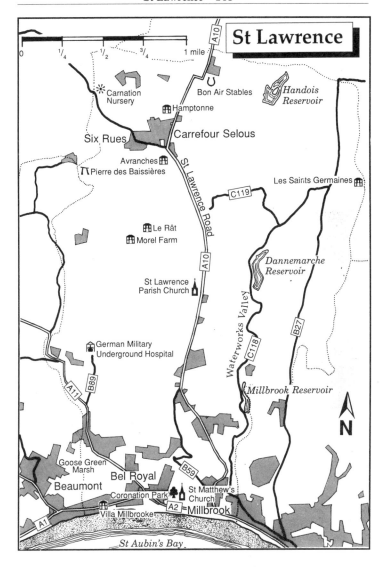

St Lawrence

0   1/4   1/2   3/4   1 mile

Carnation Nursery

Bon Air Stables

Handois Reservoir

Hamptonne

Six Rues

Carrefour Selous

Avranches

Pierre des Baissières

Les Saints Germaines

St Lawrence Road

C119

Le Rât

Morel Farm

A10

Dannemarche Reservoir

St Lawrence Parish Church

Waterworks Valley

B27

German Military Underground Hospital

C118

B89

Millbrook Reservoir

A11

N

Goose Green Marsh

B59

Bel Royal

Beaumont

Coronation Park

St Matthew's Church

A1

A2

Millbrook

Villa Millbrooke

St Aubin's Bay

a disaster and the company went bankrupt. Then, in 1882, a second enterprise, calling itself the New Waterworks Company, built three new reservoirs over a period of 40 years: Millbrook in 1892, Dannemarche in 1908 and finally, in 1929, on the site of an old china clay quarry,

Handois. It is no wonder then, that the charm that these man-made and interconnecting lakes have given to the valley should lead to it now being called Waterworks Valley.

Despite its beauty, rather a grisly legend is associated with this valley. It concerns a young girl who was going to be married in St Lawrence's church. On the day of her wedding she came down the valley, all dressed in her wedding finery, in a carriage drawn by six horses. When the poor girl got to the church, however, the bridegroom was not there — he had jilted her. So the distraught bride ordered her coachman to take her home immediately where she killed herself. Now, once a year on the anniversary of that fateful wedding day it is said that a coach and horses drives through the valley and in the distance the sound of faint wedding bells is heard in the wind. The coachman has white ribbons on his whip and the girl inside the coach is decked out in white bridal clothes. Only as she passes will those close enough to see realise that the bride has no face — the white wedding veil is draped round a fleshless skull.

Walking in St Lawrence

St Lawrence is the parish for rural walking. And not just along the half-mile which is thought to be, though there is no conclusive proof, all that is left of St Lawrence's *perquage* from the church to the sea. This short walk starts at the southern end of St Peter's Valley, goes through Goose Green where the Seigneur of Hambye (whose story is told in Chapter 3) slew the dragon and comes out on La Route de La Haule in St Aubin's Bay. The real walking is along the valley's footpaths, such as those which cross from Mont Cochon to Le Chemin des Moulins; in the north past the disused Vicart Mill, along Les Chasses, and in the south along Le Peachion and below Millbrook Reservoir. Permits are available, by the way, for coarse fishing at this reservoir at any one of three fishing tackle shops in St Helier.

Millbrook

The Boot family have strong associations with St Lawrence just as the Butlin family have with St John. Both have been equally generous benefactors to their adopted island home. Jesse Boot, the famous chemist, and his wife Florence lived in **Villa Millbrooke** which is up La Rue de Haut off the St Aubin's Inner Road in Millbrook (*Bus 7, 7b, 8a, 9, 12, 12a, 14, 15*). The site was first built on by a privateer in 1704 and when this house was demolished another was built in neo-classical style around about 1880. When this was bought by Sir Jesse Boot in 1924, it was first called Lansdowne and then Springland. The grounds of Villa Millbrooke, as it is known today, are sometimes open to the public for charity occasions.

Just over the road from Villa Millbrooke, on the south side of St Aubin's Inner Road, are two examples of the generosity of Sir Jesse Boot's wife Florence, Lady Trent, after he died. The first is **St Matthew's, the Glass Church**. This was originally built as a chapel of ease in 1840, to serve people who, despite the sand dunes which lay between what is now Victoria Avenue and the Inner Road, began to settle in the Millbrook area, then considered 'one of the prettiest of Jersey villages'. These new parishioners found it too much of a climb to walk or ride on horseback up to St Lawrence's parish church for services.

The resulting chapel was a very plain building and on the death of her husband, Lady Trent decided to beautify its interior in memory of him. As well as an architect to help her, she asked the famous glass worker René Lalique of Paris to contribute his considerable talent.

Monsieur Lalique's unique glass work starts at the main doors — in the panels of the doors are two angels. Once inside, the church is dominated at the bottom of the main aisle by the great cross behind the altar flanked by two pillars, all three illuminated. The altar of the Lady Chapel to the left is decorated by a striking quartet of angels.

Once the visitor has gained an overall impression, there are smaller details to notice. A recurring image is that of the lily, a symbol of purity, so that both the Madonna-lily and Jersey's own lily can be seen on the screens and the windows. On the glass font — probably the only one in existence — the signature 'R. Lalique' can be seen at the base.

Lalique's work is austere and executed in plain glass, so the visitor should not expect the effect of stained glass. The attraction of this glass is its form and shape and, above all, its luminescence. It is no wonder, therefore, that so many people come to see the uniqueness of the 'Glass Church' as it is so often called, for themselves.

In the vestibule, as well as religious books there are cards, leaflets and transparencies of the church and its glass. There is also a 3-minute tape to explain to visitors about Lady Florence Trent's renovation.

Three years after the rededication of St Matthew's church, Lady Florence Trent had laid out an extensive garden in Millbrook, where once there had just been scrubland. Lady Trent gave it to the island in 1937 on condition that it was always kept as a place where the young could play and the old could rest. As this was the year in which George VI and Queen Elizabeth were crowned, it is known as **Coronation Park** (*Bus as for Millbrook*).

This is an ideal spot for parents who want to sit and children who want to play. Near the Inner Road entrance there is a children's paddling pool as well as a playground, full of modern as well as traditional equipment, including a steam roller to scramble over and pretend to steer.

Close to the Victoria Avenue entrance is a wide pavilion with a view of the colourful gardens and then St Aubin's Bay beyond. At this end there is also a venture playground, specially built for the use of the disabled, which others enjoy trying their climbing skills on too. There is a refreshment kiosk in the grounds as well as toilet facilities.

To complete this area of interest at Millbrook, is a group of shops to the east of La Rue du Galet including a supermarket and a post office.

Prehistoric Remains

There are not as many remnants of the past for the public to see in this parish as there are in some others. From prehistory, two great blocks of granite from some dolmen on Mont Félard and a large block of red granite, where the parishes of St Lawrence, St Peter and St Mary meet, called Pierre des Baissières are all that remain of the menhirs. Specimens from the Bronze Age hoard of axes, knives and other implements that were dug up in an orchard on the Mainlands estate are on view at La Hougue Bie Museum.

Around the Parish

The church, the Parish Hall, the parish arsenal and the school come one after the other along La Grande Route de St Laurent, one of the major roads running north-south through St Lawrence. The oldest of these is **St Lawrence's parish church** (*Bus 7, 7b*), which started off as a chapel and was consecrated as a church on 4 January, 1199. One remnant of the earliest church on this site is a broken granite pillar — not of Channel Island origin — now displayed in the south porch. Originally it belonged, apparently, to a fourth-century Roman building. Then, in about the sixth century, its flat top was inscribed with letters suggesting a Christian memorial to a priest, though no-one now knows its meaning. Two or three centuries later, an embellished Anglo-Celtic interlaced pattern was carved down one side. In the south porch itself, which was a chantry chapel in Norman times, a plain brass cross marks the recess in the wall where the tabernacle holding the blessed sacrament was probably kept. The few fragments of medieval glass that survived the Calvinist régime can be seen in the small window above the west door.

Later alterations and additions include, in 1524, the fine Hamptonne Chapel, with its vaulted roof — unique in Jersey — and grotesque gargoyles, representing the spirits of evil driven out by the worship of the congregation. This chapel is probably the finest example of church architecture anywhere in the island. The church bell, dated 1592, is the oldest in Jersey and is still used.

In 1576, in common with all island rectors, the rector of St Lawrence signed the Discipline Ecclésiastique which imposed the Calvinist religion on the people of Jersey. Unlike the older churches, though, St Lawrence was not changed from a Huguenot temple — with white-washed walls, a long wooden communion table, and all pews facing the pulpit — into an Anglican church until as recently as 1890.

The three south chancel windows portray the story of St Lawrence and his martyrdom of being roasted alive on a grid. It is this grid which has been taken as the parish emblem. The church has been called, because of its size, and its fine architecture, 'The Cathedral of Jersey'.

Next to the church are the Parish Hall, school and arsenal, all built in the nineteenth century. Having an arsenal in which to house the artillery meant that the parish cannon no longer had to be trundled in and out of the church — through the wide door, now blocked up, at the end of the north aisle — as it had been since the time of Elizabeth I.

Other glimpses of the island's past can be seen in its old manors, of which **Hamptonne** — perhaps the finest and most interesting house in the parish — is now open to the public as a fascinating country life museum. There is a car park here, but for those coming by bus it is just a short walk from Three Oaks (*Bus 7*).

The earliest recorded owners of the farm were the Langlois family. The house that Richard Langlois owned in the fifteenth century was simply one large room, open to the roof, in which the whole family would have lived and slept. Across the road from the house is the unusual square *colombier* or dovecote, that he was allowed to build in 1445 — a rare privilege then — in recognition of his status in Jersey.

A century later, a first-floor hall was added over the ground-floor room and when Laurens Hamptonne acquired the property in the seventeenth century, there was a further extension — this time two storeys at the east end of the house. This is what visitors to Hamptonne see today — the property restored to the thatched farm with its pillared porch that Laurens, his wife Philippine and his four children lived in over three hundred years ago.

Over the open fire downstairs hangs the *trepis* or cauldron in which the family meals would have been cooked; upstairs is a replica of the curtained four-poster bed in which Laurens and his wife would have slept, as well as truckle beds for their children. Both downstairs and up are the great chests where the family kept their clothes. In each room where these objects are set out, as if waiting for the family to return, there are booklets explaining what they are and how they were used.

The next building is the Syvret's house, dating from 1830, with an exhibition called 'Living Memories'. This includes a 12-minute video with archive film and interviews with island residents, and shows how farming has changed in Jersey over the last seventy years.

Hamptonne also has a shop full of country fare, such as corn dollies, products from La Mare Vineyards and the Lavender Farm, as well as books about Jersey by local authors; a restaurant offering island dishes; and a small collection of farm animals and poultry.

Les Saints Germaines and Avranches are the other two manors: the first on the road running from the top of Mont Cochon to Sion and the second built in 1818, on the St Lawrence main road at Carrefour Selous, can both be glimpsed from the road. Avranches is set in 50 acres of ground which were used by the Germans during the Occupation as a secret store for 750,000 gallons of petrol.

Humbler dwellings of interest in the parish, both owned by the National Trust, are Le Rât and Morel Farm (*Bus 7, 7b*). These can be reached by taking the first or second turning to the left along La Route de l'Eglise. **Le Rât** is a small cottage, probably built in the seventeenth century, and is typical of rural housing used by people at that time. Nearby, on the opposite side of the road, is La Fontaine de St Martin, whose waters were once thought to have magical properties of healing.

Further to the west, along Le Mont Perrine, is **Morel Farm**, the best known farm in the island. The double roadside arch is perfectly proportioned and probably of an earlier date than the eighteenth-century building which can be seen through it across the cobblestones. Both arches have inscribed keystones: the main arch has '1666 RLG' for Richard Langlois, while the pedestrian arch has 'MLG' for his son, Matthew. By the side of the smaller arch is a mounting block.

This is a working farm, but when he has the time, the present farmer is quite happy to show visitors round it. In the bake house the bread oven and the hook for smoking bacon are still in place: in the press house the original cider press and apple crusher are still used late every autumn to transform the apples — with the help of a horse to turn the crushing wheel — into a potent cider.

The attractive inland pocket which includes Le Rât and Morel Farm also features two wooded hillsides or *côtils* both owned by the National Trust. A pleasant walk can be taken from the parish hall, through the woods to make a round trip, via La Fontaine de St Martin and back to La Route de l'Eglise again (see map page 169).

Park the car behind the Parish Hall then walk out of the back entrance of the car park and turn left on to La Route de l'Eglise. Cross the road to a footpath which goes along the side of the house called Abbey Gate. Follow the track down through woodland into the valley and along the bank on the other side. Turn right along the path which goes by Badier Farm. This is one of several fine properties on this walk. It is only a short distance to the road. Turn right on to the road and continue walking through well cultivated farmland. Turn right into the road signed La Rue de la Fontaine de St Martin. On your left pass Morel Farm. The next property is a fine granite farmhouse which also has a mounting block outside — the second in a few hundred yards.

Look for the *abreuvoir* on the left of the road which is a stone trough fed by the valley stream which then flows back through the wall until it crosses the road. Further down on the right is the well, which is called La Fontaine de St Martin. The land on the left belongs to the Jersey National Trust as does the Meadow.

Continue right up Mont l'Evesque and take the first turning right on

to La Route de l'Eglise to return to the Parish Hall car park. This is about an hour of easy walking.

Leaving the manors, farm and cottage, the visitor's attention is directed to a notorious relic of a much more recent period in the island's history. It is the **German Military Underground Hospital** (*Bus 8a*) built in 1941-5 under the valleys of St Lawrence.

To begin with, the German plan was to have a tunnel as an artillery barracks at Meadowbank to supply the main infantry base at St Peter, together with the island's coastal bunkers. In the next valley of Cap Verd there was to be a gun park. The work of drilling and excavating for these tunnels was too vast for the German army units to undertake alone, so the civilian task force, Organisation Todt, was brought to Jersey to complete the construction. This work force, founded by Dr Fritz Todt, was a motley crowd of Spanish Republicans, North Africans, Alsatian Jews, Poles, nationals from Occupied France and, from 1942 onwards, several hundred Russian prisoners of war. They were to all intents and purposes slave labour and many of them died in Jersey of harsh treatment, overwork and malnutrition.

The task of blasting the rock face to make the tunnel was also dangerous and it is believed that those who were killed in the frequent rock falls were buried where they fell. To link the tunnels of Meadowbank and Cap Verd involved excavating 43,900 tons of rock and pouring in about 20,000sq ft of concrete. But the ambitious underground network was never finished, nor was it ever used as an artillery barracks. After the British invasion of Normandy, when the Germans imagined that the Channel Islands were next to be attacked, the whole complex was turned into a military hospital to cope with the casualties.

So, the visitor to the German Underground Hospital today will see, recreated down to the last detail, a hospital ward, the operating theatre, a doctor's quarters, the Commandant's office and the important communications centre, just as they were left when Jersey was finally liberated by the British on 9 May 1945: without a drop of blood being shed. In addition, to recreate the experience of that horrific time, there is a special video, more than fifty pictorial panels and personal memorabilia, documents and photographs, belonging to that period.

Thousands of tourists come every year to the Underground Hospital in St Lawrence to learn for themselves more about the German Occupation of Jersey, the only part of the British Isles to come under the direct control of Adolf Hitler.

In the new visitor centre there is an information desk, a licenced restaurant, a tea terrace and landscaped gardens.

 Just the antidote to the grim reality of the Underground Hospital is a visit to Retreat Farm, the **Jersey Flower Centre** (*Bus 7*) on Rue de Varvots. As well as the large glasshouses in this floral paradise there is so much else to see: a flamingo lake, a wild fowl sanctuary, exotic bird aviaries and wild flower meadows, as well as floral gifts and the Café des Fleurs. There is also a section where the blooms can be bought to be taken away, or ordered to be packed and posted home. Keen gardeners can even buy carnation cuttings.

'Jersey fresh' carnations can also be ordered at any time. Visitors can watch the blooms being graded and orders being packed by the mainly Portuguese workers ready for immediate posting. Altogether over two million carnation blooms are exported every year from this, the largest mail order florists in the world.

Despite having such a small coastline in St Aubin's Bay, St Lawrence's only beach is a very popular one. The beach is sandy but kept clean by the tide; the bathing is quite safe at both high and low tide, though there is not much water left to swim in at very low tide; and the whole area is protected by the high sea wall separating the promenade from the beach. On the promenade are both refreshment and toilet facilities all along the bay. Anyone queueing for ice-cream at the

Morel Farm

Railway Café will be standing in the place of those who used to queue for tickets for the Jersey Railway that ran between St Helier and St Aubin and on up to Corbière. Millbrook was one of the stops along the line. The other relics of the past along this stretch of the beach are the two German gun emplacements known as resistance nests at Millbrook and Bel Royal. A few of the sand races organised by the Jersey Motor Cycle and Light Car Club are run at Millbrook. Visitors should see the local press for details.

Anyone with a love of horses will enjoy attending the meetings of the Jersey Horse Driving Society. As well as staging events at different venues, they hold their annual member's show every August at the British Show Jumping field, just off Mont Cochon (B27). Show jumping competitions are also held here most summer weekends.

This parish also provides excellent hacking territory and the place to find a horse is at **Bon Air Stables**, on La Grande Route de St Laurent (A10). Here they not only specialise in children's rides and lessons for novices, but experienced riders are given the thrill of riding along the

PLACES OF INTEREST IN THE PARISH OF ST LAWRENCE

Parish Church
La Grande Route de St Laurent
Twelfth century. Largest in Jersey.
Celtic remains.

Hamptonne Country Life Museum
Top of Waterworks Valley
Restored seventeenth-century
thatched farm with animals.
Restaurant and shop.

Le Rât
La Route de l'Eglise
Seventeenth-century cottage.

Morel Farm
Le Mont Perrine
Eighteenth-century building,
working farm.

German Military Underground Hospital
St Peter's Valley
Built by slave labour during
German Occupation of Jersey
1940-5, now museum of the
Occupation. Licenced restaurant.

Jersey Flower Centre
Rue de Varvots
Blooms can be looked at, bought,
sent home. Flamingos and other
exotic birds. Gift shops and café.

Villa Millbrooke
La Rue de Haut
Millbrook
One-time home of Sir Jesse Boot
the famous chemist. Open
occasionally for charity functions.

St Matthew's Glass Church
Millbrook
Decorated throughout with Lalique
glass.

Coronation Park
Millbrook
Children's paddling pool, venture
playground for disabled.

Bon Air Stables
La Grande Route de St Laurent
Riding by the hour, lessons
available.

Beaches
St Aubin's Bay between Millbrook
and Beaumont.

Activities
Promenade walk to St Helier or St
Aubin
Walks through valley and wood
land
Coronation Park — children's
playground, paddling pool,
venture area for disabled

beach. It should be remembered, however, that from May to the end of September, for the sake of the safety of other beach users, riding on the beach between 10.30am and 6.30pm is prohibited. Riding is by the hour and also takes place on bridle paths along the cliffs. Here at Bon Air Stables everything is taught from jumping to sitting side saddle and proper riding headgear can be borrowed at no extra charge.

9 ST MARTIN

Around the Parish

(*Bus 1, 1a, 1b, 3, 3a, 3b, 20, 23*)

The parish of St Martin has always been dominated by its church, its castle and its manor. So it is not surprising that the major building developments in this mainly rural parish centre round the church, Gorey Castle and the small harbour to which the manor has given its name of Rozel. It is, though, probably confusing to the visitor to find that both Gorey and Rozel are in two different parishes. Gorey Castle and harbour are in St Martin, but most of Gorey Village is in Grouville. With Rozel, the harbour and the manor are in St Martin, but the western part is in Trinity.

Though both **St Martin's parish church** (*Bus 3, 3a*) on La Grande Route de Rozel, and Grouville's are dedicated to the same saint, the former is always mentioned in records as St Martin the Old, and the earliest mention of it dates back to 1042. It was also considered to be Jersey's leading church, not just because of the size of its endowments but because it provided so many of the island's Deans.

A glance at the outside of the church will show an amazing number of buttresses, some even made of tombstones. This was because the walls were built only sufficiently strong to support the original thatched roof. When a stone roof was added, the stability of the walls was endangered and in both the sixteenth and eighteenth centuries had to be given extra support.

Another part of the church's structure which caused problems was its spire. One Sunday morning in 1616, just as the congregation were going to church, the spire was struck by lightning and broke in two. This caused a great deal of panic in the parish, as parishioners thought that this act of God was the forerunner of worse evil about to befall the island, because they fervently believed that 'Judgement must begin at the House of God'. The spire rebuilt in 1618 was struck by lightning too — in 1837. However, the spire to replace that one, which is still in place today, was supplied with a lightning conductor.

What can also be noticed from outside, by looking at the south wall, is where the earliest part of the church originally was and where a later addition was made. The chancel at the east end was the original chapel

Mont Orgueil

from which the parish church sprang and has its walls built of boulders taken from the beach. The later, western extension of the south wall is made of quarried stone and has a higher roof.

None of the original altars, statues or stained glass from before the Reformation remain, as they were all ripped out and smashed in accordance with the Calvinist beliefs which turned all the island churches into temples in the sixteenth century. The gradual restoration of the temple into a church began in the nineteenth century and the refurbished chancel, with its choir stalls and altar rails, was donated in 1877 by the then Seigneur of Rozel, the Reverend William Lemprière. His gift of stained glass for the east window and the other stained glass windows are some of the chief attractions of the church. Another notable gift tells the story of St Martin himself sharing his cloak with a beggar. It was given by Lady Florence Trent — the wife of Jesse Boot, Lord Trent — and is an ancient carving she found in the south of France.

St Martin's *perquage* or sanctuary path went from the church and followed a stream which finally came out at St Catherine's Bay. The last recorded criminal to use it was Thomas Le Seeleur, who, in 1546, preferred exile in Normandy to a death by hanging in the island of his birth. The path from the church through Rozel Woods to St Catherine's Tower makes a pleasant if rather muddy walk which can be enjoyed by holidaymakers in a rather different spirit from those for whom the escape route was originally intended.

 To walk the sanctuary path in reverse, park the car at White Tower on the B29 to St Catherine. Walk out of the car park turning left on to the B29. Take the first turning to the right and then in about 200yd take a track to the left. This leads to and by the side of the Mazeline Reservoir which was constructed by the Germans during the Occupation. The path now follows the stream through delightful woodland, where the yellow iris, foxglove, red campion and buttercup grow in profusion. In spring and early summer the woods are alive with bird song.

The stream is crossed and recrossed by stepping stones. At the walled path keep to the left and continue upwards, until the sign 'La Becterie', on the wall on the left. Now turn right into Rue de Belin, which passes the large Methodist chapel and leads to La Grande Route de Rozel, turn left and walk along to the parish church, which completes the route of the sanctuary path.

This is a good resting place, or refreshments can be taken at the local tavern. Now retrace the route until the second turning on the right, La Rue des Vaux de l'Eglise. There are some interesting properties along this lane and also a fine *lavoir*. The hinge pivots either side would suggest that this public place for washing linen once had doors, with the stonework at the side for beating the washing dry. Follow the winding lane uphill, turning left into Rue des Charriers, which continues downhill. As you are about to turn left to join the B29 to St Catherine and the

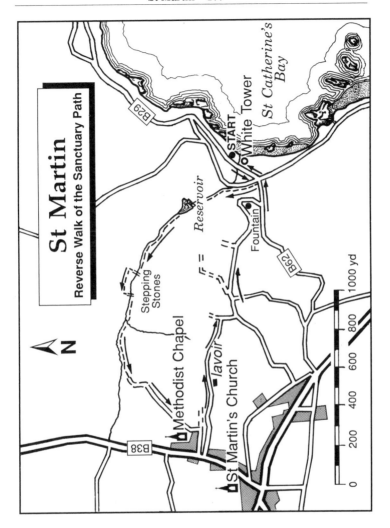

St Martin
Reverse Walk of the Sanctuary Path

car park, notice the fountain on the right, set into a wall with its tiny granite trough and 3½ft-high pillar, which would have been used as a spout for a purpose now forgotten. Walking time 1 hour. Moderate hills.

Built over 150 years later than the church was **Mont Orgueil (Gorey Castle)** (*Bus 1, 1a, 1b*), on a rugged promontory which had once been the site of a large Iron Age hillfort. Started sometime between 1180 and 1212 on the orders of England's King John, it commanded the Normandy coastline from Cap de la Hague to Coutances from where any threatened invasion would come.

To begin with, the castle was simply known as Gorey Castle, which it is still called today, but, at the beginning of the fifteenth century, Henry V's brother, the Duke of Clarence, was so impressed by the castle's unique position and great strength that he called it Mont Orgueil (Mount Pride), a name which it also bears, for this medieval island defence was one of the finest ever built. It was constructed on the concentric principle, with each stage of the fortification independent of the rest. For even greater impregnability, the walls wherever possible come straight out of the rock, so that the combination of stone wall and rock presented any would-be attacker with almost insuperable obstacles at every level. Morever, there is not just one but five gates to breach, each one higher up than the last, with drawbridges to cross to the first two, until the keep itself is reached.

Mont Orgueil's ten towers and two machicolated bastions — where boulders and pitch could be poured through holes in the floor onto the invaders coming up from below — were not in place or complete in the twelfth century. They were gradually added and modified through the next three centuries in increasing efforts to defend the island against the French. The castle was beseiged by them in 1338 and 1339; nearly taken in 1373, but an English fleet arrived just in time; French troops, however, did finally get in through the treachery of a postern being left open in 1461. The importance of the castle in the island's defence is proved by this French victory — once French troops were in the castle, they managed to stay in it for 7 years and virtually ruled the rest of the island from it. It took Richard Harliston in 1468 — with the help of the rebelling islanders — 19 weeks to get the French garrison to surrender and finally liberate Jersey from the invaders.

With the exception of this 7-year French Occupation, Mont Orgueil had proved impregnable from attack by armies which relied on bows and arrows and knights in armour. Quite the reverse was true when cannon were introduced. The castle had not been built either to withstand cannon shot nor to have cannon positioned inside it. Worse than that, it was overlooked by Mont St Nicolas, just 400ft away, from which enemy artillery could have bombarded it with impunity. So, in 1593, the English military engineer Paul Ivy suggested that no more money should be spent on Gorey Castle but that a new castle, to defend the fast growing town of St Helier, should be built in St Aubin's Bay.

In the normal course of events, Mont Orgueil would have been razed to the ground to make it unusable, but that it still exists to dominate Jersey's eastern coastline today is due to Sir Walter Raleigh. When he was Governor of Jersey, he wrote to Queen Elizabeth, whose final decision it was: 'It is a stately fort of great capacity. It were a pity to cast it down.'

La Pouquelaye de Faldouët

In the centuries following its reprieve, it has played an important role in the island's history no fewer than three times. In the English Civil War it took the part of King Charles and was under the command of the Governor's wife, Lady Philippe de Carteret, while Sir Philippe himself held out in Elizabeth Castle. Only after the king's defeat at the battle of Worcester, was Mont Orgueil handed over to the Parliamentary troops.

During the French Revolution, the castle was the centre of another band of Royalist supporters, this time of the French king. Admiral Philippe d'Auvergne made the castle both a safe haven for escaping aristocrats and also the headquarters of an unsuccessful underground movement to restore the French monarchy.

Gorey Castle's final role was as part of Hitler's impregnable fortress, during the Nazi Occupation of Jersey. The Germans constructed a large military headquarters and a machine gun post within the medieval fortification to defend the island against a British invasion.

Any visitor who goes inside the castle will soon realise from the information plaques that over the centuries it has been much more than a fort. In the early years the island was governed from here; its various lords, keepers and governors lived here. So there are two chapels inside the walls as well as residential apartments, the great hall and kitchen. Until 1693 the now ruined Busgros Tower was the island's prison, whose narrow stairs lead down to a damp and noisome dungeon in which many prisoners died before they could be brought to trial. This was where in the sixteenth and seventeenth centuries the alleged witches were held — many on a starvation diet of bread and water.

The castle was also used to detain political prisoners — in the Civil War both Cavaliers and Roundheads — and perhaps the most distinguished among the latter was William Prynne, the Puritan author of *Histriomastix*, an enormous work directed against stage plays, in which he was supposed to have cast aspersions against Charles I and his queen. He had his own cell and was eventually treated by Sir Philippe de Carteret, the then Governor of Jersey, during his 2-year stay, almost as his house guest. One of the tableaux set up in the castle to tell its history is of Prynne sitting in the cell he actually occupied, his cheek branded with the letters 'SL' —Seditious Libeller!

Inside the castle there are also tableaux with taped explanations which span more than five centuries of the castle's history. The figures are sumptuously dressed and there is background music of the period to match. The small museum near the top of the castle displays archaeological finds dating from prehistory to the nineteenth century.

As this historic building is built on a steep slope at several different levels reached by innumerable steps, it is not suitable to be visited by the disabled. However, those in wheelchairs are allowed in free to sit in the lower ward and to admire the colourful flower displays there, the views beyond the castle walls and to get some feel of the towering strength of the castle itself. There is, also, outside the entrance, a tea room and on the way to it an excellent view, to the right through the ramparts, of Gorey's harbour and floral promenade. Toilet facilities are inside the castle.

The grounds of **Rozel Manor** (*Bus 3*), off the B38, north of St Martin's church, are only open to the public occasionally for special events and charity functions. Visitors find the tall *Taxodium distichum* by the pond and the magnolia outside the chapel, both trees over a hundred years old, of particular interest. The manor itself is noteworthy both for the origin of its name and for the duties of the Seigneur to the visiting monarch.

'Rosel' is the old French for 'reed' and the Seigneurs of Rosel Castle in Normandy had three reeds as their arms. It was one of these Seigneurs in Norman times who was given a fief, a grant of land in Jersey from the King of England, and both the fief and the manor he built on it, including the bay it overlooks, were all given the name of Rosel or Rozel.

The duties of the Seigneur when his monarch came to Jersey were as follows: ' If the King come to this isle, you shall ride into the sea to meet him till the waves reach the girth of your saddle. And as long as he tarry in the isle, you shall act as his butler, and receive for your fee what the King's butler hath.' Today this duty is still carried out, but in more modern terms. When the Queen visits Jersey, after she has been received on landing by the Lieutenant-Governor and the Bailiff, the

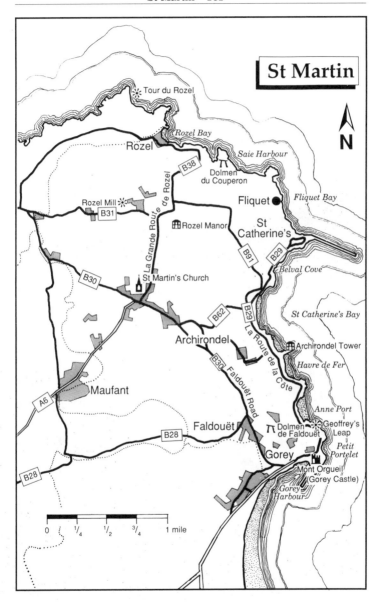

St Martin

N

Tour du Rozel

Rozel Bay

Saie Harbour

Rozel

B38

Dolmen
du Couperon

Fliquet Bay

Rozel Mill

Fliquet

B31

Rozel Manor

St
Catherine's

La Grande Route de Rozel

B91

B29

Belval Cove

B30

St Martin's Church

B62

B29

St Catherine's Bay

Archirondel

La Route de la Côte

Archirondel Tower

B30 Faldouët Road

Havre de Fer

Maufant

A6

Anne Port

Faldouët

Dolmen
de Faldouët

Geoffrey's
Leap

B28

Petit
Portelet

Gorey

Mont Orgueil
(Gorey Castle)

B28

Gorey
Harbour

0   ¼   ½   ¾   1 mile

Geoffrey's Leap

Seigneur of Rozel with the Seigneur of Augrès, who enjoys similar rights, are the first to greet her and welcome her to the island.

The present manor was built in 1770 but had the addition of the towers and turrets 50 years after. The *colombier* or dovecote and the chapel, both in the grounds, are much older, part of the latter going back to the twelfth century. Rozel Manor is off La Grande Route de Rozel, on the number 3 bus route.

Those visitors who are interested in prehistory have two dolmen to visit in this parish. The oldest is **La Pouquelaye de Faldouët** (*Bus 3a, ask for top of Gorey Hill*), which goes back to about 2500BC. It is a developed passage grave with an intermediate design between the passage grave and the later simpler designs. So the chamber with its 25 ton capstone recalls the passage grave, but the area which opens up from it before the passage is a new feature. The small cists in this open area were found to have cremated bones and late Middle Neolithic objects in them and originally had their own capstone.

The term 'Pouquelaye' to describe this dolmen at Faldouët needs explanation. 'Pouquelaye' or 'pouclée' means fairystone. Long after the menhir and dolmens on the island had ceased to be ritual centres for prehistoric man and his later descendants, many of the stones were still venerated for their enormous size and continued to have a role to play in the supernatural beliefs of islanders, right up until comparatively recent times. As the original purpose of the stones, standing in their isolation at several places in the island, had long been forgotten, their presence was explained by later generations as a result of fairy magic. The stones were thought to have been borne through the air by fairies — carried in their magic aprons! Thus have come about the place names associated with these so-called fairystones, such as La Pierre de la Fételle (The Stone of the Fairy) in Trinity and La Pouquelaye de Faldouët in St Martin and the road south of this dolmen, La Rue de la Pouclée.

Anyone approaching the dolmen along La Rue de la Pouclée et des Quatres Chemins will pass on their left an imposing building called Peirson House. Once called Haut de la Garenne and built as a children's home, it was used in the later *Bergerac* series as the Bureau des Etrangers. There is then a clear sign ahead to the dolmen.

The burial place is on the left along La Rue des Marettes, up some steps and at the end of a narrow bush-lined lane. The grave itself is dominated by its huge capstone and beyond, through the trees, there is a view of the sea, as there so often is from these prehistoric sites.

Plant lovers, while they are in the Faldouët area, might like to know that there is a Garden Centre here and that plants can be taken from Jersey to the UK. The garden centre is on the B30 La Grande Route de Faldouët.

The other dolmen in St Martin is to the north of the parish at Le Couperon, the **Dolmen du Couperon** (*Bus 3 to Rozel*). This gallery grave dates back to about 2400BC and is only one of two of its kind in Jersey, the other being in St Helier. Originally the parallel-sided chamber was covered by a long, low mound, with the other stones forming a supporting wall at its base. The tomb was once divided by the porthole stone at the entrance, which because of its size would indicate that bones rather than bodies were laid in the upper part of the chamber.

Even someone not particularly interested in prehistory should try to visit this last resting place of some of Jersey's earliest inhabitants, with its wide view of the sea round to Telegraph Tower. It is reached by taking the road down to Le Saie Harbour and walking up along the bracken-lined footpath which branches to the left at the small space for car parking. Above the dolmen, Rozel Bay can be seen to the north-west, Le Saie Harbour just below, and everywhere the scent of wild flowers, as broom and wild honeysuckle grow in profusion in this tranquil spot.

Further south down this rocky coast is a place which has associations which are not nearly so pleasant. It is the large rock which stands just south of the café with the same name known as **Geoffrey's Leap** (*Bus 1b*). The legend tells of a criminal named Geoffrey who was found guilty of a crime whose punishment was death. He was to be thrown off the high rock overlooking Anne Port into the sea below. Crowds came to witness his spectacular death plunge. But Geoffrey survived the huge drop and was seen by the crowds to be swimming back to shore. The sight of him still alive then began to divide the crowd. Some, mostly the women, said that he should be thrown over the edge again; the executioner had not done his job properly. Other islanders protested that the sentence had been carried out; that justice had been seen to be done and that Geoffrey should be allowed to return home a free man.

Geoffrey himself decided between the two factions in the crowd. He would throw himself off the rock to show those watching how easy it was to survive the fall. This time, unhappily for Geoffrey, he mistimed his leap over the cliff top and dashed his head on a rock as he plummeted towards the sea and drowned. Ever since that day centuries ago, that particular spot has been known as Le Saut (The Jump) or Geoffrey's Leap. There is a café of the same name nearby for those who wish to recover their spirits after seeing his fearful drop for themselves. Geoffrey's Leap is off La Route d'Anne Port.

Harbours and Beaches

GOREY HARBOUR AND THE SURROUNDING AREA
St Martin is just the right parish for beach combers and harbour hunters, for, between Gorey and Rozel and including them, there are at least ten delightful sea shores to track down.

Gorey Harbour

On the south-east of the parish is **Gorey Harbour** (*Bus 1, 1a, 1b*) with its dominating backcloth of Mont Orgueil. The growth of this port from a mere fishing jetty to the harbour it has now become — boats ply between Jersey and the Normandy ports of Carteret, Granville and Port Bail from here — is the reason for the development of the whole area. It all started in the nineteenth century with oysters.

There had always been an oyster bed just out to sea from Gorey which Jerseymen fished without competition until, at the beginning of the nineteenth century, they were joined by English boats from the south of England. By the mid-1830s at least 2,000 men and hundreds more women and girls were engaged in what had become such a profitable industry that oysters were served free at all hotel meals.

Oysters too were the cause of a famous riot in the parish. The States had thought to encourage the oyster industry further by laying down new beds in Grouville Bay, but they had to be left until they had established themselves sufficiently to be dredged. In April 1838, however, the crews of 120 boats decided to ignore the prohibition and raided the beds. When the Constable of St Martin tried to stop them, they took no notice, so the following day he arrested the ringleaders. This seemed to make no difference to the unrepentant fishermen, as 4 days later they were illegally raiding the beds yet again. This time the Constable of St Martin decided to appeal to the Lieutenant-Governor, who marched out at the head of the St Helier militia and the 60th Regiment to quell the rebels. A couple of cannon balls fired out across the bay and all the fishing boats slunk back into harbour, where the authorities were waiting to arrest the ninety-six captains of the boats. This rebellion in St Martin has since been popularly known as 'The Battle of the Oyster Shells', the only casualty being the Lieutenant-Governor, who died a month later from the chill he caught while supervising the suppression of the rioters.

The oyster industry lasted only 40 years or so — it destroyed itself by overdredging — but the effects of it on this country parish were permanent. To accommodate the many English people engaged in the industry who could not understand a word of the French services held in the parish church, a church was built near the harbour specially for them, where the services would be in English. Many of the houses and cottages in Gorey also date from this time.

Shipbuilding was the next industry to bring prosperity to the parish with no fewer than seven shipyards stretching along the coast. By 1890, though, with the increasing use of steam powered, iron hulled boats, Jersey's shipbuilding boom was over. There is still, today, in the colourful gardens that line the promenade, a tangible record of Gorey's boatyards — a stone monument represents the keel of a ship on the stocks.

So, as well as a picturesque and lively harbour, where the **Jersey Diamond Centre** can be found, Gorey has a nineteenth-century church, a small shopping area and a delightful walk along the flower-lined prom. What it does not have is ample parking space, so it might be as well to park somewhere along the common in the free parking zones and walk the short distance in.

After Gorey, going north along the coast, come several beaches before St Catherine is reached. **Petit Portelet** (*Bus 1b*) just behind the castle is tiny, pebbly and an ideally secluded picnic spot. It is reached by a footpath to the north of the fourteenth-century *mâchicoulis* (machicolation), misnamed by the Victorians 'Caesar's Fort.' Half a mile further along La Route de la Côte is the charmingly situated **Anne Port** (*Bus 1b*) with a beach extending both sides of the slipway. Here there is shingle and a wide stretch of sand with rising ground on three sides providing perfect shelter from all but an off-sea east wind. The bathing is also safe. There are toilet facilities but the parking — on one side of the slipway only and on one side of La Route d'Anne Port — though free, is limited.

Parking is not quite so much of a problem at **Archirondel** (*Bus 1b*), the next beach round, for there is a new car park to the left of the narrow lane leading to the cove, as well as parking space at the bottom of it. This delightful and sheltered spot with its rocky outcrops for scrambling, its shelving shingle and stretch of sand at low tide is certainly worth a visit.

The eighteenth-century defence tower on the left of the cove, now painted red as a landmark, juts out from what was once going to be the southern arm of a great harbour planned by the British Government for St Catherine's Bay as part of the war effort against France. The plan was, however, found to be impractical and never finished. Now only cormorants and other sea birds keep guard on the offshore rocks.

There is a small café here with toilet facilities, making this a good family beach. For walkers there is a coastal path to Fliquet which starts in the new car park in the lane, down the slipway. Pausing here, one can see right round the coast to Gibraltar slipway, where several local boats are moored, and beyond to Belval Cove. The unspoiled countryside that slopes gently away from this coastline, with its handful of classically proportioned houses, has probably hardly changed at all over more than a hundred years. For the technically minded, the large notice 'Power Cable', immediately to the left of this slipway at Archirondel, refers to the island's recent connection with the French electric grid, which enters Jersey at this point of the coast and goes to the rest of the island via the electricity station in the lane.

Archirondel is down a well signposted lane on the right of La Route de la Côte (B29) going towards St Catherine. This road, known as the pine walk, which leads to St Catherine is charmingly wooded with views of the bay through the trees. There are barbecue sites above Gibraltar slipway and just beyond Belval Cove where there is also a small car park on the other side of the road. Gibraltar itself is worth stopping at for

Archirondel

the marked and photogenic contrast between the dark woods which come down to the right of the slipway with its bobbing boats and the lighter colour of the sea. In the woods in St Catherine's Valley grow plants unusual for Jersey, such as dog's mercury and yellow archangel.

ST CATHERINE AND THE SURROUNDING AREA

St Catherine (*Bus 1b*) is reached by a one-way system, on which are one or two laybys for parking and barbecue sites. Once at the headland, one's view is dominated by the almost $^3/_4$-mile-long breakwater. This was begun in 1847 and completed in 1855, at the instigation of the British Government, to be the northern arm of a large safe harbour for the British fleet in any altercation with France. The whole enterprise proved impractical and now all that remains of the grandiose scheme is St Catherine's breakwater, which now belongs to the States of Jersey, and the short sea wall at Archirondel.

Today the breakwater is popular both for strolling along and fishing from. As it is built with two levels it is possible to walk out to sea on one level and come back on the other. On the way out Fliquet Bay and La Coupe Point can be seen on the left, the Ecréhous islets on the left horizon and the sweep of St Catherine's Bay to the right. There are plenty of seats *en route* from which to enjoy the seascape, as well as coin-in-slot rotating binoculars. For keen as well as casual anglers there are rods to hire and bait to buy.

There are also on the headland a café and a sailing club, where

Rozel Harbour

holidaymakers can try their hand at dinghy sailing. Walkers can join the Archirondel to Fliquet walk to the left of the one-way system into St Catherine, just before the café, by the side of the layby. It is best to go along to Fliquet by the lower path and come back down the upper path — not so much of a climb. On this path there is a seat from which to see nearby France — not too clearly, though, or that would be a sign of coming rain!

At **Fliquet** itself there is a ridge under the eighteenth-century defence tower which makes an ideal picnic spot and limited parking on the roadway above. The beach is pebbly with rocks and suitable for picnics and exploring rather than bathing. There are no refreshment or toilet facilities but not being much frequented is part of Fliquet's charm. Just beyond the tower, on the road which winds out of Fliquet there is a house like a fairy-tale castle on the corner, which incorporates many of Jersey's typical granite architectural features. Walkers will pass it on their way back to St Catherine by the footpath which starts again up the hill, on the left, marked by a wooden stile and from which panoramic views of France can be glimpsed. For drivers, Fliquet is down a well signposted turning on the right, off the B91.

Up the twisting road from Fliquet, the road to the right at the first crossroads leads to two more secluded spots — **La Belle Coupe** and Saie Harbour. The first turning to the right, Rue de la Coupe, winds down with Telegraph Hill rising up at the end of it. Here there is restricted parking with one footpath leading to the cliffs and the other down under

PLACES OF INTEREST
IN THE PARISH OF ST MARTIN

St Martin's Parish Church
La Grande Route de Rozel
Eleventh century. Fine nineteenth-century stained glass.

Gorey Castle (Mont Orgueil)
Gorey
Twelfth century, final addition by Germans 1940-5. Guided tours, café. Includes museum.

Rozel Manor
Off La Grande Route de Rozel
Eighteenth century. Only open to public on special occasions.

La Pouquelaye de Faldouët
Developed passage grave from 2500BC.

Dolmen du Couperon
Le Couperon
Gallery grave from 2400BC.

Jersey Diamond Centre
Largest selection of diamond jewellery in Jersey.

Beaches
Gorey, Petit Portelet, Anne Port, Archirondel, Fliquet, Saie, Rozel

Activities
Woodland walk from St Catherine to St Martin's church

Promenade from Gorey Common to Gorey Harbour

Coast walk from Archirondel to Fliquet

St Catherine's breakwater, ¾-mile walk

Saie Harbour to Rozel, along La Rue des Fontonelles

Sailing, fishing, barbecues on special sites

hawthorne arches to La Belle Coupe. The tiny shingle and sand beach has a few steps leading down to it and is at its warmest in the morning, as it faces east. This is really the place to get away from it all.

Returning back up La Rue de la Coupe, the first turning to the right, La Rue de Scez, leads to **Saie Harbour** (also spelt 'Scez'). This beach is more open than La Belle Coupe and is not so good for bathing. It too, though, is not much frequented and affords plenty of opportunity for rock scrambling, collecting shells, winkling and limpeting and finding a sheltered niche in which to enjoy the expanse of sea stretching to the horizon. Brambles, sloe bushes and bracken go right down to the edge of the beach. An eye should always be kept on the tide, so that there is no danger of the sandy path along Saie Harbour leading to the slipway being covered by the swift inrush of the sea. A narrow track cut out of granite and the granite cobbled slipway were once used for collecting vraic (seaweed) with a horse and cart for growers to fertilise their *côtils*.

More back-tracking is needed up La Rue de Scez for those in cars who wish to go on to Rozel, but for those on foot there is a public path called La Rue des Fontonelles — up the headland of Le Couperon, with its view across to the French coast, and past the dolmen which leads across the cliffs to the top of Rozel Hill.

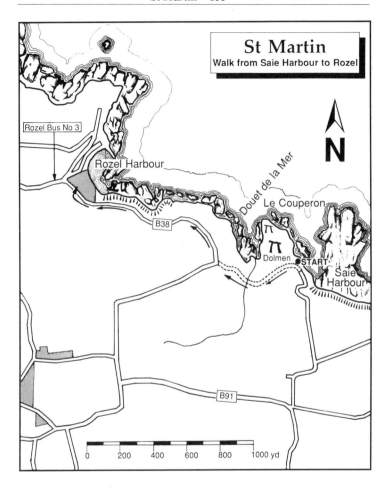

Take the footpath, leaving the dolmen on the right, over the fast-flowing stream where watercress grows abundantly. From the top of the hill, a moderate climb, there is a good view across the bay to Rozel Fort above Rozel Harbour. Turn right into La Route de Rozel, passing Bistro Frère and then there is the sweep down into **Rozel Bay**, one of the most attractive bays in Jersey. This walk should take about an hour.

ROZEL

Rozel (*Bus 3*) itself lies in what appears to be a wooded amphitheatre and it has all the charm of a fishing village, including a couple of small cafés along the waterfront as well as fishermen's cottages. It looks its best when the tide is up, with pleasure and fishing boats anchored in the harbour. When the tide goes out, it leaves a sandy beach along which waddle geese and ducks. There is also a rocky part of the beach away from the harbour which offers seclusion. Bathing is safe at all stages of the tide. Parking is often the worst part of visiting this north-eastern bay but there is parking just above the village up Le Chemin de Guet. Just follow the signposts. While up this hilltop, to the west of the bay, note the great earth rampart about 20ft high and 30ft thick, the remains of a prehistoric promontory fort, called Castel de Rozel.

Back down in Rozel, it is well worth finding the road called Vallée de Rozel where the buses stop, just opposite the road leading to the beach in front of the hotel. This is a nature walk in miniature, especially in the spring, for over the road branch two spectacular trees — a pink tulip tree and the aptly nicknamed handkerchief tree, whose flowers resemble hankies. At the end of the road are fine examples of primulas growing by a tiny roadside stream at the approach to a private garden. The peaceful atmosphere all along this road was once shared by the whole of Rozel before it became so popular.

The rural charm of this walk can continue by turning left and going up Vallée de Rozel, past the willows grown specially for the making of baskets and the sweet chestnut trees that overhang the road. At the top of the steep hill is one of Jersey's remaining windmills, now sail-less and standing in private grounds. It dates back at least to the sixteenth century and was adapted by the Germans during the Occupation as an observation post. Nowadays it is used as a landmark.

Bannelais

St Martin's is the only parish which has kept up the ancient custom of *bannelais*.This means that throughout the year the road sweepings of leaves and twigs from this heavily wooded area of the island are stored for auctioning by the Constable in October. These *bannelais* or road sweepings which are stacked at the top of St Catherine's Hill and at Carrefour Baudains can bring in as much as an extra £400 to the parish — no wonder that Grouville has recently decided to renew this ancient Jersey custom.

The Ecréhous Reef

Just as Grouville administers the offshore Minquiers, so St Martin administers the Ecréhous reef, which can be seen so clearly to the east of St Catherine's breakwater. The reef, with its three main islands of Maître Ile, Marmoutier and Blanche Ile, had a priory built on it in the thirteenth century; later it became a good place to gather vraic or sea-weed; and in the eighteenth century it was a smuggling centre, as well as an excellent place to dump voters who supported the wrong political

St Catherine's breakwater

party, until the election was over!

The Ecréhous have twice had a 'king'. In the nineteenth century Philip Pinel and his wife lived for 50 years in a small cottage he had built on Blanche Ile and were 'crowned' by visiting Jersey fishermen.

In the 1960s Alphonse le Gastelois fled to the Ecréhous to avoid the malicious gossipers in St Martin who said that he was the perpetrator of several attacks on island children. Alphonse le Gastelois stayed on Marmoutier for 14 years, acclaiming himself King of the Ecréhous. During this time the actual attacker of the children was found and convicted.

Recent excavations on Maître Ile have revealed flints from the Neolithic and Bronze Ages, including the stone head of an axe thought to be 5,000 years old, together with extensive buildings on the site of the thirteenth-century priory. Anyone wishing to visit the Ecréhous should apply to one of the fishermen at Gorey or sailors at St Catherine for details of any boats going out there.

10 ST MARY

Inland St Mary

(Bus 7, 7b, 8, 9)

O ne of the most renowned visitors to the small parish of St Mary was John Wesley. The bicentenary of Wesley's visit here was celebrated in 1987 in Les Marais, where the then 84-year-old founder of Methodism had preached 200 years before. As his Jersey congregation were all French-speaking, Wesley had to address them through an interpreter. John Wesley spent 8 days in the island altogether, as part of his Channel Islands tour to meet and preach to the increasing number of his followers.

Methodism, after initial, often violent, opposition, was particularly well received in Jersey as its many large, typically nineteenth-century Methodist chapels bear witness. The Methodist place of worship in St Mary is Bethelem in Le Haut des Buttes. This was built in 1829 to replace the small chapel which had been erected on a different site 28 years after Wesley's visit.

The original centre of worship in St Mary, though, was **St Mary's parish church** (*Bus 7, 7b*), which old documents name as St Mary of the Burnt Monastery. Such evidence as there is, including place names, suggests that this was on or near the site of the present church. How it was burnt down can now only be a matter of conjecture, but it is quite possible that Viking raiders set fire to the monastery. The oldest part of the existing church, now the north-east chancel, dates from the twelfth century, and if it is the site of the burnt monastery, then people have worshipped there for about a thousand years. A fine chapel was added to the south side of the original chapel in the fourteenth century. Then, during the Reformation, any relics of its Roman Catholic origins were destroyed, as happened in all the island churches, and the building was transformed into an austere, whitewashed church, frequently described as 'Le Temple'. So it remained until the nineteenth century, when the old pews, which had been rearranged to face the central pulpit, were replaced by the present pews of Gottenburg pine and part of the south aisle was built on.

Sometime in the island's Christian past, it became a tradition in the three western parishes to ring the church bell all through Christmas day — without stopping once. The custom probably arose because, during

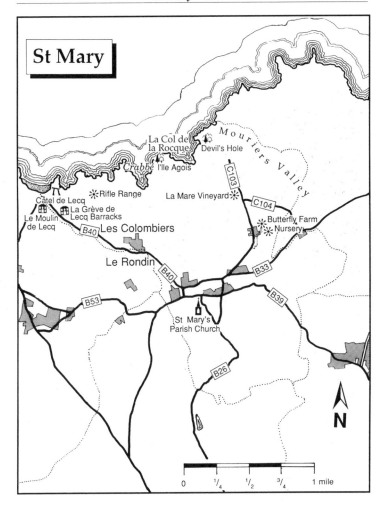

the French occupation of Jersey in the fifteenth century, St Mary, St Peter and St Ouen were the last to come under the control of the conquerors and the first to be free of them.

Whatever its origin, the custom in St Mary proved to be a contentious one on two counts. The first was that the thirst provoked by all the bell ringing was generously quenched with cider; the second, that once church services were reintroduced on Christmas Day — they had been forbidden by the Calvinists — no one could hear the rector for the noise

Grève de Lecq

of the bell. Matters came to a head in the eighteenth century, when three different rectors complained to the authorities. Two locked the church doors on Christmas Eve, but the ringers merely took the doors off their hinges and carried on bell ringing. In the nineteenth century the rector went even further, not only did he fit new locks on the doors but he removed the bell clapper, the bell rope and finally the ladder that led to the belfry.

The bell ringers were then doubly determined that they would ring the bells, despite all the rector's efforts, so they first distributed a handbill to all the parishioners. This read: '*Enfants de Ste Marie, vos droits sont envahis*' ('Children of St Mary, your rights are threatened'). To restore the bell — once they had broken the new locks and left the church doors in the rectory garden — the blacksmith forged a new clapper and a new rope was brought from town. The custom was kept; the rector was spoken of in the next parish assembly as 'pigheaded'; and the three western parishes still keep up the bell ringing tradition, although nowadays the bell ringers do stop while the Christmas services are being held!

St Mary's church gives its name to La Route de Ste Marie and the visitor will be interested to notice the austerity of its interior, the retention of its box pews and the wooden carving of the Annunciation to the left of the main door. The acoustics are good and visitors are welcome to the concerts which are held on some Sunday afternoons in the winter.

St Mary's Coastline

This parish may have the smallest population, under 3,000, but it has the most remarkable stretch of coast (*Bus 7, 7b*) in the island. The 1½ miles of precipitous and frequently indented cliffs from Le Mourier to Grève de Lecq give the visitor a coastal path through gorse and bracken with stunning views, particularly from the promontory called Le Col de la Rocque; caves to marvel at, such as the one that tunnels through L'Ile Agois and the one called the Devil's Hole; and the largest beach on the north coast, Grève de Lecq, although only about one-third of it is in St Mary.

The visitor walking from east to west will probably pick up the coastal path at Sorel in St John and follow it into St Mary up the western slopes of Le Mourier. The stream in this valley used to turn three of the island's watermills but the water is now diverted to Handois Reservoir in St Lawrence. Once a tranquil haven for the keen walker, Le Mourier is now often the noisy resort of motor scrambling enthusiasts, but from the top of La Plaine to its east and La Falaise to its west, there are spectacular views of the island's north coast in both directions.

From La Falaise the path leads west to the **Devil's Hole** (*Bus 7*),a natural crater in the solid cliff measuring about 100ft across and plunging 200ft down. It has been caused by the sea gradually eroding the roof of what was once a cave, until it collapsed and formed a crater. The name 'Devil's Hole' is a dramatic one but only invented in the nineteenth century. Formerly it was called 'Le Creux de Vis', 'Le Creux de la Touraille' or Spiral Cave. One possible derivation for its modern name is connected with the shipwreck of a French boat in 1851. Its figurehead was thrust by the tide straight into the hole and someone had the idea of getting a local sculptor to transform the torso into a wooden devil, complete with horns. Today this devil's metal replica stands in a pool on the way down to the crater, to lend atmosphere to the winding — and in one place quite steep — path down to the Devil's Hole itself. The hole can be peered down into from two safe vantage points.

Access to the Devil's Hole is through the grounds of the Priory Inn, which are open all the year round, and is free. Here there are parking and toilet facilities and a wishing well. The Priory can be reached via La Grande Rue or Le Chemin des Hougues for those who are not walking to the Devil's Hole along the cliff path.

After the Devil's Hole, there is the promontory — carpeted in spring with lent-lilies and bluebells — owned by the National Trust and known as **Le Col de la Rocque** where breathtaking views of the cliffs either side can be seen from Plémont Point to Ronez Point. To the north and east all the other islands and the Normandy coast are visible on a clear day. The path then goes on to the cliff above L'Ile Agois, under which is a tunnel. This cave can only be explored at low tide and then only in dry conditions, as the beach is often flooded by the stream which crosses it after heavy rain. **L'Ile Agois** is a 500sq yd islet separated from the mainland by a narrow gorge, about 250ft below the cliffs along which the footpath runs. Evidence in the way of pottery, flint heads and coins suggests that L'Ile Agois was inhabited in Neolithic times and again in the ninth century AD. As well as blackthorn, primroses and bluebells covering the cliffs here in the spring, wood small-reed (*Calamagnostis*), rarely seen in Jersey, grows on the summit of L'Ile Agois.

There is another fine viewing point from **L'Ane**. Beyond this head- land the footpath runs further inland south of the rifle and clay pigeon ranges at Crabbé and joins the lane which leads to the most popular beach on the north coast — Grève de Lecq. The walk to here from the Devil's Hole is about 2 miles. From Le Câtel there is an almost aerial view of the beach and the densely wooded valley leading to it, with the distinguishing mark of the defence tower — actually in St Ouen — in the car park between the two.

For anyone interested in shooting, **Crabbé**'s clay pigeon and rifle ranges can be reached by following the signposts to Grève de Lecq from St Mary's school (B40) and then turning right along La Rue du Rondin. At the T-junction turn left and look for the signpost 'Clayshoot', where the track leads straight to the ranges.

Visitors are welcome to join in sporting, skeet, balltrap and down the line shooting and to enjoy the club facilities. Both guns and tuition by a qualified coach are available. Other shooting here includes the Rifle Association, the Pistol Club and the Smallbore Rifle Club.

LA GREVE DE LECQ

Arriving at Grève de Lecq (*Bus 9*) either by the footpath from Crabbé or down the valley from Le Rondin, the visitor finds more than just the most popular beach on the north coast. First of all, the name 'La Grève' means the beach, and 'Lecq' probably derives from the Norse for a creek. This break in the north cliffs comes at the meeting place of two valleys, to the west from St Ouen and to the east from St Mary. The stream, which flows down the valley from Le Rondin and into the sea through the sea wall, is the dividing line between the two parishes. This means that buildings to the east of Le Mont de Ste Marie, such as Grève de Lecq Hotel, which used to be the married quarters for officers in Napoleonic times are in St Mary, while those over the road, such as the watermill, known as Le Moulin de Lecq, are in St Ouen.

The whole area of Grève de Lecq is full of historical titbits from the Iron Age to the present day. To begin with the headland to the east of the bay, known as Le Câtel de Lecq (Lecq Castle), the extensive earthworks here were raised to protect the Iron Age inhabitants of Jersey from their enemies. They also served as a refuge for their descendants right down to medieval times.

One of the surviving watermills which ground the flour for these medieval inhabitants still exists. It is **Le Moulin de Lecq** (*Bus 9*) — first mentioned in 1299, standing in meadow and woodland on the way into Grève de Lecq and now converted into an inn. It was in use as a mill right up until 1929, thus serving the area for over 600 years. During the German Occupation, however, the power of the huge 18-ton waterwheel was harnessed for a different purpose — to generate electricity for the searchlights the Germans had positioned round Grève de Lecq Bay. This outside waterwheel, which has a diameter of 21ft, works entirely by the weight of the water that rushes past the mill.

Inside the inn, on the ground floor, in the Mill Room, the machinery which worked the mill from inside has been preserved as part of the decor. Upstairs in the Granary Bar, where all the grinding took place, is much of the mill's old equipment as well as corn-sack style cushions and paraffin lamps.

Though Le Moulin de Lecq is just over the border in St Ouen, it is really an integral part of the Grève de Lecq scene and adds the soothing splash of water, as well as flood lighting at night, to this photogenic spot. It also has a children's play area.

The Germans were only the last in a long line of defenders of the bay.

In fact, such a natural vantage and defence point as Grève de Lecq was used for warlike purposes at several different times over the centuries. The fort overlooking the bay and battery on the summit of Le Câtel de Lecq, the round tower in what is now the car park were all three built as part of the eighteenth-century defences all round the island against a threatened French invasion.

Further building continued into the next century, with the construction of the **Grève de Lecq Barracks** (*Bus 9*) which have the protection of Le Câtel de Lecq to the north of them. They were begun in 1810 at the height of the Napoleonic invasion scare and were completed in 1815, the year of Napoleon's defeat at the Battle of Waterloo.

The barracks included rooms for the soldiers, the NCOs and their officers, together with the quartermaster's stores, stables and harness rooms for the horses. The only item in the two tiny whitewashed prison cells was an uncomfortable iron bedstead.

There are occasional open days — publicised through the media, when visitors can look over the barracks and see an exhibition of horse-drawn vehicles from the time when the barracks were in use: everything from an old Jersey milk cart to an 1875 four-wheeled dog cart, in which the four passengers would have sat back to back.

Even when the barracks are not open, there is an interpretation centre in Block 1 for further information about the north coast area.

Also built in the last century was the pier at Grève de Lecq, which jutted out much further from the western headland than it does now. Thirteen years after it was built, a severe storm broke it up and the granite stones which were strewn across the beach as a result have been used to build a breakwater and to repair the stump of pier that remains. Today it makes an ideal place for a bit of fishing and gives, as one looks back, a good view of the beach in its rural setting.

The circle of concrete at the west end of the harbour wall in St Ouen marks one of the many twentieth-century defences constructed to guard the bay. It is where the Germans put a tank turret during their nearly 5 years' Occupation of the island. On both sides of the bay they also constructed gun emplacements. On the eastern side, by Café Romany, there is the reinforced concrete casemate for a 7.5cm gun and, behind it, a large air-raid shelter; on the western side, by Café Casino, the fortress-type concrete casemate housed a 10.5cm gun.

Looking seawards from the beach, the points of a rocky outcrop can be seen around which the white surf breaks. This reef was first called **Les Pierres de Lecq**, and was the scene of a terrible shipwreck. In 1565, after Queen Elizabeth I had given Helier de Carteret of St Ouen the authority to colonise the then uninhabited island of Sark, he chose thirty-five Jersey families and five from Guernsey to go with him. Tragically, as the Jersey contingent were crossing the Channel to start their new life in Sark, one of the ships foundered on Les Pierres de Lecq.

Among those drowned were women and children and since that day, whenever there is a storm, their terrified cries as their boat first struck the rocks can apparently still be heard. Fishermen call the plaintive sound '*les cris de la mer*' — the 'cries of the sea'. Sailors throughout the ages have recognised the dangerous nature of the reef and said an 'Our Father' or 'Pater Noster' as they passed the treacherous Pierres de Lecq, both for the souls of those who had drowned there and for their own safety. Hence the later name for the rocks — Paternosters.

 There are, however, natural as well as historic features to enjoy at Grève de Lecq. Beneath Le Câtel de Lecq there is a cave some 60ft long, 15ft wide and up to 20ft high in some places which opens onto the sandy beach of Le Val Rouget to the east. This cave can only be entered when the tide is extremely low and visitors should make quite sure of tide times before venturing to explore it.

The bay itself — most of which is in St Ouen's parish — is popular with families, because of its fine sandy beach and its several cafés and kiosks. It is also sheltered by the cliffs to the west and east, while the wide expanse of dark, rock-coloured sand is ideal for spreading out on or for ball games. Swimmers should note that the beach shelves steeply into deep water and extra care should be taken if there is a heavy swell. There is ample parking.

For the walker, as well as the 2-mile cliff path back to the Devil's Hole there is also a further extension of the coastal route westwards. This starts behind the Prince of Wales Hotel and goes along La Charrière Huet, the original track down to the watermill, towards Plémont. From the headland looking back east is the long stretch of the northern cliffs back to Sorel. The bus to Grève de Lecq is the 7b or 9 and for those who want to walk there from either east or west, the 7 goes to the Devil's Hole and the 7b or 8 to Plémont. There is a return service from all three points to St Helier.

Other Places of Interest

In St Mary, as well as the more traditional farms with their cows and *côtils*, there are two farms with a difference which are well worth a visit. The first is the **Butterfly Centre** (*Bus 7 to Devil's Hole*) at Haute Tombette, with parts of the farm house dating back to 1670.

The immediate impression for the visitor to the glasshouse in the farm grounds where the butterflies are kept is of a myriad colourful creatures, hovering and darting freely together in a large flight area planted with nectar-heavy plants such as buddleia and lantana. Then there is the section where butterflies lay their eggs on the special plants set out for them and where the giant caterpillars emerge. Here, too, when a caterpillar is replete, it climbs to the top of the cages to pupate.

PLACES OF INTEREST IN THE PARISH OF ST MARY

Parish Church
La Route de Ste Marie
Twelfth-century chancel. Wooden carving of Annunciation.

Devil's Hole
W of La Falaise
100 x 200ft crater caused by cave collapse. Access through the Priory Inn grounds.

Clay Pigeon and Rifle Range
Crabbé
Skeet, balltrap, down-the-line shooting etc, guns for hire, tuition.

Le Câtel de Lecq
Grève de Lecq
Remains of Iron Age earthworks.

Le Moulin de Lecq
Grève de Lecq
Ancient, working watermill, just in parish of St Ouen, now an inn.

Butterfly Centre and Carnation Nursery
Haute Tombette
Shop and licensed café. Parts of the farm of 1670.

L'Ile Agois
Crabbé Bay
Neolithic remains found.

La Mare Vineyards
La Rue de la Hougue Mauger
Vineyards, café, shop. Learn the stages of wine-making and explore the Vineyard Trail.

Grève de Lecq Barracks
Nineteenth century, built at height of Napoleonic invasion scare. Interpretation centre in Block 1.

Beaches
Grève de Lecq.

Caves
Devil's Hole, Le Câtel de Lecq.

Activities
Cliff path walk from Le Mourier to La Grève de Lecq

Swimming, surfing, fishing, shooting

Children's playgrounds at Priory Inn, La Mare Vineyards and the Butterfly Centre.

The whole of the butterfly farm is a series of well laid out flower beds, with exotic orchids and waterfalls and there is a leaflet available for those who would like to identify the butterflies. But a word of advice — do not wait until a rainy day to come to Haute Tombette, as when it rains the butterflies have a tendency to fly to the top of the glasshouse and stay there. Like the tourists, butterflies are liveliest when the sun shines.

There are other attractions at Haute Tombette as well as the butterflies. There are the nurseries where the visitors can see carnations in their various stages of growth and buy them or have them sent to the mainland. There is also the fully licensed Granite Tea Lodge, for which the farm proper supplies most of the vegetables and fruit, especially strawberries. Here the visitor can relax for morning coffee, afternoon tea or a lunchtime snack. Finally there is a large souvenir shop, where many of the items for sale are decorated with a butterfly motif.

Haute Tombette is certainly a place where an hour or two could be spent. Admission is free to the gardens, tea lounge and nurseries but there is an admission charge to see the butterflies and the other insects. Haute Tombette is 10 minutes' walk from Devil's Hole, on La Rue de la Grosse Epine.

❄ The second farm, **La Mare Vineyard** (*Bus 7 to Devil's Hole*) has a fine house built at the end of the eighteenth century and is set in several acres of land. It too, though, is not a typically Jersey farm, although a working one. It is, in fact, a vinery which produces the island's only wine — a fresh and fruity white.

This farm is not only beautifully laid out but is practical too, so that one can appreciate to the full all the stages of vine growing and wine-making. There is ample parking and then, just by the admission gate, there is the Video Reception House, which not only gives a brief history of the original farm, but shows the whole work of the vinery from the growing of the vines to the bottles of wine being stacked.

With this interesting information in mind, the visitor is then free to wander as he or she will, or to follow the Vineyard Trail, which is given to each visitor on arrival. This leads through the vineyard itself, round the orchard — and eventually to the building which houses the Vintry, where there is also the distilling of Jersey apple brandy and wine-tasting and the Vineyard Shop. In the Vintry are amusing notices explaining the process of pressing the grapes in the autumn; while in the charming bow-windowed shop there is everything from animal masks, Jersey wine and cider to Jersey mustard, marmalade and preserves — all made in the farm kitchen.

After a leisurely stroll round, home-made food and, of course, Jersey wine is available in the Buttery and Tea Garden, where there is a cider press dating back to 1850. There is a Tarzan Trail for visitors of all ages. For the toddlers there is a wobble-board, while for those who are older there is the Burma Bridge, the Swinging Steps, as well as an area for the spotted ponies and other family animals.

So, although, St Mary is a small parish, there is plenty to do there, including walking along its coastline, swimming, surfing and fishing and visiting its two unusual farms. There is magnificent scenery to enjoy as well as historic buildings. La Rue des Buttes (B53) is worth noting for any visitors wanting a post office — which is also a general stores — or a garage.

The late-night visitor to Jersey, who comes here after the Battle of Flowers in August, or during early September, will have the extra delight of seeing two National Trust properties floodlit. The first is Grève de Lecq Barracks and the second the headquarters of the National Trust for Jersey, at the 'The Elms' farmhouse, on La Chève Rue (A6).

11 ST OUEN

(*Buses 7b, 8, 9, 12a*)
C overing the whole of the north-west corner, St Ouen (pronounced 'wan') is the largest of the island's twelve parishes. Unlike the other eleven, the parish is divided into '*cueillettes*' and not '*vingtaines*', which date back to the time when dues had to be 'gathered' (*cueillir* means to gather) from each of the districts. As about half the parish is still largely uncultivated, consisting of heathland and sand dunes, and it is surrounded on three sides by the sea, it is not surprising to discover that the whole area is one of outstanding natural beauty.

The Coastal Path

Starting at Grève de Lecq, where the north-east boundary of St Ouen divides the valley, there is a coastal path going west towards Plémont Holiday Village, then continuing above the beach of Grève-au-Lançon and on to Grosnez Castle. This section of the coast is rich in caves and stunning rock formations; it is also an ideal spot for bird watching. There is a cave in the small and charming bay of Douet de la Mer, the so-called Smuggler's Cove, one further along at Le Grand Becquet and a third at Le Petit Becquet, to mention just a few. As for the birds to be watched, fulmar petrels have colonised the north-facing cliff ledges between Grève de Lecq and Plémont and can mostly be seen from May to September. Early morning and evening are the best times to catch sight of the breeding puffins and razor bills and the cliffs are often hovered over by kestrel. Looking out to sea, feeding gannets and tern can sometimes be spotted.

Grève-au-Lançon (or Plémont beach as it also called)(*Bus 7b, 8*) is St Ouen's largest north-facing beach and is popular because of its sand and the shelter it has from the rocks surrounding it on three sides. Care, though, should be taken when swimming near the rocks at either side of the bay, especially if there is a heavy swell. When the tide is out, this compact bay has a stretch of sand approximately a mile wide and a quarter of a mile deep — ideal for sun bathing and family games. For small children there are rock pools to explore, for adults a network of caves. These include the unusual Waterfall Cave, to the left of the steps down, where a stream of water falling from the cliff above makes a transparent curtain, and a large cave, immediately to the right of the steps, whose seaward view is divided by the famous long and pointed Needle Rock, which so appealed to the imagination of Victorian visitors. As the old name for this beach, Grève-au-Lançon, means sand eel beach, perhaps even a little low water fishing could be included. From June to September beach guards are on duty 10am-6pm.

One disadvantage for elderly or disabled visitors could be that this beach can only be reached by a steep path, a narrow bridge and down some steps. At the top of the path, before the climb down to the beach, are refreshment and toilet facilities and limited parking.

The coastal path continues from Grève-au-Lançon and on the way to Grosnez, passes the archaeologically famous **La Cotte à la Chèvre**, or Goat's Cave, perched several feet above present-day sea level at the west end of Plémont Bay. Recent excavations suggest that man was living here as early as 100,000BC and the flints and coarse stone tools found in the cave area are as important as those Palaeolithic remains found in a cave in St Brelade. These finds are now on display in the museum at La Hougue Bie.

Following the path round the headland one comes to **Grosnez Castle** (*Bus 8*), standing in isolated ruins 200ft above sea level. The entrance to this north-western refuge is all that is now left standing, but one can still trace where the rest of the walls and buildings would have stood. Carved corbels from the castle are on display in the museum at La Hougue Bie. No records say when the castle was built or how it came to be destroyed — all that is known is that it dates from the fourteenth century.

There is plenty to see from the headland at Grosnez (which means 'big nose') depending on the weather and the time of day. Bad weather and there will be many passing birds to spot, including the fulmar; a clear day and the other Channel Islands can be distinguished, starting with Guernsey to the north-west, then Jethou, Herm, Sark, the Paternosters and, farthest east, Alderney. On a summer evening this is a favourite spot to watch the spectacular sunsets for which St Ouen is renowned. There is parking on the headland for those who want to explore the castle ruins, walk down to the lighthouse, or start walking along the cliff top path that goes south to L'Etacquerel and the start of that magnificent stretch of coastline, St Ouen's Bay.

On the way from Grosnez to L'Etacquerel, one passes the wild open plateau of **Les Landes** (*Bus 8 to Grosnez*) where there are no trees to break the winds that sweep across from the Atlantic Ocean. This is the largest area of continuous heathland in Jersey, with bracken, gorse and dry acidic as well as maritime grassland breaking through the predominantly dwarf scrub heath.

Naturalists might spot the rare Glanville fritillary butterfly, or the

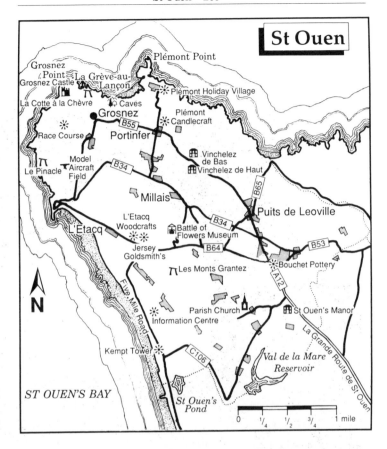

Dartford warbler which nests here in quite significant numbers. Just to the north of the Pinnacle Rock, in the wetland area of Le Canal du Squez, is the habitat of the equally uncommon and protected agile frog. In this bogland thrive purple moorgrass, St John's wort and the bog pimpernel. Casual walkers will notice, on the outcrops of rock, natural rock gardens with white sea campion, pink thrift and the pale yellow spikes of the pennywort, while, in the spring, almost underfoot is the lilac sand crocus in the turf and all about, the unmistakable fragrance of the gorse.

In the extreme north of Les Landes, to the west of Le Chemin du Château which leads to Grosnez Castle and La Mare Route de Grosnez, is the island's mile-round race course. The Jersey Race Club hold about eight meetings here a year, with the first one on Easter Monday and the last in August. Each meeting has five races, including one

Grosnez Castle

hurdle race, and starts at 2.30pm except at a Sunday meeting, when the first race is off at 3.30pm. The rest of the races are spaced at 35-minute intervals. All facilities are available at the course and the picturesque setting, together with the thrill of watching the races themselves, make for the most pleasant afternoon out.

This is also the part of the island where enthusiasts can sail kites and fly model aircraft. Walkers, though, will just wish to wander along the paths through the yellow gorse and purple heather and enjoy the cliff top peace and the views over the sea. From time to time there are reminders of a less peaceful period in the island's history, with the remains of the fortifications that the Germans placed all along this western coast during the island's Occupation: gun emplacements and bunkers still showing through the wild vegetation, together with a concrete observation tower overlooking the Atlantic to the west of the race course.

Walkers taking the cliff path from Grosnez to L'Etacq will pass on their right the long slope down to **Le Pinacle** (*Bus 8 to Grosnez*), the almost 200ft Pinnacle Rock right on the edge of the sea. Despite its exposed position, excavations have revealed that there have been no fewer than five different settlements at its foot, the first dating back to the Neolithic period, the last to Christian times. For there is no doubt that the islanders' veneration of large rocks continued here until about the second century AD — there are the remains of a pagan shrine to the god of the rock from this period to prove it.

The slope sweeping down to Le Pinacle is a special treat for spring visitors because of the wild flowers that cover it. These include, as well as the expected bluebells, sea pinks with their honey-scented blossoms, creeping broom and the spreading horseshoe vetch — both yellow. Below the rock itself is a cave which is only safe to be explored when the tide is going out — even then extreme care should be taken.

St Ouen's Bay, Les Mielles and the Surrounding Area

Walking south from Le Pinacle, the path descends steeply on to Mont du Vallette at L'Etacq, a huge circular mass of grey rock rising from the beach at the northernmost tip of St Ouen's Bay (*Bus 12a*). Here, right on the shore, an old German bunker has been transformed into a *vivier* where many locals, including restaurateurs, buy their fish. In the large tanks of sea water are live crabs, lobsters, mussels, oysters, clams, whelks and other shellfish. The *vivier* is open 8am-5pm Tuesdays to Saturdays and 8am to 1pm on Mondays.

The 5-mile stretch of the bay and the dunes behind it are divided between the parishes of St Ouen, St Peter and St Brelade, but the

interpretation centre with information about the area's prehistory, its ✳
flora, fauna, birdlife and footpaths, is at Kempt Tower, a converted
martello tower, in St Ouen. This strip of coast is, in fact, the island's mini-
National Park, known as **Les Mielles**. Admission to the centre is free but
it is not suitable for the disabled as it has to be reached by steps.

The displays at the interpretation centre have a strong natural
history bias but information can also be found about the area's prehistory. It tells, for example, of a fine example of a passage grave, **Les
Monts Grantez** (*Bus 8, 9 to St Ouen's church then walk to Le Chemin* Π
des Monts). This megalithic monument has a rounded almost polygonal
end chamber at the end of a narrow passage. Many of the capstones
are still in place but that over the end chamber was destroyed. Several
of these massive stones originate from the southern end of St Ouen's
Bay, so the huge effort involved in transporting them to the plateau
overlooking the sea, would suggest quite a sizeable Neolithic population in the area. The remains found at this prehistoric burial site include
the bones of at least eight people, together with bones of ox, deer,
horse, pig and goat. There were also piles of limpet shells, stone
artefacts, and coloured pebbles from the beach. The site is surrounded
by a granite wall and is on land overlooking the sea owned by the
National Trust, in direct line with the spire of St Ouen's church.

The sand dunes along this west coast are the ecological focus of Les
Mielles and have an extraordinary diversity of plant life. Over 400
different species have been recorded growing here, thirty of them
locally rare or scarce plants, such as the strange-looking (and smelling)
lizard orchid and the great sea stock with its night fragrance. More abun-
dant are the soft fluffy hare's-tail grass, often dyed and used on Battle
of Flower floats, the tree lupin, with its yellow or white blooms scenting
the air from July right through to October, and the prickly bluish green
sea holly which has small powder-blue flowers in July and August. At
the end of the day, there is the fragrant evening primrose to enjoy.

Dune flora and fauna can be observed along the whole of this
coastal strip between the sea wall and the coast road, some plants,
such as the yellow small hare's ear, are so tiny that you have to be on
your knees to see them. Here the green lizard, unique to Jersey, can be
found. Where the sea washes over the wall, the plants found there are
more typical of saltmarshes. The large mauve blue patches of flowers
round Kempt Tower itself are of the Alderney sea lavender, which
blooms from June through to August. In fact, there are few times in the
year when a plant cannot be seen in flower somewhere in Les Mielles.

Keen ornithologists can get a bird guide from the interpretation
centre with a check list to tick off any sighting of the many wild birds that
feed and breed in Les Mielles. Many of the birds seen on the dunes,
scrub and open grassland are likely to be permanent residents in
Jersey, but any large concentrations of water birds are more likely to be

Mont du Vallette at L'Etacq

wintering visitors. So that lover of gorse, the stonechat, and Jersey's only resident falcon — actually breeding in St Ouen's Bay — the kestrel, belong here, while the common snipe, which prefers open marshy fields, and the grey heron are only overwintering here. Birds wading along the edge of the sea include the oystercatcher, the dunlin and turnstone, while two regular inland visitors are the wheatear and the yellow wagtail. Bird lovers may like to know that in La Mielle de Moro, beside one of the reed-enclosed ponds, is the RSPB/YOC bird hide, with room for ten, which can be used by members of the public.

The only large, natural, open stretch of water in Jersey is also in St Ouen and a part of the conservation area of Les Mielles. This is La Mare au Seigneur or **St Ouen's Pond** (*Bus 12a*)— now owned by the National Trust — which is surrounded by extensive reed beds, with sharp rush and great fen sedge on their outer edge, and is therefore an important site for both migrating and overwintering birds.

The Cetti's warbler, with its excited bursts of song, skulks here and during the winter flocks of brent-geese can be seen on the pond itself or in the fields to the east of it. This is the natural habitat too of the breeding coot, moorhen and tufted duck as well as a breeding site for the delicate-looking dragon fly which can be seen anywhere in the summer within Les Mielles.

Also in these wet fields, towards the end of May, grow the unique-to-Jersey, loose flowered orchids with their tall spikes of rich purple, widely spaced blossoms, together with several other varieties. These

St Ouen's Bay

orchid meadows are open to the public in June and are well signposted to advertise the fact. From the Interpretation Centre a further checklist can be taken to help identify butterflies such as the large, small and green veined whites that can be seen throughout the summer and the painted ladies settling on thistles in the area.

On **St Ouen's Beach** (*Bus 12a*), sand races are held on one or two Saturdays a month throughout the season, and there are $\frac{1}{4}$-mile standing sprints held on the Five Mile Road just behind the beach. For further details of these events see the local press.

In the water of this, the largest bay in the Channel Islands, one can enjoy swimming, surfing, windsurfing, wave skiing or catamaran sailing. As the Atlantic ebbs and flows into St Ouen's Bay, swimmers should always obey the instructions of the lifeguards on duty and only swim between the flags. They should also take great care in heavy surf and avoid bathing when the tide reaches the slipways and wall. Non-swimmers should never venture into the surf alone.

Surfing has become one of the island's most popular water sports and in St Ouen's Bay some of the best waves in Europe can be found. 'belly boards' can be hired from several different outlets along the bay, or a full-size board, plus tuition on how to use it, if required. Although most of the windsurfing is done in the bays of St Aubin, St Brelade and Grouville, some intrepid sailors enjoy the great challenge offered by St Ouen, but use should not be made of an offshore wind. Boards can be hired for those who are competent in surf.

There are plenty of free parking areas along the length of St Ouen's Bay, as well as refreshment and toilet facilities, so this is an ideal beach for families to spend a whole day on.

Inland St Ouen

St Ouen has the distinction of having four manor houses. La Brecquette was built in L'Etacq Valley close to the shore and had large forests of oak trees on the east and to the north of it. Then, in 1356, La Brecquette and the forest that surrounded it were, as an early chronicler put it, 'overwhelmed and swallowed up by a terrible hurricane', when 'the sea engulfed a large area of fertile land'. Over 600 years later, when there is an exceptionally low tide, the stumps of the once proud oak forests are still visible but of the manor there is no sign.

There is a saying in the parish — 'Who says St Ouen says de Carteret'. This is because the de Carteret family have provided a continuous line of Seigneurs of **St Ouen's Manor** (*Bus 9*) for the last 800 years and up to the present day. The Seigneur of St Ouen is the most senior of the island's Seigneurs and his manor is arguably the most historic in the island.

In the twelfth century the manor house probably resembled more of a castle than a home and from that building only the oldest parts of the two towers remain. The central part of the manor, with its finely proportioned door dates from the sixteenth century, while in the seventeenth century the two wings and a huge kitchen were added.

When Colonel Malet de Carteret inherited the manor in 1856 it had, however, become a ruin and the building visitors see today owes much to his ambitious plans of restoration. He topped the two medieval towers and built a porch on to the main entrance. Inside the manor, with the help of local craftsmen, he created a grand hall, with a staircase and gallery.

In the grounds, de Carteret restored St Anne's chapel, in which the Seigneur and his family would, throughout the Middle Ages, have heard mass daily, but which had been used as a hayloft since the eighteenth century. Mass is once again held in the restored chapel most Sundays. He also built the lodge and the *colombier* and repaired the imposing avenue to the manor.

During the Occupation of Jersey, 1940-5, the German troops had their quarters in the manor and turned St Anne's chapel into a butcher's shop for the troops, using the altar as a chopping board. They also burnt down the south wing by misusing a stove. This has now been rebuilt.

Some stories connected with the manor are heroic, others tragic. There is the legend of the large black horse — its picture still hangs in the manor — which, in the fifteenth century, saved its master's life. When French invaders crept up on Philippe de Carteret when he was fishing in La Mare au Seigneur, he leapt on his horse to make his getaway. But, before he could reach the safety of his manor, another troop of French soldiers came to the top of the hill to cut off his escape. So he had to change course towards Val de la Charrière. Here, 'he made his horse leap the sunken road at its deepest place where it is twenty-two feet wide, and, spurring towards Les Landes, so made his escape. But ere he could reach the manor, his horse fell dead beneath him.' The horse was buried in the manor grounds out of respect for his spectacular leap which had saved his master's life.

Thirty years later, a heroic deed was carried out by a woman, Margaret, wife of another Philippe de Carteret. When her husband was thrown unjustly into Gorey Castle prison by the Governor of Jersey and challenged to 'trial by battle', by one of his henchmen, Margaret decided that the only person who could see justice done was the King of England himself, Henry VII. So despite the Governor's ban on anyone leaving Jersey, and despite the fact that she had just given birth to her twenty-first child, Margaret begged a fisherman to take her as far as Guernsey and from there she took a boat to England.

Margaret eventually arrived at Henry VII's court at Sheen just 24 hours before the Governor of Jersey himself arrived, to tell the King of Philippe de Carteret's supposed treachery. The King was so impressed by her courage that he agreed that her husband could be tried by the English Privy Council instead of 'trial by battle' in Jersey. So Margaret rushed back to Jersey with the Royal Seal and arrived just in time to stop the rigged 'trial by battle'. When Philippe de Carteret was eventually tried by the Privy Council for treason, he was acquitted — so Margaret's brave journeys had undoubtedly saved her husband's life.

It is to a seventeenth-century member of the de Carteret family that Jersey owes its American connection. For his loyalty to the exiled Prince of Wales, later to become Charles II, Sir George Carteret was richly rewarded by being granted lands off the Virginian coast which he named New Jersey. However, when the territory was occupied by the Dutch, in 1664, Sir George was granted the land between the Hudson and Delaware rivers instead, which he again named after his birthplace, New Jersey. A connection between the US territory and the Channel Island still exists and one or two inhabitants from New Jersey, with typically island names like Cabot, Picot and Poingdestre, come to Jersey every year, or write to La Société Jersiaise to search out their ancestors who left these shores in the seventeenth century to settle in the New World.

A fourth tale connected with St Ouen's Manor belongs to our own time and had a tragic ending. In March 1941, when the Germans occupied both France and the Channel Islands, a young Frenchman of 20 called François Scornet organised a party of French lads to escape from France to join the Free French forces in England. They sailed from Brittany and got as far as Guernsey, which they mistakenly thought was the Isle of Wight and so immediately began to sing the *Marseillaise* in

Plémont beach

PLACES OF INTEREST IN THE PARISH OF ST OUEN

La Cotte à la Chèvre (Goat's Cave)
Near Grosnez. On coastal path from Grève-au-Lançon.
Flints and coarse stone tools found.

Grosnez Castle
Grosnez
Fourteenth-century ruins, standing 200ft above sea level.

Le Pinacle
Les Landes
200ft-high rock, Neolithic and Roman remains found at its foot.

Kempt Tower
Interpretation centre for island's mini-national park, Les Mielles. Originally a martello tower.

Les Mielles
Behind St Ouen's Bay
Jersey's mini-national park with wonderful flora and fauna and places of interest.

Les Monts Grantez
Le Chemin des Monts
Passage grave where human and animal bones have been found from Neolithic period.

St Ouen's Manor
La Grande Route de St Ouen
Twelfth-century towers, sixteenth-century central section. Open once a week and for charity fêtes.

Plémont Candlecraft
Portinfer
Decorative and carved candles.

Bouchet Agateware
Behind Parish Hall
Shop for unique agateware made on the premises.

L'Etacq Woodcrafts
Woodwork centre, carnival market and Jersey giant cabbage products.

Channel Islands Military Museum
Five Mile Road
Wartime equipment in restored German bunker

Micro World
Five Mile Road
Minute objects created by Manuel Ussa of Spain.

Parish Church
On the C117
Mentioned before 1066. Memorials to de Carteret family, silver plate.

Jersey Goldsmiths
L'Etacq
Craftspeople at work, showroom, gardens, licensed restaurant with barbecue. Disabled facilities.

Jersey Shire Horse Farm Centre
La Route de Trodez
Old farm implements and machinery, pets corner, gift shop, tea room. Country Life Museum.

Battle of Flowers Museum
La Robiline, Mont des Corvées
Past winning floats made from hare's-tail grass. Tearoom.

Beaches
Grève-au-Lançon or Plémont, St Ouen's Bay.

Activities

Walk over Les Landes — the island's largest heath

Cliff path walks — Grève de Lecq to Grosnez; Grosnez to L'Etacq

Birdwatching at St Ouen's Pond, Plémont Point, La Mielle de Morville.

Sand racing, swimming, surfing, windsurfing, wave skiing, catamaran sailing triumph. They were straightaway seized by the Germans and sent to Jersey for trial.

At his trial, François Scornet admitted full responsibility and so for 'favouring the actions of the enemy by wilfully supporting England in the war against the German Empire' he was sentenced to death. On 17 March he was made to stand in front of an oak tree in the grounds of St Ouen's Manor and was shot by a firing squad. Every 18 June his death is commemorated by the laying of a wreath on the spot, marked by a plaque, where he died shouting — 'Vive Dieu! Vive La France!' The manor grounds are only open to the public on Tuesday afternoons.

At Vinchelez are the last two of the parish's four manors — over the road from each other. Travelling west along La Route de Vinchelez, also known as Vinchelez Lane, the manor of **Vinchelez de Bas** is on the right and the manor of **Vinchelez de Haut** is on the left. That there are two manors for the one fief of Vinchelez, stems from the fact that in 1607 the fief was divided between two sons. But when it came to claiming possession of the huge whale that was washed up on St Ouen's beach at Le Pulec in 1726, the Seigneur of Vinchelez de Bas' claim won and so, to this day, parts of the jaw bones of the huge whale stand at the main road gateway and can be seen from the road. Neither of the two manors, though, is ever open to the public.

Continuing along Vinchelez Lane, said to be one of the island's most picturesque roads, one arrives at Plémont, the headland plateau that overlooks Plémont beach, or Grève-au-Lançon. **Plémont Point** (*Bus* *7b, 8*) by the way, is an excellent spot for birdwatching: the auk from May to the end of July; the nesting fulmar and shag on the cliffs; linnet, meadow pipit and stonechat in the gorse and bracken.

Just inland from Plémont Holiday Camp at Portinfer (*Bus 8*) on La Route de Plémont, is **Plémont Candlecraft** which has been attracting increasing numbers of visitors ever since it opened in 1980. This is a delightful cottage industry run by a local family where craftsmen and women can be seen producing decorative and carved candles in traditional ways. Watchers will be amazed to see a basic mould being dipped into the hot wax more than a hundred times before it takes shape and intrigued to follow the process of making a large eagle candle or a small onion one. The results of the makers' skill are all on colourful display — including their speciality of a moulded hand-coloured candle representing the Jersey toad or *crapaud*—and are for sale. Entry is free and next door is Plémont Stores, ideal for holiday shopping requirements. Limited parking is just over the road.

Travelling southward from Plémont along the B56, B54 and A12 down to the centre of the parish, one comes to the main shopping area round the Parish Hall and down the C117 to St Ouen's parish church. Opposite the Parish Hall is a supermarket and a post office. Two special tourist attractions are also here — a pottery and a craft centre.

✳ **Bouchet Pottery** is behind the Parish Hall and specialises in agateware, a type of marbled pottery. Bouchet Original Agateware has been researched and perfected over 20 years and its originality lies in the fact that the team making the pottery had a breakthrough in the mixing of agateware clay, thus producing — with white clay stained with metal oxides — a type of agateware never seen before. Some pieces contain up to eighty shades of colour.

As this process is a carefully guarded secret, visitors can not actually see the pottery being made, but there is an eye catching display at the Pottery of all the items made from this unique agateware, from jewellery to ornaments.

St Ouen's parish church (*Bus 8, 9*) is to the west of the A12, La Grande Route de St Ouen along the C117. When the first church was built in St Ouen is not known, but it is thought that there was a small thatched chantry chapel on the site of the present chancel. St Ouen's church was mentioned in a charter signed by William the Conqueror before he invaded England, so it must have been in existence before 1066.

This same Norman duke had as his most binding oath, 'By St Ouen I swear it', so it is not surprising to learn that the saint to whom the church was dedicated, and whose emblem of a gold cross on a blue ground is the parish crest, was Dadon, the Bishop of Rouen, the capital of William's Normandy. A tiny splinter of the saint's bone is supposed to be built into the main altar.

From the twelfth century onwards, many enlargements of the church were carried out to accommodate the increasing population, so, for example, a chapel was added in both the thirteenth and fourteenth centuries. Later came the extended nave, the tower and the south and north aisles.

During the sixteenth century, the church was changed, as were all island churches, into a Huguenot temple, where all the pews were turned to face the central altar at which Holy Communion was celebrated by the whole parish only four times a year. Transformation to an Anglican church came in the nineteenth century, to which period belong most of the stained glass windows.

St Ouen's is one of the most picturesque of the island's parish churches, with its view across the sea from the churchyard. Of special interest to the visitor is the unusual stone staircase leading from the centre of the church to the belfry, the fine seventeenth-century silver plate, and the several memorials to the important de Carteret family — including their coat of arms in stained glass in the north aisle — whose large railed-in plot in the churchyard is to the right of the entrance gate. The daughter church of St George, built in 1880, is near Portinfer, to the north of the parish.

At the L'Etacq end of the Five Mile Road is the first of the craft

A Battle of Flowers float

centres which this north-west corner of the island has seemed to inspire. This is **Jersey Goldsmiths** (*Bus 12a*), where the visitor can not only watch craftsmen fashioning the gold but also browse at leisure round the largest selection of gold items on display in the whole of the Channel Islands.

There is an air of opulence as soon as the visitor walks into the open-plan display centre. At one end is 'Bergerac's' shining red car, for followers of the TV *Bergerac* series to admire, and there is also another car on show which every visitor to the Gold Centre has the chance of winning, simply by entering a free draw which is held once a year.

There is the opportunity to buy anything here, at one of the many showcases, from a simple gold chain, cut to any length required, to a gold Swiss watch. There are also complete sets of matching jewellery on view and commissions to make any special item are willingly undertaken. As well as the making of up-to-the-minute fashion jewellery, alterations can be done on the premises. And there is the fascination of watching the craftsmen at their intricate task.

And what an ideal setting the Gold Centre is for spending a couple of leisurely hours, for the colour of the beautifully laid out gardens is continued through the showroom into the well appointed licensed restaurant, where anything from a cream tea to a full meal — even a barbeque, weather permitting — can be sampled. These can be enjoyed either indoors, or under a covered patio area round a refreshing fountain.

Almost opposite the Gold Centre is a new attraction that has to be seen to be believed — **Micro-World**. Here you can discover, with the aid of a microscope, such wonders as Tower Bridge in the eye of a needle, or a pyramid on a grain of sand — all created by Manuel Ussa of Spain.

Still in the crafty corner of L'Etacq, one comes to a long established woodworking centre **L'Etacq Woodcrafts** (*Bus 12a*), which now incorporates many new and exciting tourist attractions. Here you can see being made, and buy, anything in wood, from a thimble to a walking stick and experience much more besides.

At the entrance to the woodcrafts centre, there is a café and also an explanation of what there is to see in the complex itself upstairs. Visitors are given their own personal Touchwood, selected from whichever of the fourteen trees of the Celtic calendar matches their birth date. First, there is the Lost Forest of Brecquette to explore, which is simulated with the aid of holograms and the sounds of thunder and water falling to bring back the magic of those long gone days. There is also a fascinating history of L'Etacq which appears as a vision between the trees. Visitors are then free to browse at their leisure round the showcases in the gallery, which not only display a selection of the items made at L'Etacq but also a visual account of the craft of working with wood as it is carried out at the centre.

In the workshop the craftsmen themselves can be seen at their centuries' old skills of carving, turning and cabinet making; perhaps carving out the letters for a marriage lintel or a house name; or fashioning, from the strange elongated stem of the 15ft tall Jersey giant cabbage, a shiny knobbly walking stick and from its roots a ghostly figure: or making other items such as paper weights and games from differently textured and marked woods, all obtained from sustainable sources and, as far as possible, locally. Anyone wanting to try their hand at growing the Jersey giant cabbage — *Brassica oleracae longata* (*Acephela* group) — in their garden back home can buy a packet of seeds here to sow between mid-August and mid-September. Best results come from sowing at full moon!

As well as the skilled craft of the wood carvers, there is also a carnival market in the complex, full of handmade gifts such as sweets, toys, and woollen goods, ideal to take back as presents. Finally, there is another craftsman to be watched — the potter. There are also additional attractions which change from year to year.

Next door to L'Etacq Woodcrafts is Leatherland where, though nothing is exactly made on the premises, there is a wide range of fancy leather goods on show.

For a rural treat in St Ouen's, the visitor could not do better than go along La Route de Trodez to the **Jersey Shire Horse Farm Centre** (*Bus 8*) at Champ Donné, where there is so much more than the gentle giant horses. Horse lovers will enjoy a 20-minute ride round the country lanes in a carriage drawn by one of the shire horses, or even an hour's hack on one of them; and a browse, when they come back, round the coach house with its faithfully restored carriages, such as its 1880 Brougham and a ten-seater wagonette for a pair of horses to draw. In the **Country Life Museum** there are horse brasses and tack down- stairs and antique farm tools upstairs. Every Wednesday morning there is the unique chance to see a genuine blacksmith at work, whose tasks include shoeing the horses. Twice daily visitors are introduced to the shire horses individually.

For animal lovers in general, there is an aviary and a dovecote, while enjoying free range round the refreshment area are peacocks, their broods and tiny fluffy chicks. In the fields at the back are different types of sheep and goats.

To complete this great day out for the whole family, there is a pet's corner, a children's play area, a gift shop where books and souvenirs can be bought, a tea room, where refreshments can be enjoyed outside, and toilet facilities. An added bonus is free parking in a large car park, though there is an admission charge.

Another must for visitors to St Ouen is the **Battle of Flowers** **Museum** (*Bus 9a to Five Roads*), off the road that leads from the Parish Hall down to St Ouen's Bay. Here is every Battle float, all prize winners, entered by Miss Florence Bechelet since 1953. Though only made of dyed hare's-tail and marram grass, these floats can depict any scene from the fun of *101 Dalmatians* and the stolid strength of buffaloes on the plain, to the delicate detail of a dovecote, complete with birdseed. The graceful flamingoes on the float entitled 'A Bevy of Beauties' are of particular interest, as they were made by Miss Bechelet specially for the Queen's visit to Jersey in June 1978 and then entered for that year's Battle of Flowers in August.

The Lakeside Tearoom is just beside the Battle of Flowers Museum and part of it. This is open for light refreshments, views of the lake, in or out of doors from May till September. A larger car park serves both the museum and the tearoom.

Finally, for an accurate insight into the events of the German Occupation, visit the restored German bunker on the Five Mile Road. Here the **Channel Islands Military Museum** has a fine collection of wartime optical equipment as well as an Enigma decoding machine.

12 ST PETER

(*Bus 8, 9, 12a, 14, 15*)

S t Peter may only have a couple of short coastlines — in the bays of St Aubin in the south and St Ouen in the west, but what a host of other attractions this parish has to offer inland. There is the natural beauty of St Peter's Valley and its various tourist spots. Then there is the heart of the parish, with several different places to visit, centred round the church. Perhaps, even more importantly for the island's visitors, it is the parish where Jersey's airport is sited.

St Peter's Valley

St Peter's Valley (*Bus 8, 8a*) is one of the five picturesque valleys that cut across the island from north to south and for many centuries it was considered the most beautiful of them all. In fact, when Queen Victoria asked to see the loveliest view in Jersey on her visit here in 1857, she was taken for a drive through St Peter's Valley.

It still has its rural charm, especially in the early months of the year: its hillsides dotted with lent-lilies and other wild flowers; the tall iris marking the course of the stream, with its splash of yellow; the distinctive catkins of the sweet chestnut yellow in the woodland; the red squirrels sometimes glimpsed round the fine oaks searching for hidden acorns. Regrettably, though, the German Occupation has left more than one ugly mark on the valley. For here, in the centre of the island, the occupying forces built not only their Underground Hospital in St Lawrence but also a power station, a pumping station and three huge ammunition tunnels. Some of the thousands of tons of rocks and rubble removed in these excavations were used, 7 years after Jersey had been liberated, in the construction of the runway at the airport. What was left in the valley is now almost completely grown over with natural vegetation and is no longer the eyesore that once it was.

At the top of the valley are the aptly named **Fantastic Tropical Gardens**, a full day out for the whole family. Just in front of the entrance there is a car park where courteous attendants help drivers make the most of the space available and a notice welcomes visitors and outlines the delights that await them. These include a 'passport' on admission

226

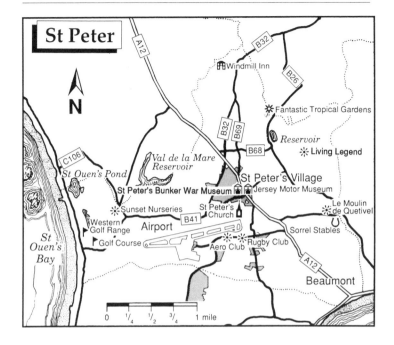

which is stamped at the borders of the various 'countries' into which the extensive gardens have been divided. In them is a licensed restaurant by the lake, a patio café for light refreshments and special amusements.

These entertainments include such delights as a troup of Thai dancers, a birds of prey show, Country and Western music, a Lillie Langtry spot, as well as donkey and hay rides, scavenger hunts, minigolf and swing boats. There is a wishing well which echoes what is said to it; prehistoric monsters standing about on the forested hillsides; a shrine to a breathing Buddha; a 'choose your own' sweet shop, with such almost forgotten delights as gobstoppers and aniseed balls; a serenade as you sip your morning coffee, lunch, afternoon tea; unusual souvenirs to buy, such as clam purses, kites and paper dragons.

For the children, 'Africa' has drums for them to play and a gently swaying Uhuru bridge to cross. In the 'Mexican' section not only is there a talkative minah bird but a tree house, swings and a slide.

Yet there is also something for the admirer of special water effects and seekers of exotic plants. There is the row of fountains, a sheet of water; there is the tree whose buds are the source of friar's balsam; the wound-healing rose of Sharon; the Japanese iris which originated the phrase 'blue blood'. For those who just want to wander round colourful flowerbeds and through winding woodland paths, this is just the place and no-one minds how long you stay. Umbrellas are even provided should your visit coincide with an unexpected shower!

 Travelling south down St Peter's Valley, on the right are signposts to the **Living Legend** in Rue de Petit Alva — another place for all the family to enjoy. This £8 million all-weather attraction (Bus 8a) is an innovative mixture of education and entertainment set in a typically beautiful island landscape. Through Jersey-style granite archways, past well laid out gardens and across a sunken courtyard is the entrance to the audio-visual experience which gives the purpose-built complex its name.

Once inside, with the help of the latest lighting and sound effects, the adventure through Jersey's past begins. Here are figures from the island's folklore — St Lawrence's Dragon, the ghost of Waterworks Valley; the history of the island's seamen and farmers; the sounds and fury of the Battle of Jersey in 1781; the story of Lillie Langtry; the Royal Square filled with German troops during the 1940-5 Occupation, and much more.

This fascinating journey back through 2,000 years is complemented by the gift centre, where books by local authors and island-made gifts can be bought. In the spacious restaurant area, or outside on the cloistered terrace, traditional home-baked fare is on offer. All around the complex local performers entertain visitors with their own brands of street theatre, while there is a special play area for children, as well as facilities for the disabled.

Nearly at the southernmost tip of St Peter's Valley, on the B58, Le Mont Fallu, is the third attraction, open three days a week. This is **Le Moulin de Quetivel**, a National Trust property, which was mentioned as one of the island's forty-seven watermills as early as 1309. It was also one of the eight mills which, at one time or another, were served by St Peter's Valley stream which still powers it.

The mill was worked from the fourteenth century right down to the nineteenth century but then fell into disrepair. By 1934 only the iron rims of the watermill remained in the way of machinery and the building itself was badly in need of repair. But, during the German Occupation, Le Moulin de Quetivel had a reprieve — the Germans ordered local craftsmen to repair it so that once again it could grind grain.

After the end of the war, the mill was of no further use until, in 1979, it was decided that it should be restored and become fully operational again. It would grind locally grown corn that would then be sold as stoneground flour. Today visitors can see Le Moulin de Quetivel once more in action and buy what it produces. There is also a display on the top floor showing the milling process through the ages and charting the history of the mills in Jersey. The shop on the ground floor sells the flour, together with locally made preserves and craft items such as prints and

Le Moulin de Quetivel

cards. A helpful leaflet which is given out on admission explains what happens on each floor. The steps up to the different floors of the mill are steep, though, and would not be suitable for anyone who is disabled.

The pastoral setting of Le Moulin de Quetivel, however, should not be missed, with its yellow irises in spring and many wild flowers colouring the meadows in the summer. The mill can also be reached by a rustic path. This starts by the car park almost directly opposite the Victoria Inn and goes through the woods until it comes to the second of the mill's car parks, opposite Sorrel Stables and Saddlery. This is a short peaceful walk, past the mill pond with its ducks and other water fowl, through the trees, several with nesting boxes on them and where sometimes a red squirrel can be glimpsed, and down some steps to the mill itself. This walk now extends down to Tesson Mill.

There is also an authentically restored windmill in the parish which is well worth visiting, which has been turned into The Windmill Inn. It was built in 1837 and many of the original features have been put to an unusual use: the hayloft is now a special area set aside for children above the main lounge, while the former mill wheel — 15ft in diameter — is the bar counter. Not only do its graceful sails dominate the skyline during the day but they make a specially fine sight when floodlit at night. The Windmill Inn is off the B53 on Les Chenolles, going west after St Mary's parish church.

For horse riders there are stables in St Peter's Valley. **Sorrel Stables and Saddlery Centre**, (*Bus 8a*) at the bottom of Le Mont Fallu as it comes into St Peter's Valley, have their own two large outdoor sand schools. In one sanded field ½-hour lunge lessons (a long rope is attached to the horse) can be given by experienced staff to young children and beginners; in another there are jumping and cross-country facilities. Riding gear, such as hat and wellies, can be hired at no extra charge. Also available at Sorrel Stables is a complete range of equestrian equipment for sale, as well as gifts with horse lovers in mind. What better way to discover the rural beauties of this western parish than from the saddle!

St Peter's Village

The second centre to visit in St Peter's parish is the village (*Bus 9*), which clusters round the church. Here there is the Parish Hall, with its typical Jersey architecture, the Youth and Community Centre, a large park, a supermarket, a food hall and a post office. Also within a short distance from the church are two popular places for holidaymakers to visit, with a hotel backing on to both where light refreshments and toilet facilities are available.

The chapel from which **St Peter's church** originated is now the chancel which, in common with others on the island, is older than the rest of the church. The chancel walls, which are nearly 4ft thick and built of stones from the beach, probably date back to before 1066. The major enlargements came in the twelfth century — when the building took the shape of a cross with the additional nave and transepts — in the fourteenth and fifteenth centuries and, finally, in the last century, when the north aisle was added.

Its spire of 120ft is the tallest in Jersey and has been struck by lightning three times since it was added to the church tower in the fifteenth century. Today, unique among church steeples, it carries at its tip a warning red light for planes using the nearby airport.

Notable features inside the church are a triptych featuring the Virgin Mary, the altar in the arched niche of the Lady Chapel and a finely carved altarpiece depicting the Last Supper.

For visitors who are staying in one of the hotels or guest houses near St Peter it is good to know that the Youth and Community Centre welcomes holidaymakers. Outdoors there is a tennis court; indoors there is badminton court available and bingo once a month, as well as a Friendly Club which meets every Wednesday afternoon. There are also several barn dances during the year.

Opposite the Community Centre behind St Peter's parish hall is the **Western Miniature Rifle Club**, open from September to March only. Markets are held every Wednesday all year round.

Then come two popular venues sharing the same car park. First there is the **Jersey Motor Museum** (*Bus 9*), with its carefully restored and highly polished veteran and vintage cars, includes many other items to intrigue lovers of cars and machines of all kinds. There is a Jersey railway carriage, dating back to 1878 which houses a steam railway exhibition, as well as a display of several different types of motor cycle. This includes a 1933 Sunbeam combination, which was artfully kept hidden from the Germans throughout the Occupation.

Among the shining car classics of a bygone age are an Austin Chummy and a Model 'T' Ford, both from 1926, a 1929 Peugeot, a 1930 Bentley, and a 1936 MG Midget. From the war years there are several British vehicles which saw active service on D-Day, including an armoured scout car; on the German side a 1942 VW Kubelwagen, a German version of the Jeep, bearing the insignia of the 319th Division, part of the Occupation force which took over Jersey. Two specially prized possessions are Sir Winston Churchill's Hillman Husky, and the 1936 Rolls Royce Phantom III that was used by General Montgomery whilst he was planning D-Day operations in 1944.

Children will love the bright red fire engine which worked for the St Helier Fire Brigade from 1935 to 1964. They will also be drawn by a whole cabinet full of tiny model cars, as well as several cars on show specially scaled down in size for children: including the 1926 Bugatti Type 35 and the 1952 Austin J 40.

From the motor souvenirs in the shop in the foyer, to the once familiar advertisements for Firestone Tyres and Pratts Perfection Motor Spirit; from mascots, including the elegant 'flying lady', to the complete old style AA box, every inch of this motor museum will appeal to the car enthusiast.

Sharing the same ample car park with the Jersey Motor Museum is **St Peter's Bunker War Museum**. This underground bunker was built in 1942 by Russian and other slave labour used by the Germans in their huge building programme to turn the island into an impregnable fortress. The specific purpose of this bunker was to guard the important crossroads leading to the island's west coast and the airport.

Thirty-three men lived and slept in this strong point — which could be air- and gas-sealed in case of attack — throughout the Occupation. They manned a heavy machine gun to cover the main road at ground level — the stand is still in position, as well as an anti-aircraft gun on the roof of the adjoining hotel. A complicated telephone communication system was installed to ensure contact with the other fortifications on the rest of the island.

The bunker now contains an exhibition of German equipment and Occupation relics and visitors can immediately sense the way in which islanders were restricted in their daily lives during the Occupation, by reading the first notice on display 'No admission without permit from the Standortkommandantur'. As visitors go round the seven underground rooms, they can hear an outline of the main events of the Occupation, together with some of the songs the Germans used to sing as they marched through the streets of Jersey.

As well as original proclamations and death warning notices lining the walls, there are models wearing the full uniforms of Army and Air Force personnel, as well as displays of German uniform, badges and medals. Weapons are also exhibited, from the officers' ceremonial swords to a twin-barrelled anti-aircraft gun.

To remind visitors of how Jersey was changed in 1940 from a holiday resort there are two telling photographs. Both are of St Ouen's beach opposite La Rocco Tower: the first in peacetime, with the dunes as they are now, and the second, when there was a gun emplacement guarding that part of the bay against a possible Allied attack.

More horrific reminders of the Occupation are a striped cotton suit such as were worn in concentration camps, and letters from informers. These letters were sent by a small number of Jersey residents who informed on their neighbours. The authentic letters from informers that can be seen in St Peter's Bunker Museum are those that fortunately never reached the German Kommandant, thanks to the bravery of the Jersey postal workers who intercepted them at great risk to themselves.

Some of those Jerseymen and women who were informed against by their fellow islanders were fined, others were put into the prison in Newgate Street, St Helier. A few, though, were sent away to concentration camps in Germany. In fact, the only British survivor of Belsen was a Jerseyman — sent there on a neighbour's information that he and his sister were sheltering a Russian who had escaped from a German slave camp.

In this bunker, is the largest collection of military and civilian memorabilia of the German Occupation in the Channel Islands, for not only are there the material accoutrements of the German forces, but also examples of how the islanders themselves had to manage without adequate resources: saucepans and jugs made from biscuit tins; a comb made of wood; the contents of the Red Cross parcels islanders depended on in the last months of the war, after the Allies had reconquered France.

For those who would like refreshments before or after, or even between visiting Jersey Motor Museum and St Peter's Bunker, there is a hotel backing on to the same car park.

Around the Parish

This parish, which has St Peter's keys of heaven for its emblem, does not only have relics of World War II, there is a cannon at Beaumont crossroads, on the way up to the airport from the south coast, which is

PLACES OF INTEREST IN THE PARISH OF ST PETER

Fantastic Tropical Gardens
St Peter's Valley
Exotic plants, birds, dancers,
restaurants, café, shops, children's
section.

Living Legend
Rue de Petit Alva
St Peter's Valley
Special audio-visual effects
recreating island's past.
Restaurant, shop, play area.

Le Moulin de Quetivel
B58
The island's only working watermill, shop.Worked from the
fourteenth century. Open Tues-
day-Thursday only.

Windmill Inn
Off B53 on Les Chenolles
Nineteenth-century windmill,
restored, now an inn.

**Sorrel Stables and Saddlery
   Centre**
Le Mont Fallu
St Peter's Valley
Lunge lessons for beginners as
well as equipment hire. Riding
equipment and gifts for sale.

Jersey Motor Museum
St Peter's Village
Veteran and vintage cars, railway
carriages, steam railway exhibition, fire engine, shop. Cars
belonging to Churchill and
Montgomery.

St Peter's Bunker War Museum
St Peter's Village
Military and civilian memorabilia
from German Occupation.

St Peter's Parish Church
St Peter's Village
Eleventh-century chancel, tallest
spire in Jersey.

Sunset Nurseries
Top of lane from Western Golf
Range, St Ouen's Bay
Exotic plants and flowers, trout
pool, aviary, shop and café.

Val de la Mare Reservoir
Off La Grande Route de St Pierre
Arboretum.

Western Golf Range
Centre of St Ouen's Bay
Par 3, 12-hole golf course and 18-
hole putting green, driving range,
crazy golf.

Beaches
St Aubin's Bay, St Ouen's Bay.

Activities
Walk through St Peter's Valley

Walk round Val de la Mare
   Reservoir

Windsurfing, surfing, sailing,
   riding, golf

Shooting, flying, tennis, badminton,
   bingo

over 400 years old. It was originally built in Houndsditch and is only one of two of the same kind still in existence. On it are the words: 'JHON [sic] OWEN MADE THIS PESE ANNO DNI 1551 FOR THE PARYSHE OF SAYNT PETER IN JERSSE.'

St Peter also has the unhappy distinction of being the parish where, during the English Civil War, Cromwell's forces successfully invaded the island and kept it under Parliamentarian rule for 9 years. It happened in 1651, on 22 October, when Cromwell's Admiral Blake, with a fleet of eighty ships, sailed up and down — some say waiting for the heavy surf to subside — the whole length of St Ouen's Bay for 2 whole days. Ready to repulse any landing, the Royalist Jersey Army marched up and down the coast between L'Etacq and St Brelade to keep a wary eye for an enemy attack. So by the time the Parliamentarian forces eventually landed on the beach in the middle of the night, de Carteret and his Jersey soldiers were quite worn out. Though the island's defenders put up a desperate fight, they finally had to retreat to Elizabeth Castle. By December that year, St Aubin's Fort, Mont Orgueil Castle and Elizabeth Castle were all forced to surrender and the commander of the English invasion forces, the Roundhead Colonel Heane, was made Governor of Jersey.

Sunset Nurseries (*Bus 12a*) is a mile inland from St Ouen's Bay at the top of the lane from the Western Golf Range. On sale in this flower centre are not only Jersey lily bulbs, seeds and dried flowers, but also an extensive range of quality gifts including leatherware, soft toys and costume jewellery. From here it is also possible to send carnations or freesias by post to any address in the UK or Europe, or even have a box made up to carry home.

Visitors can enter the glasshouses where carnations and Peruvian lilies grow; try to find their way through a passion flower maze; look into the rainbow trout pool and aviary; have home-made food in the flower-festooned covered tea garden and enjoy the miniature tropical garden where the summer air is perfumed by Stephanotis and there is the constant sound of running water.

As a charming bonus, each visitor is treated to a complimentary button hole.

The main operation of the nurseries is the production of cut flowers and the most important crop are the carnations. Rooted cuttings are planted in peat troughs and picking begins after 4 or 5 months. An automatic irrigation system gives the plants all the water and fertiliser they need for their 2-year life span. The correct temperature is kept constant by automatic heating and ventilation.

Jersey's second largest reservoir, partly in St Peter and partly in St Ouen, is just the place for nature lovers and walkers alike. In 1962, above the site of an old watermill, the island's waterworks company built a dam, above which is the reservoir known as **Val de la Mare** (*Bus 9*).

It is past St Peter's church on the left, going north along La Grande Route de St Pierre and is clearly signposted.

For tree lovers there is an arboretum that stretches down both sides of the path that leads from the car park to the reservoir. This was opened in 1977 and features trees from various parts of the world set out in their separate sections.

Once the reservoir itself, the largest on the island, comes into view, it is possible to take a short walk, by climbing a path to the right, looking across the water and to St Ouen's Bay from the north. This gives a magnificent view of fresh water and woods right to the surf breaking in the distance. For a longer walk, of about an hour, continue along the footpath until it reaches La Rue de Coin, turn left along Les Ruelles and then to the right up La Ruelle du Coin. From here it is possible to reach the main road, La Grande Route de St Ouen. The entrance to Val de la Mare and its car park are just a little down the main road to the right.

Another long walk is to follow the reservoir right the way down to the wall of the dam. Here the path goes down some steps, under the dam wall and up steps the other side, past the site of the old watermill, Le Moulin de la Mare. Continue to follow the path on the north side of the reservoir, cross the bridge and rejoin the path which leads back through the aboretum and to the car park. These are particularly sheltered walks if the wind is in the north-east.

There is one activity in St Peter which takes full advantage of the terrain of sand dunes on the western coast — golf. The **Les Mielles Golf Course** (*Bus 12a*) is to be found in the centre of St Ouen's Bay, where the Five Mile Road makes the corner with La Route de la Marette. Here there is a par 3 12-hole golf course, and 18-hole putting green. For those who want to perfect their swing, there is a driving range; for those who just want a bit of fun, there is crazy golf. All this sport with the continued sound of the Atlantic breakers in your ears!

There are refreshments such as hot snacks and ice-cream, together with toilet facilities on the same site and an ample car park.

The spectator sport to watch in this parish however, is rugby. All important games are played at the **Jersey Rugby Club** (*Bus 9*), on the left of the B36 on the way up to the airport from St Helier. Details of forthcoming matches can be obtained by dialling 1882 for the Daily Diary, or 1886 for special events; by looking at the sports pages of the *Jersey Evening Post* or by listening in to Jersey Today on the Radio 2 wavelength between 8 and 9am each weekday morning. At Easter the Hockey Festival, also involving teams from away, is played here too.

For the majority of visitors, St Peter is the first parish they set foot in because it was here, in 1937, that the States built the island's **airport** (*Bus 15 every 15 minutes*). But Jersey's aviation history does, incredibly, go right back to 1790 when a hot air balloon was launched from the hospital grounds and flew over the island. Islanders had to wait over 120 years, though, before they saw a real aircraft in Jersey. That happened in 1912 when one of the competitors in the St Malo-Jersey-St Malo Race landed his Sanchez-Beza biplane mid-route in St Aubin's Bay before — appreciably delayed by inquisitive islanders who had never seen a plane before — continuing on his way. Seven years later, today's routine of flying the UK newspapers daily into the island had a forerunner, when *Lloyds Weekly News* was flown in during a rail strike in England.

It was the 1920s and 1930s which saw the start and great acceleration of passenger air traffic to the island. The landing strip was the beach in St Aubin's Bay; the aircraft were seaplanes, de Havillands, Dragons and Rapides and the destinations Portsmouth, Southampton and London; the price of a return ticket from St Helier to Victoria Station — a 3-hour journey — was £5, quite a sum between the wars. In 1936 alone, 30,000 passengers were flown in and out of the island.

Plans for an inland airport — the disadvantage of landing on the beach was that it could only be done at low tide — had begun as early as 1930 but it was not until 1937 that the 218 vergee site earmarked by the States in St Peter had been transformed into an airport, with four grassed flightways, at a cost of £128,000.

Only 3 years after the Bailiff's wife had opened the airport, Britain and Germany were at war. Then passenger services were severely restricted and for a time the airport was used by a squadron of the Fleet Air Arm for training purposes. Later on, it was used by the RAF for a nightstop and refuelling base on bombing raids in Germany and Italy.

Once Churchill had declared, after the fall of France in June 1940, that the Channel Islands were demilitarised and would not be defended by British troops in the event of a German invasion, the airport had yet another new role to play. It mobilised its ten- and twelve-seater aircraft to evacuate, in just 2 days, over 300 islanders who wanted to spend the rest of the war in the UK.

Then came the final blow for Jersey. At 11 o'clock on 1 July, a German plane approached the airport. When it landed, a German Air Force Officer told the airport officials — in perfect English — that he wanted to speak to the Bailiff, to make sure that he had received the Nazi ultimatum, demanding the surrender of Jersey to the Occupation force which would be arriving that same afternoon. So it was that the Bailiff, in the company of the Attorney General, met the first Germans on British soil at the airport.

Today, Jersey's airport, in terms of aircraft movements, is one of the busiest in the British Isles. More than a million passengers pass through the terminal every year on their way to or from the UK and Europe. Instead of the fifteen staff employed in 1936, the States now have between 240 and 275 staff to man the airport, with the air companies employing a about 500 extra at the height of the season. No wonder the airport has an annual turnover of about £20 million, but it still remains one of the cheapest airports in the British Isles to fly into. All its many operations can be watched from the promenade decks on the roofs, free of charge, and there is also a fully licensed restaurant. Jersey's own meteorological station, whose regular weather forecasts can be heard on Radio Jersey, is also part of the airport complex.

Any visitors interested in taking to the air themselves, can apply for flying lessons to the Aero Club, just east of the airport, on the B36. Those who are interested in plants, which can be taken back to the UK, will find a large garden centre on the same side of the B36 as the Aero Club, just a little further along the road going towards St Helier.

To complete this survey of St Peter where it began, with its coastline, there is good safe swimming on its sandy southern beach in **St Aubin's Bay** (*Bus 12, 12a, 14, 15*) between Beaumont and the Gunsite slipway.

St Peter's western coast is part of the magnificent sandy sweep of **St Ouen's Bay** (*Bus 12a*), shared by three parishes, where the Atlantic rollers break and where the surfers have their fun. There is a surfing school and hire facilities as well as windsurfing equipment at the Sands Surf and Sail Centre.

SELECTED BIBLIOGRAPHY
Balleine's History of Jersey, Syvret & Stevens
The Bailiwick of Jersey, Balleine (Revised J. Stevens)
The Biographical Dictionary of Jersey, Balleine
The Birdwatcher's Jersey, M. Stentiford
Flora of Jersey, F. Le Sueur
German Occupation of Jersey 1940/45 Maps, Howard Butlin Baker
Jersey Witches, Ghosts & Traditions, S. Hillsdon
Jersey Occupation Remembered, S. Hillsdon
Old Jersey Houses Vols I & II, J. Stevens
Victorian Jersey, M. Binney and C. Loth

FURTHER INFORMATION

BUILDINGS OF INTEREST

Corbière Lighthouse
Corbière, St Brelade
Built 1873, first concrete lighthouse
in the British Isles. Public free to
wander outside only.

Elizabeth Castle
L'Islet, St Aubin's Bay, St Helier
☎ 23971
Open: daily mid-March to end
October 9.30am-5.30pm.
Admission charge.

Grève de Lecq Barracks
Grève de Lecq, St Mary
Information centre in Block 1.

Grosnez Castle
Near Grosnez Point, St Ouen
Ruins, date from fourteenth century.
Public free to wander.

Hamptonne
Country Life Museum
Near St Lawrence church
St Lawrence
☎ 863955
Open: daily 10am-5pm. Reduced
admission charge for senior citizens
and stuents; under 10 free.

Mont Orgueil Castle
Gorey, St Martin
☎ 53292
Open: daily mid-March-end October,
9.30am-5.30pm. Admission charge.
Includes museum of archaeology.

Morel Farm
Along Le Mont Perrine, St Lawrence

Portelet Tower or Janvrin's Tomb
Ile au Guerdain, Portelet Bay
Public free to wander.

Les Prés Manor
Grouville
Grounds open occasionally for charity.

Le Rât
Left off La Route de l'Eglise
St Lawrence

The Royal Court
Royal Square, St Helier
Public entrance to Public Gallery
when court sits Monday-Friday,
starts 10am. Not otherwise open

Rozel Manor
Off La Grande Route de Rozel,
St Martin
Open for special events only.

St Aubin's Fort
On island in St Aubin's Bay
Public free to wander only.

St John's Manor
Near La Hougue Boëte, south of St
John's Village
Open for charity functions only.

St Ouen's Manor
St Ouen
Manor grounds including St Anne's
Chapel are open every Tuesday
from 2-6pm and sometimes at
weekends for charity. Home of the
Seigneur of St Ouen.
Admission charge.

Samarès Manor
Inner Road, St Clement
☎ 70551

Open: daily beginning April to end of October 10am-5pm.
Shop stays open till Christmas.
Admission charge.

States Chambers
Royal Square, St Helier
Public entrance to Public Gallery when States sit on Tuesdays, starting at 10.15am. Not otherwise open.

Town Hall
York Street, St Helier
Not open to public, but anyone wishing to view pictures in Assembly Room, go to reception.
☎ 25251

Trinity Manor
Trinity
Open on charity occasions only and for special exhibitions.

Villa Millbrooke
La Rue de Haut
Millbrook, St Lawrence
Home of Sir Jesse Boot, famous chemist.
Open: occasionally for charity.

CHURCHES IN JERSEY

Each of Jersey's twelve parishes has its own parish church. Some parishes, particularly St Helier, have been sub-divided to provide more than one centre for Anglican worship. There are Roman Catholic and Methodist churches in most parishes, and St Helier provides a wide range of Free Church worship. Where the street name only has been listed, this refers to the town of St Helier.

Church of England
The twelve parish churches plus:-

All Saints, Parade
St Andrew's, First Tower, St Helier
St Aubin on the Hill, St Aubin
St George's, St Ouen
St Luke's, Route du Fort, St Saviour
St Mark's, David Place
St Matthew's Glass Church, Millbrook, St Lawrence
St Nicholas, Grève d'Azette, St Clement
St Paul's, New Street
St Peter La Rocque, La Rocque, Grouville
St Simon's, Great Union Road
Gouray, Gorey Hill, St Martin

Ecumenical (Anglican/Methodist)
Communicare, St Brelade

Free Churches
Advent Christian Fellowship, St Saviour; Baptist, Vauxhall Street; Belmont Hall, Belmont Road; Christadelphians, Grove Street; Christian Scientist, St Saviour's Road; Evangelical, Halkett Place; Elim, Stopford Road; Evangelical, Les Quennevais; Greater World Christian Spiritualist, Dorset Street; Jehovah Witnesses, Roseville Street; Jewish Synagogue, St Brelade; Latter Day Saints, St Mary's Hill; Mitspa Gospel Hall, Trinity; New Church (Swedenborgian), Victoria Street; Salvation Army, Minden Street; Church of Scotland, Midvale Road; The Society of Friends (Quakers), 71 Colomberie, St Helier; United Reformed, St John

Methodist
Wesley Grove, Halkett Place
Bethesda, St Peter
Ebenezer, Trinity
First Tower, St Helier
Georgetown, St Saviour
La Rocque, Grouville

St Martin, St Martin
Samarès, St Clement
Aquila, Aquila Road
Bethlehem, St Mary
Eden, St Saviour
Galaad, Millbrook, St Lawrence
Gorey, Gorey Village, Grouville
Philadelphie, St Peter
St Aubin, St Aubin
St Ouen, St Ouen
Sion, St John

Roman Catholic

St Mary's & St Peter's,
    Wellington Road
St Thomas, Val Plaisant (services in
    French and English)
St Patrick's, Samarès
St Martin's, St Martin
St Matthew's, St Peter
St Anne's, St Ouen
St Joseph's, Grouville
St John and St Anthony, Ville à
    l'Evêque, Trinity
Our Lady of Assumption, Gorey
    Village, Grouville
Our Lady of the Universe, Millbrook,
    St Lawrence
Sacred Heart, St Aubin
St Bernadette, St Brelade

CRAFTS

Bouchet Agateware
Behind Parish Hall, St Ouen
☎ 482345
Open: October-end April Monday-
Friday, 9am-5pm; May-end Septem-
ber 9am-5pm, 7 days a week. &

Forge
Route d'Ebenezer, Trinity
See wrought-iron work.
Open: weekdays from 8am-5pm
(4.30pm on Fridays).

Jersey Goldsmiths
Five Mile Road, St Ouen

☎ 482098
Open: Monday-Saturday March to
Christmas 10am-5.30pm. Free. &

Jersey Pearl
Route des Issues, St John
☎ 862137
Open: Monday-Saturday late
February-Christmas 10am-5pm. &

Jersey Pottery
Gorey Village, Grouville
☎ 851119
Open: Monday to Friday 9am-
5.30pm, all year. (Closed Bank
Holidays.) &

Lower Mill Pottery
Queen's Valley, Grouville
☎ 854052
See the work of Robert Boissière
and by local artists.

La Mare Vineyards
Near Devil's Hole, St Mary
☎ 481178
Open: early May to early October,
Monday to Friday 10am-5.30pm (last
admission 5pm). Admission charge.

Le Moulin de Quetivel
(National Trust)
St Peter's Valley, St Peter
☎ 483193 (mornings only)/45408
Open: mid-May to mid-October,
Tuesdays, Wednesdays, Thursdays,
10am-4pm. Admission charge for
non-members of Trust.

L'Etacq Woodcrafts
L'Etacq, St Ouen
☎ 482142
Open: Easter to end October,
Monday to Saturday 9am-5.30pm,
Sunday 10am-5pm; November to
Easter, Monday to Saturday 9am-
5pm, closed Sunday. Admission
charge.

Plémont Candlecraft
Route de Plémont, Portinfer, St Ouen
☎ 482146
Open: daily April to October 9.30am-
5.30pm; November, December,
March, Monday to Friday only. No
admission charge.

ENTERTAINMENTS AND SHOWS

Cabarets
As well as several night spots,
mostly in St Helier, several hotels
provide cabaret and dancing for the
general public. See the *Jersey
Evening Post* for details.

Cinemas
Ciné Centre
Lido de France
St Saviour's Road, St Saviour
☎ 71611

Odeon Film Centre
Bath Street, St Helier
☎ 30915

Approximate times of performance:
weekdays 2.30pm & 8.30pm,
Sunday 8pm only. Films are, from
time to time, also shown at the
Jersey Arts Centre, Phillips Street,
St Helier. ☎ 68080, the headquarters
of the Jersey Film Society.

Discothèques
These are mostly in St Helier but
discos are also held in St John, St
Ouen, St Saviour. Details from the
Jersey Evening Post.

Fort Regent Entertainment Centre
St Helier
☎ 500200 (or 500227 for credit card
bookings for concerts).
Gloucester Hall: Tickets for Piazza
evening shows are available from
the Booking Office, Main Reception,
Fort Regent.

Live Music & Dancing
Ballroom dancing:
Royal Hotel, David Place, St Helier
☎ 26521

Country Music:
Wolf's Caves, Frémont, St John
☎ 864602

La Moye Ballroom & Bars
Route Orange, St Brelade
☎ 41561

Folk Music:
Priory Inn, Devil's Hole, St Mary
☎ 485307

Theatre & Concerts
Jersey Arts Centre
Benjamin Meaker Theatre
Phillips Street, St Helier
Box Office ☎ 73767 ♿

Gloucester Hall and Piazza
Fort Regent, St Helier (see above)

Lido de France
St Saviour's Road, St Saviour
☎ 73102

Opera House
Gloucester Street, St Helier
☎ 22165

OTHER PLACES TO VISIT

Eric Young Orchid Foundation
Victoria Village, Trinity
☎ 861963
Open: Thursday, Friday, Saturday
only 10am-4pm. ♿

Fantastic Tropical Gardens
St Peter's Valley, St Peter
☎ 481585

Open: daily, Easter-October 9.30am-6pm and evenings. Admission charge. Exotic birds, dancers, bazaar, donkey rides, licenced restaurant.

Glass Church
St Matthew's church, Millbrook, St Lawrence
Open: weekdays 9am-6pm (or dusk in winter);Saturday 9am-1pm; Sunday June to September, 8.30pm community hymn singing.

Jersey Butterfly Centre and Carnation Nursery
Haute Tombette, St Mary
☎ 481707
Open: daily May-October, 9am-6pm. Admission charge.

Jersey Lavender Farm
Rue du Pont Marquet, St Brelade
☎ 42933
Open: beginning of June to end of September, Monday to Saturday 10am to 5pm. Closed Sundays. Admission charge. &

Jersey Shire Horse Farm
Champ Donné
La Route de Trodez, St Ouen
☎ 82372
Open: daily Apri-October, 10am-6pm. Includes Country Life Museum. Admission charge.

The Living Legend
Rue de Petit Aleval, St Peter
☎ 485496
Audio-visual history of Jersey. Admission charge.
Craft and souvenir shop, sun terrace, restaurant, play area, car park, no admission charge. &

Jersey Wildlife Preservation Trust (Jersey Zoo)
Les Augrès Manor, Trinity
☎ 864666

Open: daily 10am-6pm (or dusk in winter). Closed Christmas Day. Admission charge. &

Jersey Pearl
La Route des Issues, St John
Open: all year Monday-Saturday 10am-5pm, also evenings June-August.

Kempt Tower Interpretation Centre
Five Mile Road, St Ouen
☎ 483651
Open: May-October, Thursday and Sundays only 2-5pm; June-end September daily 2-5pm.

Jersey Flower Centre
Retreat Farm, Rue de Varvots, St Lawrence
☎ 865665
Open: daily 9am-4.30pm, all year. Shop & café April-October only. & Flamingo lake, wild bird sanctuary.

Sunset Nurseries
St Ouen's Bay, St Peter
☎ 482090
Open: daily 10am-5pm in season. Winter: Monday-Friday, 10am-5pm only except Christmas & New Year. Tropical gardens, aviary, souvenirs.

Wolf's Caves Complex
Near Frémont Point, St John
☎ 864602
Open: 9am-11pm all year and on Monday, (plus Tuesday and Thursday in season) the Marlboro Country Music Club hold their meetings in the lounge bar.

Youth and Community Centre
St Peter's Village, St Peter
☎ 483011
Open: Monday-Friday 9am-1pm, 2pm-11pm; Saturday 9am-1pm, 2-6pm; Saturday and Sunday 2-6pm.

Friendly Club meets 2-3pm Wednesday afternoon.

MUSEUMS AND ART GALLERIES

Battle of Flowers Museum
La Robiline
Le Mont des Corvées, St Ouen
☎ 482408
Open: March-end October 10am-5pm, daily. Admission charge.
Large car park, café. ♿

German Military Underground Hospital Museum
Meadowbank, St Lawrence
☎ 863442
Open: daily, March-early November 9.30am-5.30pm (last admission 4.45pm). February-March and early November-late December, Thursday 12noon-4.15pm, Sunday 2-4.15pm.
♿

Island Fortress Occupation Museum
9 Esplanade, St Helier
☎ 34306
Open: daily Easter-November from 10am-10pm.
Admission charge. ♿

Jersey Arts Centre and Berni Gallery
Phillips Street, St Helier
☎ 68080
Arts Centre office open 9.30am-5.30pm, Monday-Friday.
Gallery 10am-10pm.
Restaurant open Monday-Saturday 10am-2.30pm and 5.30pm onwards. Lunch 12noon-2pm and theatre dinners from 6.30pm. ♿

Jersey Motor Museum
St Peter's Village, St Peter
☎ 482966

Open: mid-March-end October, daily 10am-5pm. Last admission 4.40pm. Admission charge. ♿

Jersey Museum & Art Gallery
The weighbridge, St Helier
☎ 30511
Open: Monday-Saturday 10am-5pm, all year except for 2 weeks in January for cleaning. Admission charge. Toilet facilities. Café. ♿

La Hougue Bie Museum
La Hougue Bie, Grouville
☎ 53823
Open: mid-March-end October, Tuesday-Sunday 10am-5pm.
Includes **Archaeological Museum** and **German Command Bunker**.
Admission charge.

Pallot Steam Museum
Rue de Bechet, Trinity
Open: Monday-Saturday 10-5pm.
Railway rides 3 days a week.

Sir Francis Cook Gallery
(Jersey Heritage Trust)
Route de la Trinité, Augrès, Trinity
☎ 863333
Open: during exhibitions only 2-5pm daily. Admission free.
Disabled visitors welcome.

St Peter's Bunker Occupation Museum
St Peter's Village, St Peter
☎ 481048/484111
Open: daily March-November, 10am-5pm (last admission 4.40pm). Admission charge.

PARKS AND GARDENS

La Collette Gardens
La Collette, St Helier

Coronation Gardens (CP)
Millbrook, St Lawrence

First Tower Park (CP)
St Helier

Gorey Gardens
St Martin

Howard Davis Park
Don Road, St Saviour

Lower Park
Victoria Avenue, St Helier

Mount Bingham (CP)
St Helier

People's Park (CP)
Cheapside, St Helier

Pont Marquet Country Park
St Brelade (CP opposite)

Royal Parade (CP)
Parade Place, St Helier

Shell Garden
St Aubin

Sir Winston Churchill Memorial Park
St Brelade's Bay

Victoria Park
Peirson Road, St Helier

Westmount
West Park, St Helier

CP indicates children's playground. In summer certain private gardens are open to the public in aid of charity. For details contact Tourism, Weighbridge, St Helier ☎ 500700.

PREHISTORIC SITES

La Belle Hougue — Trinity

Les Blanches Banques Menhirs — St Brelade

Le Câtel de Lecq — St Mary

La Cotte à la Chèvre — St Ouen

La Cotte de St Brelade — St Brelade

Le Couperon — St Martin

La Dame Blanche — St Clement

Green Island - La Motte — St Clement

La Hougue Bie — Grouville

La Hougue Boëte — St John (on private land)

La Hougue des Platons — Trinity

L'Ile Agois — St Mary

Les Monts Grantez — St Ouen

Le Mont Ubé — St Clement

The Ossuary — St Brelade

La Pierre de la Fételle — Trinity

La Pierre des Baissières — meeting point of St Peter, St Mary, St Lawrence

Le Pinacle — St Ouen

La Pouquelaye de Faldouët — St Martin

Les Quennevais Menhirs — including Les Blanches Banques — St Brelade

La Sergenté — St Brelade

La Table des Marthes — St Brelade

Les Trois Rocques — St Ouen's Bay

La Ville ès Nouaux — First Tower Park, St Helier

The White Menhir — St Ouen's Bay

SPORTS (*Indoor*)

Fort Regent
St Helier (leisure centre)
Badminton, squash, table tennis,
snooker, bowls
☎ 500200
Access via Fort Regent multi-storey
car park, Pier Road. Road Train (Le
Petit Train) from Snowhill.
Open: Fort Regent 9am-11pm all
year; most other attractions 10am-
5.30pm; swimming pool Monday-
Friday 8.45am-7.30pm, 10am-
5.30pm weekends. Amenities vary
according to time of day and season,
so check with reception.

Lido Fitness Centre
Hotel de France Complex,
St Saviour's Road, St Saviour
☎ 75568
Karate, weight training, aerobics,
gym, dance studio, solarium, sauna
and squash.

Squash
Jersey Squash Club, Jersey
Recreation Grounds, Grève d'Azette
(temporary membership available to
members of visiting squash clubs).
☎ 35773

Snooker/Pool
*St John's Sports & Recreation
   Centre*
La Route de Mont Mado, St John
☎ 863574

142 Snooker Club,
Wharf Street, St Helier
☎ 21923
Open: weekdays 11am-1am.

Funland, Esplanade, St Helier
☎ 31287
Open: 10am-10pm all year.

Watersplash,
Five Mile Road, St Ouen
☎ 482885

SPORTS (*Outdoor*)

Athletics
Meetings take place during the
summer months.

Sports Complex,
Don Farm, Les Quennevais
Sporting activities available to
visitors during school summer
holidays mid-July-beginning August
from 9am-10pm. Advanced bookings
should be made through Education
Department.
☎ 509500

F.B. Playing Fields
Plat Douet Road, St Clement
☎ 509500
Track can be used by visiting
athletes, payment per hour.
Available daily 8am-dusk — floodlit
Tuesdays & Thursdays until 8.30pm.
Block bookings to Education Dept.
☎ 509500

Bowling Greens
Jersey Bowling Club
Westmount Road
☎ 32133
Open: Monday-Saturday 2.30-5pm
and 6.30pm.

St Saviour's Bowls Club
Grainville, St Saviour
☎ 66815

Canoeing
Jersey Canoe Club
St Catherines's Bay
☎ 855188.Tuition and equipment is
available.

Paddles Canoeing School
(BCU approved)
☎ 854189

Shooting
Crabbé Clay Pigeon Club
Shooting all day Sunday from 10am,
Thursday evenings during summer
from 6pm, Saturday afternoons from
2.30pm. Visitors welcome. Club

grounds are at Crabbé Range, St Mary, off the B40. Details from Mr M. Gotel ☎ 54022 or 76588. Guns and tuition by qualified coach available.

Rifle Association
☎ 36585

Pistol Club
☎ 33725

Small Bore Rifle Club
☎ 23882

Crazy Golf (*18 hoop*)
Les Mielles Golf Course
Five Mile Road,
St Peter
☎ 482787

Cricket
Matches played at the FB Playing Fields, Grève d'Azette; Victoria College Grounds or at Grainville, St Saviour's Hill, St Saviour.

Cruising and Yacht Charter
Jersey Cruising School
New North Quay,
St Helier Marina, St Helier
☎ 888100.

Dive and Ski Sports
5 Francis Street, St Helier ☎ 36209
Diving school with qualified instructors. Equipment hire and bottle filling facilities available.

Fishing
Coarse Fishing
Covers Millbrook Reservoir and South Canal, St Ouen's
Permits from:
Stewart Hunt, 71 King Street/
28 Broad Street, St Helier

PJN Fishing Tackle,
7 Beresford Market, St Helier

Freshwater Angling
For rudd, roach, perch, carp, bream, tench, chubb, eels and trout.
Maggots not allowed in reservoirs.

Sea Angling
All year round, fish of all varieties from places such as Bouley Bay, Bonne Nuit, Rozel, and St Catherine's breakwater where rods and reels can be hired, plus bait at the kiosk on the breakwater . These spots are in the north of the island.

On the south coast, St Helier town harbour, Elizabeth Castle breakwater, St Aubin's harbour, and St Brelade's jetty, all produce some good fish. For beach fishing, try St Ouen's Bay, St Aubin's Bay, and Grouville Bay for bass.

The island has a number of sea angling clubs who organize shore and boat festivals in the summer. Tackle shops have details of boat trips which show excellent catches including British records.

As Jersey has some of the highest tides in the world, before fishing from rocks ask local anglers if it is safe to do so.

Trout Fishing
(Fly only). Covers Val de la Mare Reservoir, St Ouen.
Permits from PJN Fishing Tackle, 7 Beresford Market, St Helier.

Flying
For flying lessons (and trial flying lessons), PPL and all other ratings contact Jersey Aero Club, St Peter
☎ 43990

Football
The principal matches are played at Springfield, Janvrin Road; other matches at the FB Playing Fields.

Golf (*18 holes*)
La Moye Golf Club
St Brelade
☎ 43401
Starting times available after 9.30am.

Royal Jersey Golf Club, Grouville
☎ 854416

(Visitors must be members of a recognised golf club and produce a certificate to that effect).

(*9 holes*)
Jersey Recreation Grounds,
Grève d'Azette
☎ 21938
Open: 9am all year, closes at 3.30-4pm winter and 8.30pm Monday-Friday in season with earlier closing 6.30-7pm Friday-Saturday in season. (No clubs hired.)

(*12 holes par 3*)
Les Mielles Golf Course,
Five Mile Road, St Peter
☎ 482787
Open: daily throughout the year from dawn-dusk. Tuition and equipment to buy and hire. Clubs hired.

Golf Driving Range
Les Mielles Golf Course
Five Mile Road, St Peter
☎ 482787

Horse Riding
Riding on any beach is prohibited 11am-7pm May-September.

Bon-Air Stables
La Grande Route de St Laurent, St Lawrence (Mrs J. Sebire)
☎ 865196

Brabant Riding School,
Brabant, Trinity
☎ 861105
Open: all year weekdays 9.30am-12.30pm and 2.30-4.30pm.

Le Claire Riding and Livery Stables,
Sunnydale, Rue Militaire, St John
☎ 862823

Sorrel Stables & Saddlery Centre
(tuition, livery, hacking, saddlery and riding wear), Mont Fallu, St Peter
☎ 42009
Open: daily 8am-5.30pm.

Jersey Carriage Driving Centre
Mont Mado, St John☎ 862748

1-hour drives, ½-day picnics, fun sessions for children, lessons, pony rides.

Mini Golf
Les Mielles Golf Course,
Five Mile Road, St Peter
☎ 482787

Motor Racing
The principal events, organised by the Jersey Motor Cycle & Light Car Club, take place at St Ouen's Bay and on Bouley Bay Hill.
☎ 22662

Putting Green (*18 holes*)
Les Mielles Golf Course,
Five Mile Road, St Peter
☎ 482787

Rugby
All important games are played at the Jersey Rugby Club Ground near the airport, St Peter.
☎ 42255/72752

Sailing
Gorey Watersports Centre,
Grouville Bay
☎ 852033/853250
Tuition and hire of Lasers, Mirror & Skipper dinghies. Also 14ft & 16ft Hobie catamarans and all equipment.

Sub-Aqua
Contact Mr J. Webster for skin diving, boat dives and hiring gear at Watersports, First Tower ☎ 32813 or Bouley Bay ☎ 861817/861829 for Scuba Diving School and hire of windsurfers, canoes and diving equipment. Bottle filling facilities are available at Watersports, First Tower and Underwater Centre, Bouley Bay. Diving schools recognised: PASS, BSAC, NAUI, SAA, PADI, CMAS.

Jersey Sub-Aqua Club
British Sub-Aqua Club
Club Room, La Folie,
South Pier, St Helier.

Bottle filling service and general enquiries, Mr M. Chatel ☎ 33820 after 7pm.

Surfing

Surfing school and hire facilities at:

Watersplash,
St Ouen's Bay (seasonal)
☎ 4828845

Sands, St Ouen's Bay (all year)
☎ 483707

El Tico, St Ouen's Bay (seasonal)
(No lessons.)

Surf Jets

Jersey Seasport Centre,
La Haule Slip, St Aubin
☎ 45040 or 863725
Jet powered surf boats for hire.

Pilot Watersports, St Aubin's Bay
☎ 863538
Jet skis for hire.

Tennis

Caesarean Tennis Club
Grands Vaux
☎ 22011
Courts available to visitors week-days 9am-5pm; pay court fees to the steward before play starts. Professional coach available Monday-Saturday, April-September.

Jersey Recreation Grounds
Grève d'Azette
☎ 21938

Water Ski School

Jersey Seasport Centre,
La Haule Slip, St Aubin
☎ 45040 or 81301
Water skis and sea sleds for hire. Lessons and tows. Fully qualified instructors.

Wind Surfing

Jersey Wind and Water Windsurfer Schools, St Brelade
IWS schools with qualified instructors.
☎ 853250

Gorey Watersports Centre,
Grouville Bay.
Tuition and hire. Large selection of boards for all ages
☎ 853250
Open: daily June-September 9.30am-6pm.

Watersplash, St Ouen's Bay
☎ 482885
All types of sailboards available.

Yachting (visiting yachtsmen welcome)

Royal Channel Islands Yacht Club,
St Aubin ☎ 41023/45783

St Helier Yacht Club
South Pier, St Helier ☎ 21307

TRANSPORT IN THE ISLAND

Bicycle Hire

Simple, inexpensive. Deposit usually required.

Kingslea,
70 Esplanade, St Helier
☎ 24777
One of several cycle centres where bikes can be hired.

The Hire Shop,
St Aubin's Road, Millbrook
☎ 73699
Pushchairs and wheelchairs for hire.

Jersey Cycle Tours
Get to know Jersey by bike.
☎ 482898

Bus Service

Jersey Motor Transport buses operate from a central bus and coach station at the Weighbridge, St Helier ☎ 21201.
Visitors who wish to use this service are advised to buy a timetable from the JMT office at the Weighbridge.

Car Hire
Rates, usually including insurance and petrol, are less expensive than on the mainland. Cars delivered to and collected from hotels, harbour or airport at no extra charge. Hirers must be over 20; a current driving licence (held for at least a year and no endorsements for dangerous or drunken driving for the last 5 years) must be produced when hiring.

AA Office
11 Esplanade, St Helier ☎ 23346

Coach Tours
A number of coach companies operate morning, afternoon or full day tours. Also evening drives to shows, cabarets and pubs. Information from hotels, guesthouses or direct from the coach companies — telephone numbers in Yellow Pages, under Coach Tour Operators.

Motorcycle/Scooter/Moped Hire
Hirers must be 18+ with a valid driving licence for at least 6 months. Crash helmets compulsory. Helmets and third party insurance included in hire cost. Deposits required.

Public Taxi Ranks
Airport, St Peter ☎ 41420
St Helier at: Broad Street, Snow Hill, Weighbridge.

There are also about a dozen private hire cab depots — numbers can be found in Yellow Pages under Taxis.

TRAVEL TO & FROM JERSEY

By Air

To Paris (Charles de Gaulle)
Jersey European Airways
Jersey Airport ☎ 45661

To Dinard
Jersey European Airways
Jersey Airport
☎ 45661

To Cherbourg
Aurigny Air Services Ltd
Jersey Airport
☎ 43568

Holiday House, Weighbridge, St Helier
☎ 35733

To Guernsey
Aurigny Air Services Ltd
Jersey Airport
☎ 43568

Jersey European Airways
Jersey Airport
☎ 45661

To Alderney
Aurigny Air Services Ltd
Jersey Airport
☎ 43568

By Sea

Passenger Services
Ferry Centre for all sea services
5 Esplanade, St Helier
☎ 26452

To St Malo
'Condor' Hydrofoils
Commodore Travel
28 Conway Street, St Helier
☎ 601100/607080

To St Malo, Carteret, Granville and Port Bail
Emeraude Ferries
Albert Quay, St Helier
☎ 66566
Gorey Pier
☎ 856792

To Guernsey/Sark/Herm
'Condor' Hydrofoils
Commodore Travel
28 Conway Street, St Helier
☎ 601100/607080

Emeraude Ferries
Albert Quay, St Helier
☎ 66566
Gorey Pier
☎ 856792

Car/Passenger Ferries

To Guernsey/Poole
British Channel Island Ferries
New North Quay, St Helier
☎ 38300

Commodore Travel
28 Conway Street, St Helier
☎ 601100/607080

To St Malo
Commodore Travel
(Crane on/Crane off car ferry service
— no passengers)
28 Conway Street, St Helier
☎ 601100/607080

Emeraude Ferries
Albert Quay, St Helier
☎ 66566
Gorey Pier
☎ 856792

Day Excursions to France
A valid passport or British Excursion
Document (valid for 1 month) —
which should be obtained before
arriving in Jersey — is essential for
even a day trip to France.

USEFUL ADDRESSES

AA Office
11 Esplanade, St Helier
☎ 23346

Education Department
PO Box 142, Highlands, St Saviour
☎ 509500

Jersey Heritage Trust
Jersey Museum
Weighbridge, St Helier
☎ 30511

Queries about museums, historic
sites etc.

National Trust for Jersey
The Elms, St Mary
☎ 483193 (mornings only)

States of Jersey Tourism
35 Albemarle Street
London WIX 3FB
☎ 01 493 5278

States of Jersey Tourism
Weighbridge, St Helier
☎ 500700

There are no parish tourist offices
but the telephone numbers of the
Parish Halls are as follows:

St Brelade ☎ 41141/44297

St Clement ☎ 854724

Grouville ☎ 852225

St Helier ☎ 25251

St John ☎ 861999

St Lawrence ☎ 861672

St Martin ☎ 853951

St Mary ☎ 482700

St Ouen ☎ 481619

St Peter ☎ 481236

St Saviour ☎ 35864

Trinity ☎ 865345

USEFUL INFORMATION

Banks
Hours of business are usually
9.30am-4.30pm daily. Some banks
open Saturday 9.30am-12.30pm.
Most major credit cards and
Eurocards are accepted.

There are numerous merchant banks in St Helier.

Head Offices:
Barclays Bank plc
13 Library Place, St Helier
☎ 78511

Lloyds Bank plc
9 Broad Street, St Helier
☎ 284000

Midland Bank plc
Library Place
St Helier
☎ 606606

Nat West Bank plc
16 Library Place
St Helier
☎ 72810

The Royal Bank of Scotland plc
St Helier
6 Mulcaster Street
☎ 27351

TSB Channel Islands Ltd
23 New Street
St Helier
☎ 503000

Opening hours the Jersey branches of the TSB Channel Islands Ltd are MondayThursday 8.30am-4pm and Friday 8.30am-6.30pm.

Beach Guards
St Ouen's Bay
☎ 482032 (June to mid-September)

Plémont Bay
☎ 481636 (June to mid-September)

Bureaux de Change
All banks, head post office, Jersey Airport, St Helier and Gorey harbours and several travel agents.

Caravans
Trailer and motor caravans (eg Dormobiles) are not allowed into Jersey for holiday or in transit. There are no caravan sites.

Camping Sites
All sites have adequate separate toilet facilities for men and women.

Beuvelande Camp Site, St Martin
☎ 853575

Quennevais Camp Site,
Les Ormes Farm, St Brelade
☎ 42436

Rose Farm, St Brelade
☎ 41231

Rozel Camping Park,
Sales & Hire Centre,
Summerville Farm, St Martin
☎ 856797

St Brelade's Camping Park,
Route des Genêts, St Brelade
☎ 41398

Summer Lodge, Leoville, St Ouen
☎ 481921

Duty Free Allowances
Tobacco Goods
200 cigarettes or 100 cigarillos (up to 3 grams each) or 50 cigars or 250 grams of tobacco.

Alcoholic Drinks
1 litre if the strength is more than 38.8˚ proof (22˚ Gay-Lussac) or 2 litres if the strength is not more than 38.8˚ proof or 2 litres of fortified or sparkling wine, plus 2 litres of (still) table wine.

Purchase of goods up to £36 per person can be taken through customs without being liable to tax.

Emergency Services
Fire, Police, Ambulance, Sea Rescue Dial 999.

General Hospital
Gloucester Street
St Helier
☎ 59000
Offers visitors general outpatient, accident and emergency facilities, also a morning medical clinic, free of charge.

Liberation Day
9 May public holiday, most shops closed.

Licensing Hours
At the discretion of the proprietor. Public bars are open to those over 18: weekdays 9am-11.30pm; Sunday 11am-1pm and 4.30-11pm.

Library Service
Books are available to tourists against a returnable deposit.

Jersey Library
Halkett Place,
St Helier
☎ 59991, reference section 59992
Open: Monday, Wendesday-Friday 9.30am-5.30pm; Tuesday 9.30am-7.30pm. Saturday 9.30am-4pm.

Les Quennevais Branch Library
St Brelade
☎ 42417
Monday to Friday 2-5.30pm; Saturday 10am-1pm.

Lottery
A Channel Islands lottery is held fortnightly. Tickets obtainable at most newsagents and at a kiosk in the centre of St Helier.

Marina
St Helier Harbour
☎ 34451

Markets
There are two fresh food markets in St Helier: Halkett Place for meat, fruit, flowers, vegetables; Beresford Street for fish, fruit, flowers and vegetables.

Medical Treatment
Visitors may obtain medical advice or treatment *free of charge* from the Morning Medical Clinic at the General Hospital, every morning except Sunday May-September and on Monday, Wednesday and Friday October-April. Casualty and out-patient treatment is also available at the General Hospital. Any prescriptions issued at the morning clinic will be dispensed at the hospital pharmacy for £1.50. Visitors should bring the name and address of their own GP and of any medicines they are taking. For visitor requiring hospital in-patient treatment, this is provided free of charge. Visitors consulting a private medical practitioner must *pay the full cost of their consultation and the medicine prescribed*. No reimbursements of costs can be made by the relevant Jersey Department or the UK Dept of Health. Private medical insurance might cover the cost.

Morning Medical Clinic
General Hospital,
Gloucester Street, St Helier
Open: May-September Monday-Friday 9am-noon, Saturday 10-11.30am; October-April Monday, Wednesday and Friday 9.30-11.30am (no clinic on Saturday).
☎ 59000

Newspapers
Jersey Evening Post (Town Office, Charles Street, St Helier ☎ 73333) is published on weekdays mid-afternoon and on Saturday mid-day. UK newspapers are on sale daily, as well as magazines and periodicals.

Parking in St Helier
Multi-storey: Green Street, Minden Place, Sand Street, Patriotic Street and Pier Road.
Other Car Parks: The Parade, Weighbridge, Old Fire Station (rear of Odeon cinema), Snow Hill, La Route du Fort, Midvale Road, Georgetown, Elizabeth Lane, People's Park and Gas Place.
Pay Cards: used for payment for parking in St Helier car parks displaying the special sign. Scratching off the silver foil on the card indicates the date, day and time, informing car park officials of the time of arrival and duration of stay. Pay cards are for 20p, 60p or £1.20. Parking currently costs 20p per hour 8am-5pm Monday-Saturday. Cards are available from over 200 shops, garages and post offices in Jersey.
Orange Badge Scheme: For parking for the disabled apply to the Tourism Dept for leaflet giving details.

Passports
Citizens of Great Britain and of the Irish Republic do not require passports to enter Jersey. A passport or a British Excursion Document is essential to visit France.

Post Offices
Main post office for counter services, Bureau de Change, Intelpost, Datapost, National savings, Giro Bank and enquiries is situated in Broad Street, St Helier ☎ 26262;

Open: weekdays 9am-5pm, Saturday 9am-12noon). Sunday closed all day.

Radio
BBC Radio Jersey
Rouge Bouillon,
St Helier
☎ 70111
(VHF 88.8mHZ and 1026kHZ [292m])

Channel 103
6 Tunnel Street,
St Helier
☎ 888103
(103.7mHz FM)

Speedboats, Surfboards and Sailboards
Must be registered at St Helier Harbour Office as soon as possible on arrival
☎ 34451

Speed Limit
All the island has a speed limit of 40mph. Caution — in certain signposted areas it is 20mph.

Television
Channel Television
La Pouquelaye,
St Helier
☎ 68999

Tourism Department
Weighbridge,
St Helier
☎ 500700

INDEX